Lincolnshire
COUNTY COUNCIL

discover libraries

Rural Modernity, Everyday Life and Visual Culture

Rosemary Shirley
Manchester School of Art,
Manchester Metropolitan University, UK

Routledge
Taylor & Francis Group

LONDON AND NEW YORK

First published 2015 by Ashgate Publishing

Published 2016 by Routledge
2 Park Square, Milton Park, Abingdon, Oxon OX14 4RN
711 Third Avenue, New York, NY 10017, USA

First issued in paperback 2018

Routledge is an imprint of the Taylor & Francis Group, an informa business

British Library Cataloguing in Publication Data
A catalogue record for this book is available from the British Library

Library of Congress Cataloging-in-Publication Data
Shirley, Rosemary.
 Rural modernity, everyday life and visual culture / by Rosemary Shirley.
   pages cm
 Includes bibliographical references and index.
 ISBN 978-1-4724-3143-1 (hbk) -- ISBN 978-1-4724-3144-8 (ebook) --
 ISBN 978-1-4724-3145-5 (epub) 1. England--Rural conditions. 2. England--Social life and customs. I. Title.
 HN398.E5S53 2015
 306.0942--dc23
                                                                    2014046291

ISBN 13: 978-1-138-54673-8 (pbk)
ISBN 13: 978-1-4724-3143-1 (hbk)

Contents

List of Illustrations

About the Author

Rosemary Shirley is a Senior Lecturer in Art History at Manchester School of Art, Manchester Metropolitan University. She has contributed chapters to *Affective Landscapes in Literature, Art and Everyday Life* (edited by Christine Berberich, Neil Campbell and Robert Hudson, 2015) and *Transforming the Countryside* (edited by Paul Brassley, Jeremy Burchardt and Karen Sayer, 2016). Her research centres on everyday life and visual cultures in historical and contemporary rural contexts.

Acknowledgements

I would like to offer my warmest thanks to Ben Highmore for his constant encouragement and support throughout this project. I am also grateful to the University of Sussex for their generous award of a Sussex Scholarship, to the Paul Mellon Centre for Studies in British Art for a Publication Grant, and to MIRIAD for a Research Support Grant.

The award for most patient husband goes to Nick, who I need to thank for so much, not least for his excellent bibliographic skills. I'd also like to thank my parents for their understanding and humour.

I am grateful to Joanne Lee and Claire Langhamer for their invaluable feedback, and for fascinating conversations, camaraderie and inspiration. I thank Linda Berkvens, Catherine Bate, Cameron Catiere, Sally Davies, Melanie Rose, Neeta Madahar, and James Wilkes. Thanks also go to my friends and colleagues at Manchester School of Art.

For their expertise and generosity in lending scrapbooks I thank Ann Mattingly, archivist at WI House, Winchester and the members of Micheldever and Radwinter WIs. Thanks to the National Federation of Women's Institutes for their permission to quote from their archival documents and to Hampshire WI for permission to reproduce elements from the Binsted Scrapbook. In addition, I would like to thank the staff at the following collections: East Sussex County Archive, Hampshire County Archive, Shell Art Collection, Beaulieu, in particular Nicky Balfour, and Winchester School of Art Library, University of Southampton.

Quotes from the litter trails documents in Chapter 3 are reproduced with permission of Curtis Brown Group Ltd, London on behalf of The Trustees of the Mass Observation Archive. Some material from Chapter 2 has also been published in 'Speed and Stillness: Driving in the Countryside', in *Affective Landscapes in Literature, Art and Everyday Life* (Ashgate, 2015).

1

Introduction: Beating the Bounds

In his publication *Once a Year* (1977), Homer Sykes, photographer and chronicler of the strange folk festivals practised over the British Isles, documents the Beating of the Bounds ceremony that takes place each year in Oxford. On Ascension Day (40 days after Easter Sunday) the parish priest of St. Michael's church, the choir boys, the choir master and the parishioners gather together to perform the ancient ritual. Armed with long garden canes – the type used for keeping runner beans upright – they rain down blows on each of the 22 stones which mark the parish boundary.

1.1   Beating the Bounds, Oxford, 1977. © Homer Sykes.

Taking place in spring time, the festival has pre-Christian agrarian roots, marking the change in season and providing the opportunity for symbolic or actual sacrifices to be made to ensure a fruitful growing season and harvest. In a time before parishes were established, this simply meant walking the fields. Early in its history the Christian church began to tie its activities closely to the agricultural calendar adopting seasonal festivals as their own. In his study of such festivals, Ronald Hutton shows that in eighth century England the early Christian church began to regulate these often exuberant events, prohibiting any accompanying feasting and games and decreeing that participants should instead walk exhibiting their fear and reverence towards God (Hutton 1996: p. 277). It was at this time that they were given the name Rogations from the Latin *rogare* – 'to ask' – a request to God for a good harvest and a blessing of the fields.

Such festivals also had a very real secular purpose to do with the everyday administration of the parish. In the sixteenth century parishioners became liable for certain taxes and financial duties payable to the parish and so it became important that boundaries be understood and maintained. Before most people had access to maps or the education necessary to read them, these boundaries were learnt through Rogationtide perambulations, with the brutally eccentric addition of actual beatings to ensure the younger members of the congregation were paying attention. W.E. Tate in his classic history of parochial administration, *The Parish Chest* (1983 [1946]), reveals that the practice of beating the bounds did not only refer to the beating of boundary stones but also of boys. Documents from the parish of Tunworth in Dorset show that in 1747 the ceremony included 'Whipping ye boys by way of remembrance, and stopping their cry with some half-pence' (Tate 1983 [1946]: p. 74). The idea being that having one's head hit against a stone, or in this case being beaten at the site of a stone, would instil a memory of its location and ensure the knowledge of the parish boundaries was passed on to future generations.

Varied and elaborate customs that demarcate the boundaries of a place continue to be enacted in many parts of the country.[1] While their purpose is to mark boundaries, these festivals can also have the effect of upsetting clear delineation. Temporal and conceptual boundaries between the country and the city and the ancient and the modern are shown to be mutable in festivals of this kind. In a very practical way these disturbances can be felt at the Oxford ceremony in the logistics of accessing the stones. Over the 600 years in which this ceremony has been performed the boundary markers have borne witness to centuries of civic development, deconstruction and reconstruction, meaning that they no longer simply lie in open ground but have to be searched out in shops, cellars, private property and even under the carpet of the Roebuck Inn. While the boundaries of the parish may have remained constant, the boundaries between country and city have become less distinct, and beating the bounds requires a complex negotiation of ancient markers, overlaid with modern developments, which in turn become venues for these ancient practices.

Today boundary stones are marked on Ordnance Survey maps with BS, but despite this orderly plotting they often remain unsettled. For a time I tried to discover the boundary stones of my own parish. This involved furtively trespassing onto farm land and rooting around in brambly hedgerows always to no avail. The obscure nature of these stones – present on the map but not in the field, perhaps communicates something of the mutable nature of the boundaries they describe. Alain Corbin's (1998) study of nineteenth century French villages shows how the range in which the sound of the church bells could be heard was a marker of the village territory, and that it was a matter of responsibility to ensure that the settlements in the furthest corners of the village bounds could hear the bells, which were the primary form of communal announcement at that time. In this instance of aural boundary marking, weather conditions such as winds and fog would disrupt penetration of sound therefore effectively changed the village boundaries.

An exhibition at Tate Britain called *Beating the Bounds* (2009) demonstrated the metaphorical potential of the process. To the consternation of one critic (Darwent 2009), the work on display did not centre on the festival itself, but rather used the concept as a way of thinking about embodied experiences of the world. The pieces worked to access the boundary between the viewing body and the art work itself. The works included all hit against this boundary in some way and in the process created an awareness of these different yet interconnected realms. Amongst the works was *Small Head of E.O.W.* (1957–8) by the painter Frank Auerbach, whose obsessively overworked surfaces thickly search for a visual equivalent to physical experience. A counterpoint to Auerbach's chunky canvas, Glenn Brown's flat rendering of *The Suicide of Guy Debord* (2001), is an inverted Auerbach portrait, painted by Brown as a completely smooth almost photographic surface. The disjuncture between the two pieces creates a jolt that is experienced physically. The Auerbach highlights the difference between the physicality of the sitter and their representation in paint, while the Brown accesses the difference between the fleshiness of the painting and its representation in photography (which is really a painting), both pieces creating a disturbing disparity in physical perception. 'It is in this "bump" between the living and the inanimate that something transformative occurs' (Tate 2009: n.p.).

This book has been inspired by some of the bumps encountered in an embodied experience of the English countryside: a dual carriageway shaving the edge of a bronze age burial mound, an abandoned stiletto in a wood, a pylon rendered in embroidery, and finally a wooden gallon bucket pouring flour into a supermarket carrier bag. Each of these bumps has been transformative in my development of the notion of a non-metropolitan everyday, and has been the initial impetus for each chapter.

This book endeavours to beat the bounds of the country and the city, thinking in more nuanced ways about how these realms interact. Throughout, this project is an attempt to perambulate the margins of ideas of the rural, the everyday and modernity, the bramble patches where these terms overlap and become problematic or charged. It is particularly concerned with examining and disrupting the boundaries between the country and the city; reactivating the rural as a site of modernity; and productively encountering the tension between the ancient and modern. This is done through the lens of the everyday, a perspective that allows an exploration of the 'countryside' as a populated place with lived rhythms and routines, rather than a 'landscape' which is primarily to be looked at or visited.

Everyday life has become a significant arena for critical thinking; in academic circles this interest is evident in themed journal issues (*Cultural Studies*, 18, (2/3), 2004), and a number of recent publications that work to re-evaluate the writings of many writers and thinkers through the frame of the everyday (Foley 2012; Gardiner 2000; Highmore 2002a; Moran 2005; Sheringham 2006). In the visual arts recognition of the everyday as a productive site of investigation, has also gained recent prevalence with the everyday being used as the organising principle for large scale international exhibitions (Castello di Rivoli 2000; Lyon Biennale 2009), and an edited volume bringing together artists' writings on the everyday (Johnstone 2008). However, as I will go on to detail later, so much of this current activity assumes the urban everyday as a general condition. This metropolitan focus excludes significant areas of experience, meaning that those of us living outside urban areas rarely recognise representations of these kinds of everyday. It is important to investigate how non-metropolitan experiences of the everyday can contribute to (and complicate) wider contemporary theories of the everyday, a process which in turn generates new ways of thinking about the countryside.

THE COUNTRY AND THE CITY: NON-METROPOLITAN PROBLEMS

I use the term 'non-metropolitan' throughout this book, as I think it signals some of the problematics which surround the description and theorisation of the English countryside. What it does as a term is to defamiliarise the notion of the countryside, and in this process allow for some of the otherwise generalised complexities of non-urban landscapes to emerge. Working with the idea of the non-metropolitan creates the conditions for recognition that there are multiple degrees of 'countryside' between, for example, the suburbs of the Home Counties and the hills of the Lake District. It is in this realm of the multiple non-urban geographies that this study operates.

The notion that the non-metropolitan as a term is alert to multiple experiences may seem counter-intuitive as creating this new category effectively flattens out difference, and groups manifold places under the same umbrella. However, my argument is that the multiple nature of non-metropolitan experience resists definition, and therefore is most appropriately registered using a term which is itself an anti-definition. By anti-definition I mean that it refers to a huge geographical and psychological arena that can only be a relational term – a word which is essentially defined by what it is not. In the case of the non-metropolitan, what it is not, is the metropolis, but how far does this take us? To term an arena in the negative is to define it against a perceived lack, creating a definition based on inequality. However, I would argue that this inequality already exists and the awkwardness of this term 'non-metropolitan' does some work towards highlighting this and the inadequacies of existing terminology. The vocabulary surrounding location is loaded with notions of value and power. The word metropolis is derived from the Greek for mother city, and within this definition we immediately encounter a hierarchical distinction: the idea that the city as mother, birthed, attends to and disciplines its surrounding country.

Other terms that are used to refer to the lands lying outside the metropolis are *regions* or *provinces*. Again these are relational terms and their years of usage have been imbued with metro-centric power relations. Raymond Williams, always alert to the complexities of geographical (and associated ideological) meanings, draws out these hierarchical distinctions. In his formulation of the term *regional* (Williams 1989 [1976]: p. 265), he refers to an assumed relationship between the dominant and the subordinate. An example is found in the idea of the 'regional accent', a sub-ordinate term which implies that there is such a thing as a dominant 'national accent', from which regional variations deviate. However, Williams also points out that in its modern usage, regional can have the positive association of desirable distinctiveness, especially in regard to architecture and cooking, albeit value which is often bestowed by a metropolitan audience rather than one that has been self determined.[2]

The unfortunate *province* however shares none of the region's favour, its Latin origins betray the weight of subordination; the word province refers to an administrative area of a conquered land. Williams comments that later nineteenth century social snobbery drew upon this unhappy formulation, with provincial becoming a term of relative inferiority to an assumed centre. In this way metropolitan and provincial were used respectively to indicate a contrast between refined or sophisticated tastes and manners and relatively crude and limited habits and ideas (Williams 1989 [1976]: p. 265).

The most common vocabulary used to articulate the relationship between the metropolitan and the non-metropolitan is the pairing of the *country* and the *city*, a complex binary positioning from which Williams generated one of his most engaging books. Here he usefully catalogues the cultural associations that have gathered around these locations:

> On the country has gathered the idea of a natural way of life: of peace, innocence, and simple virtue. On the city has gathered the idea of an achieved centre: of learning, communication, light. Powerful hostile associations have also developed: on the city as a place of noise, worldliness and ambition; on the country as a place of backwardness, ignorance, limitation (Williams 1993 [1973]: p. 9).

Such associations, which Williams goes on to challenge, are nevertheless very powerful and have affected the place of the country and the city in the cultural imaginary of the nation.[3]

So why not use the word country instead of non-metropolitan? Indeed country could be used in this way, one of the more obscure definitions charted by Williams is a specialised use of the word country by the metropolitan postal service, to simply mean all areas outside the capital city (Williams 1989 [1976]: p. 81), a definition which for me gets closest to the way I am using non-metropolitan. However, the more commonplace understandings of the word country place it as a term with dual meaning, containing both notions of country as a nation and country as the rural or agricultural parts of a nation i.e. the countryside. Of course these two definitions are conflated in deeply felt and quite complex ways.

The English landscape and specifically that of the southern counties of England has been made to stand as a synecdoche for the country as a whole. Most obviously in times of conflict when, during both the First and Second World Wars, stylised posters of generic rolling green hills were paired with patriotic slogans showing the population what they were fighting for (Short 1992: p. 2). In more recent times the conflation of country and countryside was famously put to political use by John Major when, as Prime Minister in 1993, he made a speech designed to reassure Euro-sceptic MPs of the security of Britain as a sovereign nation. The image which he conjured up was of the UK as one large rural community, which seemed to have been preserved as some sort of living village museum:

> Fifty years from now, Britain will still be the country of long shadows on county grounds, warm beer, invincible green suburbs, dog lovers and pools fillers and

> *– as George Orwell said 'old maids cycling to holy communion through the morning mist' (quoted in Paxman 2007: p. 142).*[4]

For this study it is with the later definition that ties country to countryside, that the problem lies, for the non-metropolitan is not an exclusively rural location. The term non-metropolitan aims to defamiliarise traditional notions of countryside and allow room for thinking about places that are more usually excluded by the term rural, loaded as it is with the pressures of the picturesque and the peaceful, places that themselves complicate the established polarities of the country and the city. This strategy aims to dislodge one of the major problems with discussing the countryside or indeed the rural: that there is always somewhere more rural than you: a market town in the New Forest may not feel 'rural' when compared to a similar community in the Lake District, then again when the Lake District is compared to a location in the Scottish Highlands the criteria for being 'rural' might change once more, a situation that leads to a feeling of being inauthentically rural, or not rural enough to contribute effectively to rural debates.

An example of this problem of positioning can be seen in a Mass Observation Archive directive on the subject of the 'The Countryside' (Mass Observation 1995).[5] The correspondents were asked if they lived in the countryside, a small town, or even a suburb that is rural. The majority did not feel able to class where they were living as rural, however many described their locations as having rural elements such as green fields and open spaces. The general feeling of confusion about what constituted 'proper' countryside speaks of the persistent problems of terminology surrounding discussion of non-urban experience. This is especially pertinent as so many areas of the UK would seem to fall somewhere in between rural and urban. It is these difficulties which have contributed to the relative invisibility of the specifics of non-metropolitan experiences in political, theoretical and aesthetic discourses.

David Lowenthal (1994) provides a useful framework for thinking about the countryside as a series of constructed narratives, arguing that the English landscape is deeply linked to national identity through a combination of four rhetorical factors which characterise how the countryside is thought and spoken about: *insularity*, *artifice*, *stability* and *order*. *Insularity* links England – or more accurately Britain's, geographical position as an island with a carefully guarded mindset of independence from Europe which often runs towards xenophobia. This is evident in the use of the white cliffs of Dover as a national symbol, specifically associated with wartime patriotism. In more recent times Britain's island nature has been celebrated in the long running BBC Sunday teatime television series *Coast* (2005–ongoing) which traces the nation's coastline, treating it as a point of national pride, and derives much of its content from spectacular aerial footage of the nation's shoreline.[6]

In Lowenthal's formulation *artifice* refers to the narrative of constant stewardship, which is expounded as necessary for the continuity of the English landscape. One way in which this is evident is in the frequent panics around the need to control invasive species of plants and animals, an instinct which also enacts the trope of insularity.[7] Considering artifice as a central characteristic of the landscape makes the important point that there is nothing natural about the way the landscape has come to look, that what might be thought of as a kind of eternal arcadia is the product of the dialectical forces of development and preservation. The work of the government funded organisation Natural England is relevant here; they provide stewardship payments to farmers in return for the implementation of schemes designed to enhance habitats for native plants and wild life and preserve the 'look' of the English landscape (Natural England 2011). What is significant here is that the custodians of the landscape are most often a landowning elite, farmers who make a significant proportion of their income from stewardship schemes, or paternalistic organisations such as the National Trust, and the narrative of essential custodianship ensures their continued role.[8]

This links to the final characteristics of *stability* and *order*. Ironically it is *changes* in how the landscape is worked and who lives there, for example the decline in agricultural employment and the subsequent middle-classing of rural places that has, as Lowenthal argues, made tourism one of the chief contributors to the rural economy. This gradual transformation has contributed to the formation of the pervasive narrative of the countryside as a place of stability and unchanging continuity. In a model based on tourism the countryside becomes heritage. Lowenthal calls it 'a vast museumised ruin' (1994: p. 24), forever a signifier of a history based in nostalgia.[9] It is interesting to note that the importance of stability is reinforced by a permanent state of alarm that it is about to be lost: ancient landscape being eroded by walkers, ancient trees becoming diseased and falling down, ancient monuments succumbing to the forces of entropy and needing funds for repair. The narrative of stability has to be anxiously defended, feeding back into the importance of the use of artifice to maintain order. Finally the characteristic of *order* draws the previous three narratives together, asserting that the orderly maintenance of the physicality of the landscape that is so important to a sense of stability, can only be carried out under the leadership of those families and institutions that have accrued so much continuous experience of land management over the hundreds of years in which they have been custodians of the land. In this way the perceived need for physical order leads to reproduction of the social order, which of course feeds back into the idea of stability and continuity.

These four persistent narratives can be seen to contribute to the idea that the countryside, or its place in the national imaginary stands in opposition to some of the major characteristics associated with modernity. The countryside's insularity is a refusal of cosmopolitanism or border crossing; its artifice is used to extinguish difference and maintain a contrived permanence; an emphasis on stability becomes denial of change; and the importance of order is an attempt to reproduce rigid social and geographical structures. This opposition to modernity can be seen in Raymond Williams assertion that 'The common image of the country is now an image of the past' (1993 [1973]: p. 297), a statement which is still true today. Popular representations of the countryside seem to derive their attractiveness from situating English rural communities and locations as alternatives to the tensions, pressures and ugliness of modern everyday life. The Sunday evening television schedule, of which *Coast* became such a stalwart, is well known for providing a quantity of relaxing escapism ahead of the working week to come (see Sanghera 2010).[10] It is therefore perhaps unsurprising that so many of these programmes are based on idealised representations of rural 'old England'. Long running examples from the mainstream channels include the *Antiques Road Show*, often held at a stately home and engaged in continuity building through heritage objects and *Midsomer Murders* in which crimes reminiscent of Agatha Christie are carried out in front of a backdrop of thatched cottages in picturesque southern county villages.

This popular portrayal of the countryside as anti-modern is echoed by Edensor (2002) in his analysis of the magazine *This England* which claims to be Britain's best-selling quarterly magazine. He notes that it exclusively contains:

> *photographs and sketches featuring little or no signs of modernity (no 'modern' buildings, hardly any cars and even television aerials are strangely absent). No youths are present in any picture, certainly no non-white locals or visitors are depicted and the urban is kept at bay. This England is located in the distant past, with little evidence of any post war development (Edensor 2002: p. 42).*

Edensor shows that editing out signs of modernity can lead to an aesthetic of rural purity as a form of nationalist identity. This is an idea that is discussed more extensively in Chapter 3 on litter in the countryside, however here it might usefully link to the less cosy side of portrayals of the countryside as anti-modern. In almost a negative mirroring of the Sunday evening genre, there is the arena of rural horror, or the anti-idyll (Bell 1997). Here isolation from modernity is both thrilling and threatening; the countryside is an arena for slavish adherence to superstition, primitive sexual practices and violent hatred of outsiders. Bell writes specifically about how films such as *Texas Chainsaw Massacre* (1974) and *Deliverance* (1972) feed into an imagined cultural geography of rural America, however this is also a well developed British genre encompassing classic rural horror such as *Blood on Satan's Claw* (1971), *The Wickerman* (1973) and *Straw Dogs* (1971).[11]

This book works to complicate these habitual representations of the countryside, asserting that it too has felt the processes and impact of modernity, and argues that in order to re-activate the rural as a site of modernity (rather than as its passive victim) it is necessary to look at the everyday – the lived and the prosaic – and how it has been registered, in order to take the rural out of the past, the pastoral or the landscape tradition and to engage it in discourses of modernity.

EVERYDAY COUNTRY

Approaching this subject through the theoretical tradition of everyday life allows an exploration of the non-metropolitan as a populated place, rather than its more usual conceptualisation as a place to be visited or looked at. Furthermore thinking about this region in terms of everyday life allows the non-metropolitan to be thought about in terms of the habits, practices, rhythms and routines from which it is constructed, a position which destabilises the notion of such places as primarily 'natural' in their appearance and use. Finally the theoretical grounding of everyday life studies has tied the emergence of a perceivable notion of the everyday firmly to processes of modernity. Relocating the topography of the everyday from its habitually urban focus out into the English Countryside, enables an examination of the non-metropolitan as an active space of modernity.

To focus on everyday life is to adopt an approach to investigating culture that attends to the ways in which the daily is woven from repeated practices and performances. It is also to attend to the ways in which these actions are shaped by societal controls and acts of resistance. It reverses the field of enquiry from the exceptional event (although exceptional events are also part of the everyday) to the boring, the routine, and the taken for granted. Yet to explore this mundane realm can in many ways be revelatory, tuning in to the background hiss of our lives and wondering if it could be different. Thinking about the non-metropolitan as a mundane space, a space of motorways and litter rather than (or as well as) waterfalls and skylarks for example, allows a shift in thinking from registers of the picturesque to a place where everyday life happens.

Critic and poet Maurice Blanchot, writing in response to Lefebvre's *Critique of Everyday Life* (2008 [1954]), asserts that:

> The everyday is human. The earth, the sea, forest, light, night, do not represent everydayness, which belongs first of all to the dense presence of great urban centres. We need these admirable deserts that are the world's cities for the experiences of the everyday to begin to over take us (1987 [1959]: p. 17).

At first this statement may seem to simply reaffirm the metrocentric nature of everyday life as a theoretical tradition. Indeed it does seem to discount elements more associated with non-metropolitan places – the sea, forests and so on, as being unable to represent or produce the required amount of everydayness. But what interests me specifically about this assertion is the idea that the everyday is human, rather than 'natural' or belonging to nature. This is a useful idea because by trying to think about the rural in terms of the everyday enables us to think about it as a populated zone. This is in contrast to the tendency to represent the rural as if it is an empty region, which is visited rather than lived in.

This tendency is particularly identifiable in the work of many contemporary artists who situate their work within the landscape tradition, an interesting example of this is land artist Richard Long. In a major Long retrospective at Tate Britain (see Wallis 2009), it is evident that many of the works on show derive much of their poetic charge from an editing out of the everyday experience of the British countryside. In recording his extensive walks through picturesque parts of the UK in the form of long poetic lists of observations, Long seems often blind to the things that are intrinsic to the specific complexities of the contemporary non-metropolitan landscape. In an echo of Edensor's notion of the countryside as being represented as 'pure space' (Edensor 2002: p. 42), contemporary elements such as car parks, traffic, litter, paths beside busy roads, other walkers, and people who live and work in those landscapes are mostly absent from Long's representation. It is important, in order to recognise the rural as a site of modernity, not to see these things as encroachments from the city into the countryside; instead they need to be seen as part of what constitutes the contemporary countryside. What I am attempting to access, by taking an approach which attends to the everyday, is a re-populated rural, which acknowledges the complexities of place in relation to modernity.

One of the aims of this book is to disrupt the habitual association of the rural with the past and to re-cast the non-metropolitan realm as an active site of modernity. Everyday life, as a theoretical tradition, is thought of as a modern phenomenon, therefore to attempt to assert that the non-metropolitan is also a site of the everyday provides a framework for investigating how the rural might be situated in these discourses of modernity.

The idea that everyday life is a phenomenon limited historically to the period of capitalist/industrial modernity experienced over the past 200 years, would seem to be counter intuitive. It could certainly be argued that throughout human history people have had everyday lives consisting of elements we would recognise today, however, as Highmore argues:

> While everyday life is not limited to modernity in any essential way, the
> qualitative changes in time and space brought about by industrialisation
> constitute a shift in the patterns of daily life. These qualitative shifts and the
> emergent culture that proceeded them (such as leisure time, commuting and
> so on) make it problematic to think of everyday life as a category that can be
> applied across history (Highmore 2002b: n. 1, p. 33).

Lefebvre, one of the key writers in establishing everyday life as an arena for critical investigation, writes that the quotidian was created by the lived conditions of industrial capitalism:

> Undoubtedly people have always needed to be fed, clothed, housed and have
> had to produce and then re-produce that which has been consumed; but until the
> nineteenth century, until the advent of competitive capitalism and the expansion of
> the world of trade the quotidian as such did not exist (Lefebvre 2009 [1971]: p. 38).[12]

The relationship advanced here between industrial capitalism and the emergence of an identifiable everyday life relates to the ways in which the daily has been shaped by the rhythms and routines necessary to reproduce this system.[13] Examples include the standardisation of time across the country, at first necessitated by railway and telegraph networks in the 1880s (Kern 1983: pp. 11–15); the development of regimented working hours by the 1840s giving rise to the division between work and leisure (Clarke and Critcher 1985: p. 58); a culture of mass consumerism driven by advertising; and the increasingly bureaucratic organisation of society.[14]

Reading modernity, in terms of standardisation, technological development and mass patterns of work and consumption, has led many theorists to situate the everyday not only as a product of modernity but also as a product of the modern city. For example in his study of everyday life in Japan, Harootunian writes that:

> In modernity, during the epoch of industrialisation and the establishment of
> mass society, the places of history are the cities, the expanding industrial sites,
> and their experiences are the everyday (2000: p. 19).

There is a clear connection to be made here, the nature of city living, working and playing undoubtedly produces the rhythms and routines that constitute an identifiable everyday life. However, the impacts of modernity have also been felt in non-metropolitan places, but in different ways. My project is not to just re-situate the rural in existing discourses of modernity, showing that it too felt this, or that it played a part, but to find different stories to tell about modernity, stories that start from a different place.

EVERYDAY LIFE AND OTHER STORIES

It is important to recognise that the everyday is not a transparent realm and a universal understanding of what constitutes the everyday can never be achieved. The designation of certain practices as belonging to the everyday – the daily commute to work for instance – is to create a league of 'others' – unemployed or retired people, parents (usually mothers) whose days are spent looking after children – who do not recognise their own experiences of the daily reflected in this description, and therefore find themselves somehow outside of the everyday (see Highmore 2002b: p. 1).

This is a scenario I recognise from my own research, in that many of the texts which broadly fall into 'everyday life studies' (Moran 2007: p. 166), privilege the city as the place where everyday life is lived.[15] As someone who has lived most of my everyday life in non-urban places I felt that were outside this analysis, I always had to bend the theory to try and make sense of my experience or attempt to rethink my experience in terms of these urban models.

A notable example of the centrality of urban living to the theoretical tradition of everyday life is Michel de Certeau's much anthologised essay 'Walking in the City' (1984). Its prevalence in the everyday life sections of many collected anthologies (During 1999; Lock and Farquhar 2007; Bridge and Watson 2010; Szeman and Kaposy 2011), has made it almost totemic in conceptions of the relationship between the individual and the societal structures which he or she inhabits, a theme which is central to investigating the everyday, and subsequently one that has overwhelmingly been thought through urban living.

However, to read de Certeau entirely as an urban theorist is to miss the wider ambition of his project. Working with the sociologists Luce Giard and Pierre Mayol, de Certeau's aim was to find ways of articulating the everyday as a site of interwoven, often hidden practices. With the intention of bringing this lived fabric of the everyday to the forefront so that '"ways of operating" or doing things, no longer appear as merely the obscure background of social activity' (de Certeau 1984: p. xi). de Certeau aimed to develop methodologies for discovering and articulating the myriad ways in which individuals – conceptualised as consumers – creatively used or 'made with' the products, systems and structures which populate the everyday. In 'Walking in the City', the urban planner's regimented aerial view of New York City is an example of just such a system. The pedestrian who might wander from the prescribed path, cut corners and negotiate obstacles, is engaged in the practice of everyday life. Through this almost unconscious processes of improvisation with the structure of the city, shaping it to his or her own needs and desires. However, as de Certeau notes 'Sly as a fox and twice as quick: there are countless ways of "making do"' (1984: p. 29), and many of the instances of 'making do' revealed in the two volumes of *The Practice of Everyday Life* (Volume 1 1984, Volume 2 1998), take place in locations other than the metropolitan centre. An example of this less urban centric perspective is the inspiration de Certeau finds in a museum in rural Vermont:

> *I remember the marvellous Shelbourne Museum in Vermont where, in 35 houses of a reconstructed village, all the signs, tools, and products of nineteenth-century everyday life teem; everything, from cooking utensils and pharmaceutical goods to weaving instruments, toilet articles, and children's toys can be found in profusion. The display includes innumerable familiar objects, polished, deformed, or made more beautiful by long use; everywhere there are as well the marks of the active hands and labouring of patient bodies for which these things composed the daily circuits, the fascinating presence of absences whose traces were everywhere. At least this village full of abandoned and salvaged objects drew one's attention, through them, to the ordered murmurs of a hundred past or possible villages, and by means of these imbricated traces one began to dream of countless combinations of existences. Like tools, proverbs (and other discourses) are marked by uses; they offer to analysis the imprints of acts or of processes of enunciation (de Certeau 1984: p. 21).[16]*

This discussion of how objects from a village become archives of their many uses and users, may contribute little to my project of disrupting the worn alignment of the rural with the past. This example does, however, play a significant role in de Certeau's thesis that sees the understanding of the practice of everyday life as being comparable to the development of language, in that language consists of formal structures of vocabulary and grammar which are manipulated, shaped and worn through everyday use and adaptation. In a similar way, the structures and products encountered in everyday life are adapted by users to suit their own needs. This is central to de Certeau's notion of the practice of everyday life and is articulated as clearly through this example from the non-metropolitan everyday, as it is in the more famous 'Walking in the City'.

Published in the second volume of *The Practice of Everyday Life* (1998), Luce Giard's investigations also find their subject matter in less urban locations. For example her essay 'Doing Cooking', finds much of its material in her own kitchen, and draws on her memories of learning to cook. Giard's research privileges the kind of knowledge that is so embedded in the everyday it attains a form of invisibility. This is a knowledge contained in the gestural qualities of cooking, in the creativity of improvising with whatever is left in the fridge, a knowledge that is transmitted not through the structured channels of formal education, but the familial environments of the kitchens of mothers and grandmothers. However, it is also a knowledge of confinement, of oppression, of dulling routine, and Giard's own ambivalent feelings are acknowledged when she says:

> *I already knew all the sounds: the gentle hiss of simmering water, the spluttering of melting meat drippings, and the dull thud of kneading hand. A recipe or an inductive word sufficed to arouse a strange anamnesis whereby ancient knowledge and primitive experiences were reactivated in fragments of which I was the heiress and guardian without wanting to be (Giard 1994: p. 153).*

In order to register these invisible qualities of the everyday, these ways of 'doing things' (de Certeau 1984: p. xi), it is often necessary to think differently about methodology, not only in terms of finding ways to bring the everyday out of its taken for granted and therefore invisible realm, but also in thinking about the most appropriate ways in which to record or envision it (see Highmore 2002b: p. 19). Giard employs research methods that might ordinarily fall outside the traditional remit of academic (sociological) investigation.[17] She examines her own journey of learning to cook, together with her childhood memories of the women in her family performing in the kitchen. Significantly in terms of framing my own investigation Giard also calls on material from visual culture, specifically Chantal Ackerman's film *Jeanne Dielman, 23 Quai du Commerce, 1080 Bruxelles* (1975). The film exhaustively maps in real time the repetitive 'feminine' gestures necessary in the maintenance of bodies, houses and appearances. Through this accumulation of gestures, Ackerman constructs the story of a woman whose daily routine of care-taking also includes the prostitution of her body to a faceless man, whom she murders. The film accesses the disturbing combination of boredom, compassion, and violence (both physical and psychological) that constitute so much of the quotidian.

Other challenges to a metro-centric envisioning of the everyday have also come from a feminist perspective.[18] In her article 'Cartes Postals: Representing Paris 1900' (1992), Naomi Schor (like Giard) takes elements of visual culture – postcards of Paris at the turn of the twentieth century – as her inspiration and as an investigative tool. Schor outlines the often binary ways of conceptualising the everyday as either belonging to a male sphere situated in the modern city street, or the female sphere located in the home, and notes their unequal presence in analysis of this field:

> Two widely shared but diametrically opposed views inform what theories we
> have on the everyday: one which we might call the feminine or feminist, though
> it is not necessarily held by women or self described feminists, links the everyday
> with the daily rituals of private life carried out within the domestic sphere
> traditionally presided over by women; the other, the masculine or masculinist,
> sites the everyday in the public spaces and spheres dominated especially, but
> not exclusively, in the modern Western bourgeois societies by men. According
> to the one, the everyday is made up of the countless repetitive gestures and
> small practices that fall under the heading of what the existentialists called
> the contingent. According to the other, the everyday is made up of the chance
> encounters of the streets; its hero is not the housewife but the flâneur ... On the
> whole, what with the current vogue enjoyed by the theoretical works of Walter
> Benjamin and the Frankfurt School, Guy Debord and the situationsists, and other
> modern urban theoreticians of the everyday, I think it would be safe to say that
> the street version of the everyday tends to prevail (Schor 1992: pp. 188–9).

Through an examination of her personal archive of postcards from this period Schor is able to effectively disrupt this opposition. She notes how the postcard images portray scenes from a triumphantly modern city – bustling streets, crowds, traffic and monumental architecture, yet on the reverse side, the written messages speak of the domestic intricacies of the everyday:

> From the backs of these cards emerges a murmur of small voices speaking of
> minor aches and pains, long-awaited engagements, obscure family feuds;

> *reporting on safe arrivals and unexpected delays; ordering goat cheese;*
> *acknowledging receipt of a bouquet of violets, a bonnet; in short, carrying on the*
> *millions of minute transactions, the grain of every-day life (Schor 1992: p. 239).*

The recto and verso planes of these slices of everyday life demonstrate that the public and the private, the excitement of the city street and the familiar routine of the home are intricately woven together and lived simultaneously. Turning our attention to the non-metropolitan produces a similarly interwoven zone where the country and the city begin to overlap and the ancient and the modern are lived simultaneously.

VISUAL CULTURE

The term visual culture gained academic circulation during the 1990s.[19] In some ways it is seen as an alternative to what are perceived as more traditional art historical practices, concerned primarily with object rather than context based analysis; such connoisseurial approaches are applied to a limited range of usually historical objects designated by elite institutions as art, whereas a methodology centred on visual culture recognises that visual experience is not confined to the art gallery or even to the cinema, but is one that permeates all aspects of everyday life. This shift necessarily acknowledges a whole new set of visual encounters as meaningful sites of analysis, establishing a field that is wider than (fine) art, film and TV, indeed necessarily wider than simply the visual, as Irit Rogoff makes clear in her formulation:

> *visual culture opens up an entire world of intertextuality in which images, sounds*
> *and spatial delineations are read on to and through one another, lending ever-*
> *accruing layers of meanings and of subjective responses to each encounter we*
> *might have with film, TV, advertising, art works, buildings or urban environments*
> *(Rogoff 1998: p. 14).*

I would challenge Rogoff's limiting of spatial visual culture to the urban – indeed this book hopes to contribute to a field of study which works from the basis that rural environments are subject to design, construction and convention in different yet comparable ways to urban environments and as such, this research broadens the territory of visual culture. Spatial locations aside, Rogoff's description of the field of visual culture not only emphasises the broad range of visual manifestations available for study, but also that visual experience is a matrix of intersecting stimuli that do not necessarily belong to the primary visual artefact. This is an approach which runs contrary to the often reductive practices of object centred art history. We are reminded that visual experiences do not exist within a pure space, but are products of context and culture.

Moving away from the rarefied air of the art gallery, into an approach which is alert to all kinds of visual communication establishes visual cultures in the terrain of the everyday. Mirzoeff states that visual culture 'is not just part of your everyday life, it *is* your everyday life' (Mirzoeff 1998: p. 3), a statement that recognises the essentially visual nature of modern (and post-modern) experiences of the world.

This shift in thinking reflects not only the increase in the prevalence of visual communications and technology that has characterised the past century but also to a shift in perspective that Mirzoeff, referencing W.J.T. Mitchell's influential *Picture Theory* (1994), sees as the potential for visual culture to disrupt the long standing Western tradition of privileging the spoken/written text over the visual representation and experience. It is however, important to remember that the prevelance of the visual does not produce a coherent world-as-picture, everyday life is characterised by multiple, fractured visual experience. The practice of visual culture offers the possibility of picking routes through this visual onslaught and seeking out 'ambivalences, interstices and places of resistance' (Mirzeoff 1998: p. 8).

The close relationship between everyday life and visual culture has been significantly reflected in contemporary cultural production. Stephen Johnstone notes the prevalence of everyday life as a theme for international biennials and exhibitions from the mid-1990s onwards, notably the same period in which visual culture as a discipline was being mapped out.[20] This popularity has led to the term everyday life attaining, in Johnstone's words 'the status of global art-world touchstone' (Johnstone 2008: p. 12). It is off course possible to trace the representation and exploration of everyday life themes in art well beyond the past two decades. Lynne Gumpert's anthology (1997) details the importance of everyday life in post war French culture, notably through Nouvelle Vague film practices which not only represented the rhythms and routines of life at that time, but also experimented with its rendering in real time. In the inter-war period artists identified with the surrealist movement were also engaged in finding ways to represent the inherent strangeness of the daily experience of modernity (Highmore 2002a: pp. 45–59; Gardiner 2000: pp. 24–42).

In his overview of how artists engage with the everyday Johnstone identifies several strategies, or ways of working with the daily. These include: finding value in the mundane or overlooked; showing how the ordinary can also be extraordinary; seeing the everyday as a site of controlled behaviour and consumption and resistance to that control; and finally working with an ethnographic aesthetic based on an observation of everyday things, people and practices (Johnstone 2008: pp. 12–13). The move towards seeing everyday life as a site of meaning can clearly be linked to a way of thinking about visual culture which does not reproduce a hierarchical system of high and low or popular culture. A position that indicates an attention to the everyday, an engagement with the overlooked, can be considered as a political strategy that works towards a displacement of dominant ideologies through representing the unrepresented. It is perhaps somewhat ironic now that current artistic enthusiasm for the everyday has created a glut of representation of the once overlooked. However, while this unrepresented realm is often realised in terms of class, gender, ethnicity, and sexuality, it is usually situated within an entirely urban context.[21] What continues to be overlooked within this myriad of cultural production is non-metropolitan everyday and as such this research has centred on seeking out the visual cultures which go some way towards addressing this under-representation.

I would like to argue that elements of visual culture can provide an alternative set of resources which enable heterogeneous experiences of the non-metropolitan everyday to be registered and communicated. I am not asserting that these resources reveal what could be referred to as a 'true' picture of the non-metropolitan everyday, as this is not particularly useful terminology. Rather these elements of visual culture make visible and activate the multi-various associations which have gathered around the non-metropolitan everyday. This methodology values the reading of objects of visual culture for what they reveal about the culture in which they were produced and important tools of analysis on themselves.

COLLAGE

Collage is made from the everyday, famously the experimental collage of Picasso and the Cubists of the early 1900s began to challenge traditional languages of representation through an amalgamation of everyday life as subject matter and everyday life as material (Ades 1993: p. 37). Collage as a visual tradition makes use of the low grade visual noise of everyday life, the litter of packaging, flyers, newspaper, advertisements, tickets, magazines, postcards, and found images. The throw away nature and the mass availability of this 'stuff' signals the over production so redolent of industrial modernity (O'Reilly 2008: p. 17).

Collage plays an important role throughout this thesis. It is directly present in many of the pieces of visual culture that feature in the following chapters such as Lord Berners' montage for the cover of the *Wiltshire Shell Guide* in Chapter 2, and the Women's Institute scrapbooks in Chapter 4. It is also indirectly present in elements such as the litter trails described in Chapter 3, which can be thought of as a form of topographical collage, and the *Folk Archive* discussed in Chapter 5, which can be seen as a constellation of disparate elements brought together through the processes of collection and display.

Furthermore, collage is a methodologically productive way of approaching and registering the everyday. Conceptually it is a medium that privileges the detail or the fragment, allowing it to maintain its integrity – its particularity, whilst also putting it into to circulation with other elements in a wider orbit of ideas and meanings. This is an approach which is particularly useful when thinking about something as amorphous but also as personally specific as everyday life – an arena that requires constant negotiation between the micro and macro poles of individual experience and structural controls.[22] To attempt to meaningfully investigate the everyday it becomes necessary to work with the detail, the specific, perhaps even the personal, seeing how they might relate to or generate new meanings on a macro-scale.[23] In this way, rather than taking the form of a broad survey of visual culture that has taken towns, villages and the countryside as its subject matter, this thesis operates through activating a constellation of everyday details – 'A' roads, litter, electricity pylons, Morris dancers – as ways of accessing wider stories about rural modernity and everyday life.

Collage has the ability to draw directly on 'reality' using fragments from everyday life, but it can also act as an agent of disruption of that reality. The combination of disparate images and materials has the potential to rupture the taken for granted surface of the everyday, revealing its illusionary nature and creating the possibility of something different. Walter Benjamin saw this potentiality in montage as practised both in epic theatre and in avant-garde art and films. He argued that it disrupts any unproblematic, immersive or purely aesthetic reading of a scene, creating visual and temporal interruptions. These bumps or jolts prevent a smooth rendering of an illusionistic surface and force the viewer to question the reality of the situation they are witnessing (Benjamin 1970 [1934]). Later, writing about her dissatisfaction with the market driven production of apolitical art, Lucy Lippard argues that the collage aesthetic is the only effective methodology in a society where 'most of us, on the most basic level, exist in a downright surrealist situation' (Lippard 1981: p. 17). Lippard saw the fundamental mechanism of collage as the placing of 'this up against that', and argued that the juxtaposition of different realities that this approach enables, creates new realities or new ways of thinking to emerge (Lippard 1981: p. 16).

In this book such juxtapositions of different realities often emerge as conjunctions of the old and new, for example the images that appear at the start of each of the following chapters are in themselves forms of collage. Collected throughout my research, they represent moments of unexpected juxtaposition which dislodged my thinking around the non-metropolitan realm. They are at once singular occurrences but could also be read as synecdoches. For instance the uncomfortable meeting of dual carriageway and Bronze Age burial mound with which the next chapter begins, challenged my assumptions about development and preservation in rural places and seems to give a sense of this wider dialectic. This combination speaks of the tensions which arise from the daily negotiations between these forces, characterising something of the multiple natures of rural modernity. The image at the start of Chapter 3 is of a single stiletto in a stretch of woodland. Its presence here forms a disconcerting juxtaposition that disrupts received notions of the use and meanings of non-metropolitan spaces, revealing narratives that provide a resistive counter current to mainstream accounts of conservation and ownership. Chapter 4 begins with an image that is more easily identified as a piece of collage; taken from one of the WI scrapbooks it shows a disembodied hand holding a kettle, a single electric light bulb and an electric fire. This image initially caught my attention for its use of modernist montage techniques, emanating not from the urban avant-garde but from the Women's Institute. However, the juxtapositions of image and text in this piece access anxieties around preservation and development; while electricity is welcomed in the village, residents are relieved that the church and its beautiful surroundings will not be besmirched by overhead wiring systems. The image with which Chapter 5 begins was taken at a local calendar custom, the Tichborne Dole. In this tradition which dates back to the thirteenth century flour is distributed to residents of the Parish of Tichborne: it was the momentary conjunction between the old gallon buckets used to measure the flour and the Tesco's 'Bag for Life', that formed a montage of ancient and modern, and challenged ideas about our relationship to the past and notions of the rural as a site of continuity.

In this way collage plays a role as a way of conceptualising rural modernity as a spatial and temporal collage. I started this chapter with a description of the Beating of the Bounds ceremony that takes place in Oxford each year. This festival accesses the idea of collage as a spatial/temporal phenomenon in that its performance (a spatial performance, where the boundaries of a space are literally enacted) accesses the simultaneous overlay of different spaces and temporalities which has become a theme of this research. This overlay is generated by the contemporary iteration of a tradition which has been practised over hundreds of years, and more literally in the overlay of the houses and pubs which have been built over the boundary stones. This way of thinking about the space of the non-metropolitan has been useful in trying to think critically about the tension between the ancient and the modern, and development and preservation, which is an important element of conceptualising forms of rural modernity.

STRUCTURE

The book looks at moments where the terms modernity, rural and everyday overlap and become problematic or charged. Rather than focusing on a historical survey of the changing patterns of everyday life in non-metropolitan places, I have identified themed sets of practices or activities that seem to highlight my primary concerns of re-thinking the rural as a site of modernity, troubling the distinction between country and city and accessing tensions between ancient and modern.[24]

The thesis is structured around four themes or occurrences: Driving, Litter, The Women's Institute, and Festivals and Folk Art. Clearly this choice of areas for investigation would appear eccentric for anyone expecting this study to be a stocktaking exercise in representing an itemization of what constitutes non-metropolitan everyday life. The logic of my choice is to focus on the very items that productively problematise holding onto a received idea of what constitutes the rural. The subject of Chapter 2 is driving in the countryside. The mass adoption of the automobile has had a tremendous effect on the way the countryside looks, is occupied, accessed and thought about. Increased personal mobility changed who occupies the countryside, making it the venue for both motorised day trippers and home for a new breed of commuters. It also radically changed the look and feel of the countryside leading to fears that the country would be enveloped by a subtopia (Nairn 1955) or megalopolis (Mumford 1940; Gottman 1961) wiping out distinctions between country and city. This chapter examines roads and driving from a non-metropolitan perspective, which recovers the experience of speed and technology as one which belongs to the realm of the rural. It critiques the popular association of the road and the non-place by reclaiming the motorway as a situated rural phenomenon. Road building and use is also a site which vividly brings out tensions around preservation and development. This anxious relationship is examined through the lens of speed and stillness in the countryside. It draws on the illustrated essay *Outrage* by Ian Nairn (1955), a film *3 hours from here* (2004) by contemporary artist Andrew Cross, advertisements from *Country Life*, and the 1930s *Shell County Guides*, edited by John Betjeman.

Chapter 3 examines reactions to litter in the countryside. Litter is a modern phenomena, and thinking about it in relation to the countryside rather than the urban environment is an act that restores something of the modern to the rural, however in an anxious problematic way. Litter is an agent of disorder and this chapter examines how it can demonstrate and disrupt boundaries between the country and the city, and access fears around change and preservation, revealing that people as well as things can be considered to be in the wrong place. By examining papers from the Mass-Observation archive on the appearance of so called 'litter trails' in the Cambridgeshire countryside during World War II, it reveals the non-metropolitan as an unstable potentially dangerous place under threat of invasion. The notion of invasion is also the basis for the anti-litter campaigns also examined in this chapter, this time however litter signals invasion by tourists and keeping Britain tidy becomes an act of patriotism while dropping litter becomes an act of treachery. This narrative is then complicated by thinking about practices of littering by residents rather than visitors by drawing on the works *Dangerous Pathway* (1999) and *Lurky Place* (1978) by artist Stephen Willats, that bring into play different notions of ownership and use of the countryside.

The central source for Chapter 4 is a set of scrapbooks produced by the rural women's organisation the Women's Institute in the 1960s. It examines the fascinating role that the organisation played as unofficial archivists of the non-metropolitan everyday through the creation of scrapbooks which record a snap shot of their villages at a specific moment in time. The scrapbooks, which are held in county archives and by the Institutes themselves, reveal something of the complexity in how modernity has been felt in non-metropolitan places, evidencing dramatic yet uneven changes in the landscape, in consumption and in the home. This chapter works towards re-situating the rural, the female and the domestic everyday as operating as part of wider networks of modernity. In particular this interconnectedness is examined in relation to the national grid, a physical and conceptual network of modernity and an element of the non-metropolitan everyday that features significantly in the scrapbook material.

Chapter 5 is based around festivals and folk art, particularly the calendar customs which are enacted annually in rural communities. Traditionally a focus for carnivalesque behaviour and communal exuberance, this chapter tracks how the contemporary function of these festivals can be thought of as enactments of an anxious relationship with the past. Drawing on an exploration of my own experience of attending a local custom together with an analysis of the work of photographers Anna Fox, Homer Sykes, Tony Ray-Jones and Benjamin Stone, it examines the notion of the 'performance of the village', looking at how both the importance and the absurdities of these festivals have been communicated. The *Folk Archive* project by artists Jeremy Deller and Alan Kane is then investigated for the simultaneity of non-metropolitan experience, which as the beating of the bounds festival mentioned at the beginning of this introduction makes clear, is an overlay of different geographies and temporalities, revealing the non-metropolitan everyday as a site of fluid, creative responses to the contemporary village.

Collectively these chapters aim to relocate the topography of the everyday from its habitually urban focus, out into the English countryside, recasting the rural as an active and complex site of modernity. They complicate established distinctions between the country and the city and explore the ancient and the modern as simultaneously experienced aspects of the non-metropolitan everyday.

Importantly, this approach theoretically repopulates the rural, thinking it not only as a space to be looked at, moved through or visited, but as a space which is practised and lived.

NOTES

1   Such as the Abbots Bromley Horn Dance, which rather than taking place in the Spring time happens in September and involves men of the village dressing in costume with headdresses made from deer antlers and dancing around the parish boundaries, a gruelling practice which starts early in the morning and goes on for around 12 hours (Hogg 1971: p. 80).

2   An example of this is Sue Clifford and Angela King's book *England in Particular* (2006), which describes itself as 'A celebration of the commonplace, the local, the vernacular and the distinctive' (front cover). This popular interest can also be seen in the contemporary enthusiasm for locally distinctive foods and farmers' markets, feeding into environmental and tourism discourses, see Holloway and Kneafsey (2000).

3   For further discussion of landscape in relation to national identity see Daniels (1994), Edensor (2002) and Matless (1998).

4   'old maids cycling … ' is from Orwell (1941). It is misquoted by Major. Orwell has it 'old maids biking to Holy Communion through the mists of the autumn mornings' (p. 11). What Major fails to note is that in Orwell's picture of England this picturesque rural image is combined with 'The clatter of clogs in the Lancashire mill towns, the to-and-fro of the lorries on the Great North Road, the queues outside the Labour Exchanges, the rattle of pin tables in the Soho pubs' (p. 11). Orwell was of course a highly vocal and committed socialist, so it is somewhat ironic that a Conservative Prime Minister would turn to him as a figure representing a cosy societal status quo.

5   This directive is taken from the post 1981 activity of Mass Observation, a more detailed discussion of the origins of the organisation and its work in 1930–1940s is made in Chapter 3.

6   Significantly, given the countryside's link with the past as discussed below, repeats of *Coast* are also being shown on the nostalgia based digital channel *Yesterday*.

7   Significantly it is the Conservative press who pursue these stories most vehemently, the most recent panics centre on crayfish (*The Daily Telegraph* 2011a), exotic plants (Derbyshire 2011) and killer shrimp (*The Daily Telegraph* 2011b).

8   The history of the National Trust as custodian of national heritage is discussed further in Hewison (1987: pp. 51–82).

9   It is interesting to note here that one of Natural England's policies is to provide funds to preserve ruined farm buildings in their ruined state (Natural England 2011).

10   A BBC report into the coverage of rural areas on the network cites the Sunday evening programme *Countryfile* as one of the broadcaster's 'rural gems' Hancock (2014).

11   Young (2010) also identifies a tendency in 1960–1970s British cinema to access an old weird Britain referencing examples such as *The Witchfinder General* (1968) set in the fields and fenlands of East Anglia.

12   While much of the writing establishing everyday life as a theoretical tradition works with this historically limited notion of the everyday, Felski has noted that the history of writing about everyday life extends from ancient Greece, to medieval England, to the Enlightenment (Felski 1999: p. 16).

13 Kaplan and Ross (1987: p. 2) note that another term for everyday life could be social reproduction.

14 Clarke and Critcher argue that this change could be considered the invention of leisure, however Borsay (2006: p. 9) draws on Burke (1995) to argue that leisure was not an invention of the industrial revolution rather that it can be thought of as a qualitative experience that can be traced back beyond 1500.

15 This focus is also reflected by much of the secondary literature on everyday life, which is centred on analysis of writers and theorists who situate their ideas within the modern urban experience such as: Walter Benjamin, George Simmel, Siegfried Kracauer, Georges Perec, and The Situationists Highmore (2002a), Moran (2005), Gardiner (2000), Sheringham (2006).

16 The Shelbourne Museum in Vermont was founded by Electra Havemeyer Webb (1888–1960), a collector of American folk art, in 1947. It continues to display its collection of Impressionist paintings, folk art, quilts and textiles, decorative arts, furniture, American paintings, and an extensive collection of seventeenth to twentieth-century artefacts (Shelbourne Museum 2014).

17 Later in the essay Giard also uses more traditional sociological methods of research such as loosely structured interviews see 'Women's Voices' in de Certeau, Giard and Mayol (1994: pp. 159–63).

18 In addition to Schor these include: Felski (1999), Ross (1995) and Smith (1988).

19 The *Visual Cultures Reader* edited by Nicholas Mirzoeff, published in 1998, attempted a preliminary definition of the field and a compilation of key areas for study. Another important moment in the development of this term was an extensive article in *October* where leading academics were asked to respond to the notion of Visual Culture (Alpers et al. 1996). During this time Visual Cultures departments have been created in universities, in some cases replacing, in name if not in practice, Art History departments.

20 Johnstone makes a comprehensive list of international biennales, site specific projects, historical overviews of modernism and themed group exhibitions based around the theme of the everyday from 1995–2007. To add to this list two more recent examples include 'Life a Users Manual', Art Sheffield 2010, and 'The Spectacle of the Everyday', 10th Lyons Biennale, 16 September 2009–3 January 2010.

21 There are of course some notable exceptions including projects which engage with how the quotidian is played out in rural places, such as Grizedale Arts, which is covered more extensively in the conclusion of this book and Griffin (2009).

22 Kaplan and Ross (1987: p. 4) note the importance of 'attempting to grasp the everyday without relegating it to either institutional codes and systems or to the private perceptions of a monadic subject'.

23 Examples of this privileging of the detail and its relationship with the macro include Giard's (1998) approach to using her own memories and experiences of cooking to think about hidden practices and knowledges of the everyday (detailed earlier), also Ross (1995) using products such as cars and soap to map the relationship between France and its colonies in the 1950s.

24 As will become apparent, although I am ostensibly engaging in what I have defined as the non-metropolitan, my study is limited to England and many of the sources reflect my own experience of non-metropolitan life which has taken place in the Midlands and the South of England.

2

Speed and Stillness: Driving in the Countryside

Just north of Winchester, in the south of England, the A34 cuts through a group of Bronze Age barrows or burial mounds. The small grassy heaps sit on each side of the busy dual carriageway, so close to the traffic that the tussocky edge of one of these structures seems to be shaved by the road surface. Travelling at speed, the majority of road users may not notice these man made bumps in the landscape, and if they do, they are unlikely to connect them to the ancient burial practices of which they are evidence. The proximity of the road to these earth works – the uncomfortable montage of tarmac and grass, reveals something of the complex relationship between the ancient and the modern, and processes of preservation and development; a relationship which lies just under the surface of everyday non-metropolitan experience.

2.1   Burial mound seen from A34, 2014.

This chapter explores how these tensions are played out through experiences of driving in the countryside. It is divided into four parts, each taking its lead from a different visual resource. First it examines how road building and increased automobility have contributed to a blurring of the boundaries between country and city, looking at the idea of 'subtopia' as expressed in Iain Nairn's publication *Outrage* (1955). Second, through analysis of *3 hours from here* (2004), a film by artist Andrew Cross, it questions the idea of the 'non-place' in relation to a non-metropolitan perspective on motorways. This section also attempts to re-think motorways as non-metropolitan places, rather than urban enclaves, and in so doing, recovers the experience of speed and technology as one which can belong to the realm of the rural. The uncomfortable relationship between speed, technology and the countryside is further explored in the third section which centres on how driving in the countryside has been conceptualised in the renowned magazine *Country Life*.

The chapter finishes with an examination of how the seemingly contradictory forces of development and preservation, technology and nature, speed and stillness are interwoven through the pages of the *Shell County Guides* produced in the 1930s.

SUBTOPIA

The A34 was the road on which architectural journalist Ian Nairn travelled from Southampton to Carlisle and onwards into the Highlands – a journey which he documented in a special edition of *Architectural Review* in 1955 called *Outrage*.[1] At this time the A34 was the major North-South route through the country, taking Nairn through the southern counties of Hampshire and Oxfordshire, into the industrial Midlands and up to the North West coast through Lancashire and the Lake District.[2] The rationale behind the journey was to document the many and various ways that the British countryside was, in Nairn's eyes, being consumed by agents of modern development. He begins the issue with an aerial view of an unidentified stretch of countryside, predominantly featuring small fields bordered by hedgerows and wooded areas, the scene presents the countryside as largely uninhabited with just three visible properties some distance from each other. With this image he overlays the text:

> *This is the first and last view of rural England to be seen in these pages. It is just a reminder of what we are squandering with all the means at our disposal, confident that there will always be some left over. What follows proves that this is a criminally feckless illusion, and that we are in fact obliterating the whole countryside (Nairn 1955: p. 364).*

This rhetoric of loss is familiar from Lowenthal's (1994) analysis of the narratives that are constructed around the countryside (see Chapter 1). However, rather than the erosion of footpaths, the invasion of alien species or the ruination of historic buildings, Nairn's outrage is directed towards spread of a phenomenon he terms 'subtopia', which he describes as:

> *A mean and middle state, neither town nor country, an even spread of abandoned aerodromes and fake rusticity, wire fences, traffic roundabouts, gratuitous notice-boards, car-parks and Things in Fields. It is a morbid condition which spreads both ways from suburbia, out into the country, and back into the de-vitalised hearts of towns, so that the most sublime backgrounds, urban or rural, English or foreign, are now seen only over a foreground of casual and unconsidered equipment, litter and lettered admonitions – Subtopia is the world of universal low-density mess (Nairn 1955: p. 373).[3]*

This quote complicates the narrative that has become familiar throughout this research: that signs of modernity spread out from the cities into the country. This is a problematic story because it casts the rural as the victim of development, rather than acknowledging the complexities of rural experiences of modernity. Nairn however sees the origin of this development as the suburbs and the movement as lateral in both directions: into the countryside and back into the inner city. Whether the suburbs can really be seen as productive of subtopia in this way is debatable, however Nairn is really focusing on the aesthetic of subtopia which he identifies as being of the suburbs – banal, ill designed, utilitarian, and standardised. What is particularly interesting here is that he identifies as a product of subtopia a state that is 'neither town nor country'.[4] In this way subtopia alerts us to the ways in which the modern developments charted by Nairn, have complicated the distinctions between town and country. Roads are agents in this process in that they join town to country, and as is argued below, development spreads along roads blurring the boundaries of brown and green field. In addition the new arterial roads of this time made commuting an option for many more people, significantly changing the demographic of rural places (Rogers 1989). In this way using the term non-metropolitan to think about places that feel unable to qualify as 'rural enough' – neither town nor country, becomes particularly relevant.

The term is clearly an amalgamation of suburbia and utopia, neatly making Nairn's point that the mediocre architecture and attitudes of suburbia were being valorised as the desirable norm (a movement towards utopian living) and were multiplying accordingly.[5] However, it is also interesting to note how subtopia relates to the other meanings of the word utopia. Philosopher Louis Marin sees as central to the definition of utopia, that it operates in between established dialectical or oppositional forces:

> It edges its way between the contraries and thus is the discursive expression
> of the neutral (defined as 'neither one, nor the other' of the contraries). Here is
> one example: More's Utopia is neither England nor America, neither the Old nor
> the New World; it is the in-between of the contradiction at the beginning of the
> sixteenth century of the Old and New Worlds (Marin 1984: p. xiii).

In the case of subtopia it could be asserted that it is in between the contraries of the country and the city, and provides a third and different formulation, a way of acknowledging a space of possibility that is neither of these things. While in Nairn's formulation subtopia is a warning call rather than an aspiration, it does provide a vocabulary for articulating the increasingly modern experience of in-betweeness. Working with More's *Utopia* ([1516] 1986) Marin discusses the geographic instability of the island, noting that its latitude and longitude are never satisfactorily revealed, writing: 'U-topia, *ou-topia*, no-place' (Marin 1984: p. 85).[6] There are links to be made here with the notion of the non-metropolitan, a geographical nonsense, a relational term, but one necessary for imagining and articulating certain forms of experience that happen as a product of being in-between the old and the new, ancient and modern, preservation and development, and speed and stillness.

Subtopia is used by Nairn to refer to many architectural characteristics of modern development but he was chiefly concerned by the growth of low density housing developments which extend the footprint of cities and towns and had started over the two decades previous to his publication, to attach themselves to villages. Many protests against the development of new housing specifically identified the building of new roads or the improvement of old ones as being a cause of a new ill, termed ribbon development. This refers to the practice of building single strips of new houses and shops alongside a main road. This was seen as an inefficient use of space as building in strips, rather than in cul-de-sacs for example, extended the foot print of habitation further out into the countryside. Books edited by Clough Williams-Ellis, a founding member of the Council for the Protection of Rural England (CPRE), such as *England and the Octopus* (1928) and *Britain and Beast* (1937), both contain various tirades against ribbon development. The front cover of the former showing the green and pleasant land being invaded by the sinuous tentacles of an enormous pink octopus. The eight legged brute was supposed to represent the modern development of roads and houses spreading through the land, as was the less specific 'beast'.[7] Moran notes that in many ways certain battles against this spread or 'sprawl' as it is often called had been won in the decade before Nairn's publication, with the introduction of the Town and Country Planning Act in 1947 which advocated much stricter controls on new development (Moran 2009: p. 137). However, even in the 1970s developments of this type persisted as a cause for concern, with Edward Hyams in *The Changing Face of Britain* citing increasing car use and rural availability of electricity as the chief reason for the continued popularity of ribbon developments (Hyams 1977: pp. 210–15).

For Nairn, however, the concept of subtopia was about more than road building and its associated developments. He asserts that a subtopic landscape represented the spread of a sort of sameness throughout the land; he feared that the country would become one large indistinguishable suburb of itself, and worse than that it would be ugly. Nairn identified this problem of sameness as a product of standardisation and economic expediency. He identifies various everyday, taken for granted details such as wire fences, television aerials, pylons and road signs, as agents of subtopia. One full page is given over to a photomontage of lampposts (Figure 2.2), which he uses to argue that rather than thinking about the introduction of lampposts into an area as a project which requires a sensitivity to the existing environment and as such should be approached on a case by case basis, he asserts that these 'diagrams of progress' (telephone/electricity poles, lampposts etc.) are 'treated by their authors as if they were invisible' (Nairn 1955: p. 317). He continues:

> That is just what all these aren't: the reason – the usual one in matters of
> England's appearance – is a combination of out-of-hand standardisation
> and expediency. Standardisation – 25 foot poles on main roads, 15 foot poles
> on minor roads produces fittings of incredible size well above the roof line.
> Expediency provides the concrete – steel shortage – and the clumsy designs …
> They stamp any scene with their apathetic pattern (Nairn 1955: p. 372).

Such standardisation is a notion that Lefebvre saw as key to an understanding of modern everyday life. Philip Wander writing in response to Lefebvre, demonstrates how our everyday relationships with the world are constructed through such standardisation driven by bureaucratic (state) and economic (capitalist) expediency.[8] Wander describes this situation with an example that speaks to some aspects of the outrage felt by Nairn:

> The shape and content of our lives is the product of a number of decisions in
> which we do not participate and about which we may or may not be aware.
> The building in which I live is the product of negotiations between builders,
> environmentalists, and bankers: its cost, which is a product of interest rates,
> a depression in the construction industry, and the efforts made by unions to

2.2   Iain Nairn, Lamp Standards, from *Outrage*, 1955. Courtesy of RIBA Library Photographs Collection and the Estate of Ian Nain.

*preserve jobs, as well as its shape – the kind of building materials used, where
it sits on the lot, its relation to the sun at mid-day. The nature surrounding me?
Every shrub is planned, its selection influenced by what is planted on the freeways
and in front of office buildings (this establishes a fashion and lowers the cost of
the plants involved). The sky, the azure blue of romantic poems, is laced with
wires the telephone company, electric utilities, and lumber interests did not wish
to bury (Wander 2009 [1984]: viii–ix).*

Wander's analysis shows that it is possible to see the spread of this subtopian
sameness, not only as a product of ill considered design, but as a product of the
many bureaucratic and economic forces structuring the everyday. One of the
illustrations by Gordon Cullen which feature throughout the book, which could
easily be an observation of many locations, both rural and urban today, eloquently
summarises these processes. It shows the telephone wires that it cost too much to
bury; the generic municipal planting schemes devised to be most efficient in terms
of cost of plants and maintenance, whilst still communicating a sufficient amount
of civic pride to attract investment/tourism and to reduce disaffection and crime;
the jumbled road signs, soon to become a product of standardisation across the
country, might point to a one-way system implemented by local government as
necessary for the increased road users to negotiate streets designed for minimal
traffic;[9] the tree in the centre has been shorn of most of its limbs, to eliminate leafy
branches obscuring traffic signs and advertisements and then shedding onto
the pavements necessitating clearance; space becomes a product sold to firms
for advertising in order for them to sell more things to us; and what we do with
the things we've bought once we've consumed them also becomes a municipal
problem with a municipal answer: the litter bin.

While all of this is eminently recognisable, something that is lacking in Nairn's
account is the resident's perspective – the actual experience of living in places
he feels are touched by subtopia. It is significant that it is not the arterial road
that is the agent of subtopia but the ribbon development that follows it, for the
road is key to Nairn's perspective on the countryside which is very much that of a
visitor. He refers to the countryside as scenery, view and background, presumably
accessed through the car window. We saw Nairn begin his book with an image of
the uninhabited countryside, this is his ideal, the rural as an empty space available
for the rest and recuperation of the urbanite. He asserts that the duty of the 'man-
in-the-street' is 'two-fold: on the one hand, to bring to the highest pitch of effective
life his man-made environment – the "city" – on the other, to put limits to it as enable
him to keep contact with the wild – the "country"' (Nairn 1955: p. 367). This idea
is tied up with cultural imaginary of the countryside as possessing health-giving
properties, a notion that is seen in the idealised body of the rural labourer found in
late nineteenth century paintings (Holt 2003: p. 6), the idea of the 'Organic English
Body' described by Matless (1998: pp. 136–70), and the idea that the countryside is
morally improving (Joad 1937).

Nairn's exploration of Subtopia usefully complicates the distinctions between
town and country, however rather than productively suggesting an alertness to
the different ways in which modernity is experienced in these zones, he instead
sees subtopia as a leveller of experience, an agent of ill designed sameness

homogenising the nation. In the next section we see how Nairn's predictions of sameness, or loss of identity have been played out in the contemporary landscape with an examination of the work of Andrew Cross and what it reveals about the non-metropolitan as non-place.

RE-PLACING THE RURAL NON-PLACE

The latest homage to the A34 has been made by artist Andrew Cross in his film *3 hours from here* (2004). The film documents a journey from Southampton to Manchester, from the cab of a heavy goods vehicle. Using a fixed camera which periodically alternates between a shot of the view through the windscreen and view through the passenger window, and with only ambient sound, a somnambulistic passivity pervades this visual and durational record of the state of the nation characterised by repetitive similitude.

The starting point for this journey is Southampton's docks. The film begins with a shot of a big yellow crane manoeuvring an anonymous freight container which we assume is to be our cargo. The choice of Southampton as a point from which to begin is a reference to Nairn's trip and perhaps more famously to J.B. Priestley's *An English Journey* (1934), in which the author made a tour of the nation visiting rural areas and industrial towns to report on a country that he perceived to be 'in crisis' (Drabble 1997: p. 7).[10] Southampton, it seems has been a popular place to leave:

> *it had no existence in my mind as a real town, where you could buy and sell, and bring up children; it existed only as a muddle of railway sidings, level crossings,*

2.3   Andrew Cross, *3 hours from here (an English Journey)*, 2004.

customs houses and dock sheds: something to have done with as soon as
possible (Priestley 1977 [1934]: p. 27).[11]

Almost 50 years later Cross' film might be seen to function as a further instalment to Nairn's *Outrage*. However, rather than documenting the spread of the kind of residential subtopia of low density housing and ill conceived municipal street furniture predicted by Nairn, it instead records the spread of a different type of development, that of the network of motorways and their accompanying 'Big Shed' warehouse complexes, which in the years following the publication of Nairn's book have become so much a part of the English landscape.[12] While Nairn's book predicted the ruination of the small towns and villages that he passed through in 1955, he failed to foresee that the most major development in the coming decades would mean that these places would no longer offend the eye of the motorist as they have been in large part literally bypassed by new roads circumnavigating awkward town and village centres.[13]

Cross' film reveals a network of sameness, a complex of wiry roads knotted together by roundabouts. Mile after mile of black-top and non-descript green embankment mean that any orientation through distinctive landmarks becomes impossible. All navigation is delegated to the standardised and highly coded road signs. Travelling in this way becomes abstract and placeless, roads are numbered rather than named, they skirt the edges of towns and cities in a state of unbelonging. Huge and abundant, blue and white hoardings provide a shopping list of places, their only meaning derived from their relative distances. When you are on the road, that's where you are: on the road and in between, 'I'm on the A34 between Newbury and Oxford' one might yell into a mobile phone.

The abdication of place, the settling for the state of in between, situates motorways and fast roads more generally in the realm of the *non-place*, a concept articulated most notably by the French anthropologist Marc Augé (1995).[14] For Augé the non-place is a product of supermodernity, a kind of hyped up, speeded up version of the modern where hollowness and disconnection are symptomatic of the accelerated processes of late stage capitalism and global being, 'If place can be defined as relational, historical and concerned with identity, then a space which cannot be defined as relational, historical or concerned with identity will be a non-place' (Augé 1995: pp. 77–8).

Augé sees non-places as essentially transitional spaces through which people and goods move on their way to somewhere else, places like airport departure lounges, supermarkets and of course, motorways (Augé 1995: p. 79). These locations appear to have no history or make no connection with their histories. In the case of new roads and supermarkets, it is often difficult to remember what occupied the space before they emerged, as if their manifestation has conjured a new piece of land into existence, their construction often appearing to seamlessly alter the landscape making it difficult to feel as if they have not always been there.[15] The ahistoricity of the non-place means they are entirely spaces of the present, in which time can seem suspended, or at least different, for example the black and orange roadside display units which hang like rectangular thunder clouds over sections of the motorway now claim time for their own purposes, conflating it with distance and progress along the road 'J9 for A34, 12 miles – 10 minutes' they might say.

Non-places offer few opportunities for human to human interaction, an individual entering a non-place remains an individual, few or no connections are made with others. While driving on motorways a few signals such as the flashing of lights or intricate indication routines represent a kind of impoverished communication, however actual interaction with other drivers is to be avoided at all costs, out of fear that an accidental catching of the eye might invite an act of 'road rage'.[16] Identity might be recorded in a non-place, but one always remains essentially anonymous. At airports passports are scanned, in supermarkets payment cards are inserted into chip and pin devices, on the road CCTV and speed cameras register number plates. However, this numerical identity does not displace anonymity between other occupants of the non-place, this impersonal identity is known only to the state – registered on a giant database.

The non-place operates through signs and messages rather than human interactions.

Orders given by illuminated over head signs are changed remotely by an unseen hand, information is communicated silently and impersonally based not on your individual journey or destination but on a system of standardised measurements and road signs. This situation is made particularly evident in a startling moment in Cross' film when after around an hour of silence punctuated only by the low level sound of the road and the occasional tick of the lorry's indicator, the driver stops at the M6 toll road and a few words of greeting from the gate operator seem to glimmer like coins thrown out into the abyssal grey of the motorway non-place.

In his essay 'Notes on a New Town', Lefebvre comments on how the newly built town of Mourenx has been planned to function through these impersonal forms of communication, becoming reduced to a set of signs:

> Mourenx has taught me many things. Here objects wear their social credentials: their function … When an object is reduced to nothing but its own function, it is also reduced to signifying itself and nothing else; there is virtually no difference between it and a signal, and to all intents and purposes a group of these objects become a signalling system. As yet there are not many traffic lights in Mourenx. But in a sense the place is already nothing but traffic lights (Lefebvre 1995 [1962]: p. 119).

Lefebvre wonders if the potential residents of Mourenx will obey these signs, will they shop in the places signed as shopping centres, ask for advice in the planned advice bureau? He asks, is this functionalist world of signs capable of creating the ideal community, or is it more likely to harden all spontaneity, and result in deadening boredom?

Boredom is certainly the dominant characteristic of Cross' filmic account of motorway travel, with hours of indistinguishable landscaping punctuated with the occasional sign communicating the rules of the road. However, Augé takes this idea further arguing that our relationship with the landscape through which we are travelling is reduced to a text of signs and symbols:

> it is the texts planted along the wayside that tell us about the landscape and make its secret beauties explicit. Main roads no longer pass through towns, but lists of their notable features … appear on big signboards nearby. In a sense the

traveller is absolved of the need to stop or even look. The landscape keeps its
distance, but its natural or architectural details give rise to a text ... Motorway
travel is thus doubly remarkable: it avoids, for functional reasons, all the principle
places it takes us; and it makes comments on them (Augé 1995: p. 97).

Such texts are available to the UK motorist in the form the ubiquitous brown sign. These pieces of roadside furniture differ from the blue or green road signs which give us the factual, day-to-day tidings of place names, distances and junctions, while the brown signs have a holiday air about them. Brown signs give the impression of not belonging to the workaday world of the motorway; commuters and lorry drivers 'look away now' this information is for Saturdays and Sundays. Days off, made for visiting the rare delights of *Birdworld*, signalled by the white silhouette of a down cast cockatoo, or a museum (Doric columns, pediment and capital 'M'), or a garden centre (six petal flower), or a theme park (carousel). However, if we follow Augé's thinking the brown sign is not meant to entice travellers to leave the motorway at the next slip road and park up at the nearest National Trust property (sprig of oak leaves). Brown signs are not meant to enable the visit, they are meant to replace it. In this way they are precisely aimed at commuters and lorry drivers, people who will never stop, they don't need to, the education they receive about a place through these signs is enough to placate any yearnings to turn away however momentarily from the primary modality of the road: placelessness.

Midway through Cross's film the lorry follows a series of road signs marked DIRFT. DIRFT is emblematic of the non-place, it is no place at all, its not even a word. It is entirely appropriate that it should be confused with the word 'drift', redolent of a non-specific vagueness. It is a location named for an obsolete acronym – Daventry International Rail Freight Terminal. This insignia is inaccurate and in many ways meaningless, for DIRFT is placeless – adrift between Daventry and Rugby (and is really closer to Rugby), and the freight is now overwhelmingly that of road rather than rail. In Cross' film this non-place represents zero on the milometer, it is where everything leaves from, it's primary value is in relation to other destinations. The DIRFT website claims that:

98% of the British population (85% of the UK) can be accessed within the 4.5 hour
drive time limit ... due to its central location and strategic road communications
(DIRFT 2010).

This geographic location – and non-places depend on their grid references – means that DIRFT has become the largest distribution centre in the UK. In Chapter 1 I referred to the non-metropolitan as a relational space, defined by its relationship to other spaces, and the everyday as a concept has also been seen as relational, filling the space of the daily when all the identifiable and specialised forms of activity has been removed, in DIRFT we find a non-metropolitan space which is entirely reliant on its relationship to elsewhere, it is not a place in itself, but is defined by its distance from other places. This floating entity is an invisible hub of the invisible rhythms of the everyday: the circulation of goods hidden in anonymous containers and the immaterial electronic transactions of international trade. It is these rhythms of the everyday that Lefebvre attempted to map in his *Rhythmanalysis* (2004 [1992])

project, here we see them manifested not in the major city stock exchanges, but in a non-specific part of the English countryside.

In Cross' film the lorry becomes temporarily embroiled in a Gordian knot of roundabouts, bordered by grey warehouses so large that it is easy to confuse them with the sky. These big shed storage units are 'containers for containers' (Bode 2004). They are made of similar materials and share the proportions and aesthetics (multiplied hundreds of times) of the corrugated metal freight containers they house. The only distinguishing marks on the warehouse in Figure 2.4 is the giant letter D, like half a battleship's grid references, its gargantuan presence simultaneously indicates an overwhelming fullness and a hollow emptiness.

Cross does not take us inside DIRFT, we are not sure there *is* an inside to DIRFT, lorries reverse towards house sized hatches, presumably goods are exchanged, we do not witness any interaction. We do not see what goes on inside these giant roadside sheds, we do not see what the driver gets up to while his freight is switched, we do not see him take a break, chat with other drivers, perhaps indulge in the hackneyed cup of tea and bacon butty. Cross's film denies human interaction, it performs the non-place in its refusal to do anything other than skim the surface, endlessly representing the same grey and green, while preventing any attempt at a deeper understanding of, or connection with the people or places of this everyday landscape.

It should be remembered that the idea of the non-place is, however, a product of a certain perspective, that of the driver, or indeed the passenger – let us say the

2.4   Andrew Cross, *Untitled (an English Journey)*, 2004.

traveller, who between starting point and destination inhabits a state of suspended placelessness. This suspension can be seen as a kind of everyday ensnarement, Lefebvre calls it 'constrained time' or 'compulsive time', time which is not quite your own and not quite belonging to the world of work, a state of in between functions as well as in between destinations (of course in Cross's film the driver is both at work and in between destinations). Lefebvre argues that this form of in between time is encroaching further and further into everyday life:

> if the hours of days, weeks, months and years are classed into three categories, pledged time (professional work), free time (leisure) and compulsive time (the various time other than work such as transport, official formalities, etc.) it will become apparent that compulsive time increases at a greater rate than leisure time (Lefebvre 2009 [1971]: p. 53).

Here we see compulsive time as blurring the edges of the otherwise carefully demarcated work time and leisure time. A difference which Lefebvre argues is key to both the impoverishment of the everyday and as an agent in its visibility. The non-integration of leisure and work, is for Lefebvre emblematic of the alienation of modern society. This integration, he argues, was lost with pre-modern agrarian cultures in which work and leisure were indivisible from the general process of living. In modern times those involved in paid employment cannot escape the tripartite of work time, leisure time and the non-place of constrained time.[17]

The feeling of entrapment generated by being in between places is also articulated by Michel de Certeau in 'Railway Navigation and Incarceration' (de Certeau 1984: pp. 111–14). While the idea of incarceration is obviously unpleasant, de Certeau also sees it as being the source of temporal escape, suggesting that rail travel provides a certain mix of freedom and incarceration which generates a situation in which the traveller can day dream. In one sense the traveller is physically unable to escape the train carriage, and is committed to the pre-ordained railway network of rails, prescribed routes and station stops, yet at the same time the statelessness of being in between meaningful locations such as home and work, creates the space in which the traveller's mind might escape into reverie, 'behind the windowpane, which from a great distance, makes our memories speak or draws out of the shadows the dreams of our secrets' (de Certeau 1984: p. 112). Of course there are differences between the rail passenger and the car driver in terms of the amount to which each can allow themselves to be distracted by day dreams. However, as is made plain by the strangely mesmeric qualities of Cross' film, when driving along a motorway, especially along a familiar route, one often settles down into what could be described as an attentive trance. To some extent one is alert to the movements of other drivers, but there is certainly the opportunity to let your mind wander with a kind of passive enjoyment that the only thing required of you is to keep your foot on the accelerator.

It is clear that the narratives of placelessness and timelessness of roads and driving are very much from the perspective of the driver. The mentality of the non-place is a product of the tyranny of the navigational road sign. Space becomes a coded text which creates the illusion that between the place names, glowing white on blue, there is nothing but a nameless space without history or meaning. But change the perspective from traveller to resident, and with it the modality from constant mobility to relative stillness, and it becomes evident that these roads are very much embedded in places. They generate an orbital belt of histories and meanings, through their influence on the shape and feel of everyday experience of place for the people who live with these roads.

If we start to claim the motorway as a feature of rural modernity, then the non-place can also be discussed as part of how the modern rural is experienced. However, it is important not just to claim the non-place as part of the experience of non-metropolitan everyday, but to trouble the idea of roads as non-places. If we shift the perspective to that of residents or residents as well as travellers, by thinking about the non-metropolitan as a place which is lived in as well as travelled through, then roads also become part of embodied, situated experience of place.

This process could begin with DIRFT. I have already noted that it is wrongly ascribed to Daventry, commentators more concerned with accuracy note its proximity to Rugby, or the part of the world just before the M42 becomes the M6, but all fail to identify its location as being just outside the village of Crick. Crick is an ancient village, it features in the Domesday book, it has a school and church and a post office. It is encircled by major roads, the transit connections that made it the ideal location for DIRFT have also made it attractive for commuters seeking to move out of the suburbs. Over the past 20 years the village has doubled in size, with large new housing developments being built on ex-farmland and a bypass taking heavy goods traffic out of its centre (Crick Village 2014). From this perspective DIRFT and the associated sections of the M42 and M6 are not non-places, they are part of the parish of Crick. I would not wish to argue that Crick is a piece of non-metropolitan England that has sadly become unwittingly host to these nameless roads and faceless distribution centre. Instead, if we are to recast non-metropolitan places as active sites of modernity it is important to recognise that the busy roads and distribution centres are part of the characteristics of this village. Rather than an upsetting anomaly in an otherwise picturesque village, this overlay of the ancient and modern is an example of what constitutes everyday experiences in non-metropolitan places. Roads and their accompanying infrastructure are widely seen not as part of the rural locations in which they are situated, but more as ribbon-like metropolitan enclaves which flap loosely across the countryside, tethered intermittently by their urban destinations. Their presence needs not only to be seen as part of a national or indeed global network of roads, but also as a feature of a local landscape. A view that challenges the more familiar narrative of the non-place.

Merriman (2004) provides a critique of Augé's formulation of non-places arguing that it 'fails to acknowledge the heterogeneity and materiality of the social networks bound up with the production of such environments' (2004: p. 147). He asserts that spaces such as motorways are replete with complex networks of meanings, histories and perspectives:

> *Roads and motorways such as the M1 may be placed through the folding of a diverse range of spaces, times, thoughts and materials into different architectures, atmospheres, subjectivities and texts. Landscape architects, Irish*

and West Indian labourers, American bulldozers, public relations, booklets
comparing the engineering of the motorway with the construction of the railways
in the nineteenth century, guide books, journalists and even artists and BBC
Radio producers are implicated in working and placing the motorway in different
spaces and times (Merriman 2004: 162).

It is however important to acknowledge that the experience of motorway travel, does not easily lend itself to accessing the complexities of place and history described by Merriman. Even given Merriman's criticisms of Augé's formulation, as too generic and focused on creating new categories of hyper modern experience, the fact remains that mesmeric propulsion along anonymous motorways can create the impression of the world as non-place, a sensation which is effectively portrayed in Cross' film. However, it is equally important to acknowledge that such journeys are relatively uncommon. Most driving takes place as part of an everyday routine, on a selection of familiar routes or 'routinized time-space paths' (Edensor 2004: p. 109), signed by self designated landmarks and embedded in everyday meaning. Edensor problematises the notion of the motorway as non-place by mapping his everyday commute along the M6 in terms of the sensual impacts of the road 'At one point, pylons cross the road, causing the radio to crackle' (Edensor 2003: p. 158), and the poetics of the landmarks he looks out for each day. These familiar features, make it possible to think about the experience of motorway driving not as one of anonymity and alienation, but one that can foster 'modes of homely comfort, provoke affective and imaginative connections to other times and places, facilitate kinaesthetic pleasures, and construct complex topographies of apprehension and association' (Edensor 2003: p. 152). For Edensor the daily commute is structured through a series of landmarks that indicate the interconnectedness of the motorway with the land through which it passes, personal stories and memories, and wider world rhythms:

Some mornings a herd of cows slowly cross over a footbridge on their way to
milking … There are a series of polythene houses, a large shed and a fleet of
lorries where bean sprouts are grown and transported … The motorway passes
over a dell, which on the east side accommodates a small, bright pink church that
looks like something Hansel and Gretel might visit (Edensor 2003: p. 158).

Edensor's study shows that for the regular traveller the road can shift from a non-place to very specific interconnected place. However, for my study it is also important to think about how motorways operate as part of the rural landscape from the perspective of the resident. In changing the perspective from traveller to resident – and it must be made clear that this role might be taken by the same person at different times, keeping in mind that residents are not victims of these roads, but often willing users – it becomes evident that one of the ways in which major roads switch from the status of non-place to becoming embedded in place is through the visceral experiences of roads which are felt by the non-traveller. Not far from my house a field path passes underneath a raised section of the M3 motorway. Here the road is suspended above the landscape by a prolonged concrete flyover, travellers on the motorway have no idea what lies beneath their tyres. On either side of the road are fields of arable crops, cattle graze, there are two villages within five minutes walk and a stately home which has been turned into a private school. Approaching the flyover the noise from the road is so loud that if in company one has to shout to be heard, the road is so wide that the passage way beneath it becomes a tunnel. Underneath the road it is completely dark, it feels cold, it smells of dry mould, feet scuff uneven aggregate, noises echo, and the vibrations of the traffic overhead resonate in one's chest. Inside the tunnel and at its edges I feel uneasy and vulnerable. Here I've seen peacock butterflies sleeping at night hanging upside down from the concrete beams. For me this road is very much a place, it is part of a place and a place in itself.

This road also has its own histories; just two miles south of my bit of the M3 the motorway carves a breathtaking channel through a piece of ancient chalk downland.[18] This is Twyford Down, the scene of extraordinary road protests in the early 1990s, which bought many of the residents of this part of Hampshire together with the Donga Tribe (a group of new age travellers) and other environmental groups, in a set of prolonged and at times violent demonstrations against the M3 extension (McKay 1996: pp. 134–48).[19] Protests against the road were grounded in environmental concerns, the destruction of habitat, ruination of the landscape and the increase in polluting car use. However, the preservation impulse of the stalwart Tory voter was also triggered, leading to an interesting situation which saw people with very different political outlooks and lifestyles occupying (sometimes literally) common ground. In addition to the new age travellers and 'ordinary' residents, some of the most vehement protestors were well heeled locals such as the Conservative councillor Barbara Bryant who wrote a book about the campaigns and subsequent legal processes (Bryant 1996). Even so, the protests were textured by class antagonism. The land for the road had been supplied by Winchester College, an extremely wealthy public school, which had also been gifted the land occupied by the old road which would no longer be in use, they seemed to be profiting from the resident's and the environment's loss (McKay 1996: p. 136).

Such protests alert us to the ahistorical illusion of roads and give the lie to the idea that roads, out of town shopping outlets and airports occupy previously 'empty space'. Protests change the perspective on roads from mobile traveller to resident (even if only temporarily resident – like members of the Donga tribe) and they re-situate the non-place as meaningful, interconnected and historical place. The need for this disruption becomes apparent in the images taken at the Twyford Down protest. These photographs devolve much of their charge from the stilling of the road space. It is perhaps obvious to align speed with development and stillness with preservation, nevertheless images of the road protestors occupying the motorway space on foot, are visually stunning because of their incongruity, both in scale and in velocity. The road or rather the building of the road is brought to a standstill, and the non-place is inhabited by a community of protestors.

It is perhaps easy to make the connection between slowing down, stopping development and returning the motorway to a rural location – however speed can also be seen as a feature of the rural landscape.

LANDSCAPES OF SPEED

Forms of haptic sensuality were actively avoided in motorway design, for the driver any feeling of friction or resistance in the form of uneven road surfaces, sharp bends or steep inclines were to be avoided. When such sensations do occur they are often deliberately engineered, perhaps most notably the rumble strip running along the boundary of the hard shoulder, which when crossed bumps the dozing driver back into awareness and back onto the carriageway.

As we have seen with the concerns of the protestors at Twyford Down, motorways occupy the cultural consciousness as other to the rural landscape, and often in direct opposition to it as its destroyer. However, debates around motorway design in England in the 1950s and 1960s reveal that motorways were originally conceived as belonging to a landscape of rural modernity.

In his fascinating research into the roadside planting of England's early motorways, Merriman shows that not even the driver's eye was to experience any resistance to the smooth flow of transit, particularly any visual unevenness which might result from overly detailed or fussy landscaping. Discussions about the type of planting that was most appropriate to the new 'landscape of speed' (Merriman 2006: p. 91) that the motorway represented were long and passionately fought. The two main players in this encounter were the Institute of Landscape Architects (ILA) and the Roads Beautifying Association (RBA). The ILA argued that the roadside landscape should be designed to be seen at speed and therefore emphasised the need for simplicity and flow, favouring the use of a limited number of native shrubs and plants. Whereas the RBA favoured the 'pretty' flowering shrubs and trees found in many domestic gardens. The ILA blocked proposals for the use of ornamental species which they felt to be too detailed, small-scale and distracting, threatening to fragment or disrupt the desired feeling of streamlined speed.

Interestingly, it is in this debate that we see that the motorway in its early conception was indeed thought of as a rural entity. Commenting on the planting scheme devised for the M1 motorway by landscape consultants employed by the construction company of Sir Owen Williams, which reportedly included the use of garden plants such as Forsythia on the central reservation and liberal use of Pyracantha elsewhere, the Landscape Advisory Committee deemed the scheme to be 'too fussy, ornamental, colourful and urban for a *modern rural* motorway' (my italics) (Merriman 2006: p. 92). In these early visualisations of the motorway the rural is playing a starring role in one of the most ambitious modern projects of the twentieth century. Merriman's research shows that the debates among the engineers and landscape architects of the time made it clear that, in contrast to accepted notions of the countryside as a place of slowness and continuity, 'Movement and speed are seen to be vitally important to the way we see, encounter and inhabit Britain's landscape' (Merriman 2006: p. 83).

Perhaps surprisingly, this conflation of the countryside with speed can also be seen, in the pages of the long running, traditional, publication *Country Life*.[20] Speed is evident in both the advertising and editorial rhetorics of the magazine, a significant amount of which is focused around cars. Every year the magazine ran a motoring special to coincide with the Earls Court Motor Show featuring a detailed description of each of the stands. In addition it regularly included features on cars and motoring called 'New Cars Described' or 'Motoring Notes'. Full page adverts for cars or car components introduce an aesthetic of speed to the magazine: in an advert for a Rolls-Royce dealership well over half the page is devoted to an image of striated tarmac giving the illusion of speed, with the highly desirable automobile perched atop, while an advert for Goodyear tyres uses images of a highly streamlined speed boat racing through maritime waters to advertise its wares.

This content gives the publication an unexpected texture in which narratives and aesthetics of speed sit next to features on standing stones and hibernating dormice, communicating a multivalent collage of speed and stillness, and by extension development and preservation.

This contrast is concisely articulated on the cover of the October 1970 Motor Show edition which features a highly polished, brand new Jaguar parked on a village street of half timbered cottages and a stone market cross. Along the bottom of the page runs the strap line 'Ancient and Modern' (Figure 2.5), producing an interesting example of how the tensions between these terms are played out in the non-metropolitan arena. This image works to equate the cottages and the car, there is no hint of incongruity, the deliberate juxtaposition situates both elements as examples of classic English design, heritage and crucially, aspiration.

The contradictions here are many and various. The car is the only one visible, there is nothing to link it with the congestion often experienced in rural villages where narrow roads and on street parking make speedy negotiation an impossibility. Equally there is little evidence of any of the changes that increased car user-ship has brought to places like this village, such as road widening schemes and the ill designed signage much maligned by individuals such as Nairn (1955) and groups like the CPRE (Matless 1998: p. 47). The image makes no concessions to the idea that national road development programmes are problematic in relation to preservation of the countryside. In addition it could also be noted that the half timbered cottages pictured here would have originally been built by and for peasant grade agricultural workers, in contrast to the luxury branded car, however given the proximity of the village to London and the date of this issue they too register as commodities in the luxury market, either as second homes or commuter residencies.

As it is portrayed in *Country Life*, speed is not associated with the building of rural motorways, instead it is part of an idealised affluent countryside in which tensions between ancient and modern are smoothed away by the timeless washing of a tide of 'old money'. A powerful image of this can been seen in a copy of the magazine which ran an advert for a new Italian sports car, dark brown and sleek, emanating speed and power, next to an advert for a fine art auction featuring a painting of race horses of the same dark brown colour. As well as obviously playing a role in creating the illusion of perpetual rural prosperity, this pairing seems to tell a story of speed in countryside as historic, and part of its heritage. From powerful horses to powerful cars – speed has always been a feature of the countryside.

This is an ideology that is perhaps responsible for *Country Life*'s otherwise baffling under-reporting of motorway building as a countryside issue. During the

COUNTRY LIFE
MOTOR SHOW NUMBER

On Sale Thursday
OCTOBER 15, 1970

FOUR SHILLINGS
(20 NEW PENCE)

ANCIENT AND MODERN: EAST HAGBOURNE, BERKSHIRE

2.5   Front cover of *Country Life*, 15 October 1970.

prime decades of English road development (mid 1950s–mid 1970s) which saw hundreds of miles of land become the venue for new roads, motorways and their associated issues do not feature heavily in its pages. One of the few features on road development focuses on the building of the West Way in London (Taylor 1971: p. 981), firmly situating the motorway as urban phenomenon/problem rather than one directly effecting the countryside.

The target audience of *Country Life* may have had residences in both the country and in London, and were easily mobile. While they may have talked the talk of preservation it was also important for them to tell a story in which the car belonged in the countryside; more specifically, that their big expensive cars belonged in the countryside, just as their families had done for many generations, whilst the smaller congestion creating cars of the newcomer or tourist were without this important heritage and therefore out of place.

So far we have seen how the ideas of speed and stillness might be used to conceptualise the cluster of anxious relationships that texture the modern, rural everyday. Concerns around development and preservation were central to Nairn's polemics on the homogenisation of country and city that ill-designed and hastily implemented development would bring about. While Cross' portrait of non-metropolitan England through the windscreen of an HGV, evidenced the realisation of Nairn's feared subtopia in the standardised and seemingly anonymous network of motorways. To complicate this picture however we have seen how the road as super-modern non-place can also be experienced as a meaningful, rooted and inter-connected place, with a shift in perspective from traveller to resident and the associated shift in velocity that this necessitates. It has also been demonstrated that roads and the experience of speed need not always be thought of in opposition to the countryside, with the rhetorics around early motorway design enabling a certain reclamation of motorways as a significant feature of rural modernity. The following section builds on these stories of the conflicting tensions between preservation and development, the ancient and the modern, nature and technology, stillness and speed through a reading of the *Shell County Guides* which focuses on their multivalent negotiation of these tensions and their influential conceptualisation of the nation as old, strange and predominantly rural.

SHELL COUNTY GUIDES

The *Shell County Guides* were a long running series of guidebooks to 35 counties of England sponsored by the Shell Oil company and produced between 1933 and 1985.[21] Initially they were designed for the market of newly mobile middle class car owners, however, over their 50 year history they became a ubiquitous addition to a large proportion of Britain's households (MODA 2008). Over this long period the design and content of the guides changed, in the 1930s they were inspired by avant-garde art practices of the time such as photo-montage and surrealism, with their authors often adopting an irreverent or entertainingly polemic tone. As the series progressed the guides became more conventional and less idiosyncratic.[22]

The guides focus on counties rather than the cities of Britain, meaning that they provide a view of England that centres on the non-metropolitan.[23]

If Andrew Cross' film *3 hours from here* could be seen as the inheritor of Nairn's *Outrage* then the *Shell County Guides* could be seen as its forbear. They share a visual and textual rhetoric railing against ill thought out design (particularly with regard to architecture), whilst also exhibiting anxieties around the modern tension between preservation and development.[24] Figure 2.6 is from the *Oxon* guide by John Piper (1938), it shows Banbury Road in Kidlington, just north of Oxford (incidentally just off the A34). It illustrates newly built housing in ribbon formation, ugly telegraph poles at odd angles and a road which is in the process of being widened (all elements that featured highly on Nairn's subtopia hit list). The collage of ancient and modern that characterises the *Shell Guides* perspective on the non-metropolitan is made apparent in the text which juxtaposes this area of new development with the village's thirteenth century church. A similar contrast is made in the *Devon* guide (Betjeman 1935) where, in what looks like a piece of photo-montage, a modern villa sits cheekily on the end of a Georgian terrace, a montage that has taken place at street level rather than the artists studio.

The *Shell Guides* also share with *Outrage* a concern with everyday detail which is presented in fragmentary ways (see Figure 2.2 for Nairn's treatment of lampposts). In the *Shell Guides* this collaging of fragments takes place in a number of ways. For example an image titled the 'tree of knowledge' shows a tree stump festooned with advertising placards all jostling for the most prominent position, forming a montage of juxtaposed signs and lettering. Montage can also be seen within the guides in the odd connections that can be made between images on a page, an example of this can be seen in Paul Nash's Dorset guide where a double page spread contains an image of twin sheep, their curly horns uncannily mirroring eachother,

2.6   'Kidlington' from *Oxon Shell Guide*, 1936. © Shell Brands International AG. Courtesy the Shell Art Collection.

together with a photograph of a Freudian looking snake. Heathcote notes that 'Nash's images could make links between the forms of objects that were suggestive of greater closeness than mere facts would suggest' (Heathcote 2011: pp. 45–6). Finally collage is sometimes present as fully realised photo-montage as in Cecil H. Greville's evocation of 'Slough Then and Now' (Figure 2.7). The effect is disorientating and unexpected, perhaps doubly so given their subject matter, which is not shocks of the modern city – so often associated with montage (Benjamin 1970 [1934]: p. 90) – but the rural villages and market towns of England's countryside.

These publications are fascinating documents which clearly evidence the early twentieth century re-framing of the English countryside as a space of leisure – rather than agricultural production (Borsay 2006: p. 186). They find much of their content in the lived material of the non-metropolitan everyday – vernacular architecture, door knockers, pub signs, conceptualising the country as a vast accumulation of everyday detail. Their use of avant-garde design to represent the English countryside aligns the non-metropolitan with modernity and the avant-garde, as does the connection with personal motoring. However, at the same time this innovation is cut through with preservationist rhetoric, a love of Victoriana, and the construction of an old weird rural.[25] It is the intertwining of these apparently incongruous positions: the valorisation of the old, with the use of avant-garde aesthetics, together with Shell's alignment with both nature and technology, that this section focuses upon.

The guides were the idea of John Betjeman, whose reputation as chronicler of the English middle classes (Taylor-Martin 1989: p. 11), together with interest in Victorian architecture are reflected in the style and perspective. It is these early

2.7 'Slough Then and Now', *Bucks Shell Guide*, 1937. © Shell Brands International AG. Courtesy the Shell Art Collection.

incarnations of the *Shell Guides*, specifically those that were produced under his general editorship, that are explored in this section.

Each guide is a unique project with its inclusions, exclusions, rationale, illustrations, photographs, typography and format, determined by its editor, together with varying amounts of input from Betjeman. Many of the guides produced under Betjeman's general editorship were written and compiled by artists. Contributions came from Paul Nash as editor for the *Dorset* guide (1936); his brother John Nash as the editor for the *Bucks* guide (1937), which included works from Stanley Spencer and Humphrey Jennings; and John Piper as the editor for the *Oxon* guide (1938). These contributions gave the publications a Neo-Romantic feeling for landscape that was cut with a Surrealist eye for the absurdities of both ancient tradition and modern development. This combination accessed the post-war nostalgic patriotism of the Neo-Romantic, an ideology inspired by William Blake's mysticism and notions of Albion (Spalding 1994: p. 129), together with a disregard for authority and an attunement to the strangeness of the everyday of the European Surrealists (Gardiner 2000: pp. 35–40; Highmore 2002a: pp. 45–59). Montagu notes the links between these different responses to the landscape, and shows how they were opposed to the functionalist concerns of artists and architects inspired by the Bauhaus and the European modernist avant-garde, stating that:

> [T]he counter or 'traditionalist', position was a ruralist fantasy that could be linked to the Romantic tradition, championing wilderness over garden and ruin over modern development. In its more modern guise, this position resembled the anti-linear, disordered and organic vision imagined by the Surrealists (Montagu 2003: p. 13).

While Neo-Romantics and Surrealists may find similar ground in the love of the wilderness and ruins, Surrealism offered an avant-garde aesthetic that passed an unexpected visual current through the guide's often preservationist rhetoric.

It is perhaps Paul Nash in particular who negotiated most skilfully between the Neo-Romantic and Surrealist positions.[26] David Mellor in his survey of British Neo-Romantic tendencies locates Nash's response to Dorset as a key moment in this re-imagining of the British Landscape (Mellor 1987: p. 11). Yet at the same time Nash was also exploring surrealism, and his famous article 'Swanage or Seaside Surrealism' centring on the Dorset resort, was published in *Architectural Review* in 1936 – the same year as his *Shell Guide* to the county. In addition to negotiating between preservationist instincts and Surrealist influences, Nash found his neo-Romanticism somewhat at odds with the modernist movement in which he was also a central figure. Harris (2010: p. 22) points out it is possible to see very clearly in certain paintings how Nash is involved in reconciling the future-facing, rationalist abstraction of the *Unit One* artists, with his love of landscape and tendency towards mysticism. In his Equivalents for Megaliths (Figure 2.8), modernists geometric forms sit within a landscape and at times seem to become part of it, perhaps as ultra neat and tidy hay bales or reflected in the ridges of a Iron Age earth work. Nash's guide to Dorset operates in a similar way, in that it makes visible the artist's processing of the conflicting but equally seductive attractions of the ancient and the modern, accessing both preservationist sentiment and surreal aesthetics.

2.8   Equivalents for megaliths, 1935, Paul Nash (1889–1946). © Tate, London 2014.

In *Dorset*, Nash portrays a county that is very old, prehistoric in fact. That time has been registered in the very earth of the county, layered with fossils, earthworks, evidence of ancient farming systems such as strip lynchets, churches and tombs. He bookends the guide with flamboyantly anti-development polemic. Starting with a dedication 'To the landowners of Dorset, The Council for the Preservation of Rural England, The Society for the Protection of Ancient Buildings and all those courageous enemies of 'development' to whom we owe what is left of England' (Nash 1936a: p. 6), and finishing with a postscript:

> *When you go to an inn ask for English food. If you are given badly cooked so-called French food kick up a row. Use your influence … to clear the simple and often beautiful interiors of country churches free from the cheap colour reproduction of sixth-rate religious paintings and other undignified rubbish occasionally to be found there. Use your influence by writing or speaking against the frequent attempts on the part of jerry-builders and those bodies which attempt to absorb whole tracts of the open countryside for their more or less destructive activities (Nash 1936a: p. 44).*

This concern for history and preservation is textured by Nash's use of images that prompt surrealist visual correspondences, giving the county often associated with comfortable seaside holidays, an unfamiliar quality. The surrealist concerns of Nash can be seen to run throughout the guide starting with the front cover, a montage that treats the coast's rock formations in a similar way to the object personages which had become a feature of Nash's surrealist works.[27] The title page features

2.9   Frontispiece from *Dorset Shell Guide*, 1936. © Shell Brands International AG. Courtesy the Shell Art Collection.

SCELIDOSAURUS HARRISONI : FORMER NATIVE

SHELL GUIDE

COMPILED

AND WRITTEN BY PAUL NASH

LONDON: ARCHITECTURAL PRESS,
9 QUEEN ANNE'S GATE, S.W. 1

a dinosaur (Figure 2.9) labelled as a 'Former Native' of the county, after which a double page spread of a ship wreck seems to take on the characteristics of a toothy prehistoric beast. There is a use of doubling as a formal device here, something which was often used in surrealist works to disrupt the easy reading of imagery and on occasion access the uncanny; the dinosaur is reflected in a pool, in the 'Flora and Fauna' section a moth is photographed with its shadow and two identical rams stare out from the page, their horns making a visual connection with the ammonite fossil pictured elsewhere. Turning the pages of this guide a different sort of rural England appears.

The physical form of the early *Shell County Guides* also marked them out as different from what had gone before, aligning them with newness and modernism. They were spiral bound with newly developed system called Spirax (Heathcote 2011: p. 15). This combined with their thin cardboard covers, and relatively few pages (averaging around 45 pages each), seemed to speak of speed. They were publications to be flicked through, looked at while on the move and due to their innovative new binding they would stay open at the appropriate page as you drove along. Photographic images were central to the design of the guides and photography's status as a newly emerging art form among the avant-garde again accessed the vocabulary of modernism. Often double pages were given over to a single image reaching right to the edges of the pages with no borders, a look which is still strikingly contemporary.

These elements made the *Shell County Guides* significantly different in content and feel from the established guides that preceded them; in particular the European Baedeker guidebooks, that were extremely popular throughout the nineteenth century and into the first decades of the twentieth, with the word Baedeker becoming a generic name for any tourists' guidebook (Koshar 1998: p. 303).[28] Travel or least leisure orientated foreign travel at this time was predominantly the preserve of the upper classes, and represented a significant undertaking in both time and resources. The Baedeker guides gained a reputation for being full of thoroughly researched factual information (rather than commentary) about places to visit, travel and accommodation arrangements. The content was devised in order to keep the necessity of negotiation with tour guides, hotel keepers and other representatives of the tourist industry to a minimum for the well informed Baedeker traveller (Koshar 1998: p. 303).

Heathcote, speaking on a radio travel show, points out the Baedecker's intended audience also influenced the selection of places of interest included in the guides – an audience of wealthy industrialists were interested in the industrial production of Great Britain, its towns and cities rather than its countryside:

> Baedecker's Great Britain is not a heritage theme park but an enormous industrial complex. It recommends great factories, markets, mines, also the life of the place, how people shop, musical culture, politics. You were supposed to really experience how the place functioned and was lived in rather than focus on museums, art galleries or stately homes. The nature of tourism and what constituted a site is very different in Baedecker than it is today (Excess Baggage 2009).

In contrast, the perspective of the *Shell Guide* is that of the (predominantly male) urban middle class motorist who wanted to visit the countryside. He too aims to be independent of the tourist industry, however his independence is granted through his means of transport, the personal motor car. Free from the restrictions of railway routes or pre-organised tour parties, the *Shell Guide* traveller cannot only devise his own itineraries (with help from the guide) but he can also 'discover' parts of the countryside, which are newly accessible to the motorist.[29]

In his guide to Derbyshire, Christopher Hobhouse makes the connection between this new form of individual motorised tourism and historical military invasions of Europe:

The motorist has an advantage that the railway traveller lacks: he can tackle
a country that is new to him as an invading general would have tackled it, as
Napoleon or Caesar would have tackled it, by its main contours, by its natural
masses and its lines of communication. Derbyshire is perfectly made for such a
method of attack (Hobhouse 1935: p. 7).

Domestic travel becomes exploration, with the undercurrents of colonialism that this also brings. The *Shell Guide* traveller is engaged in re-discovering a landscape that had never been lost. This rhetoric of exploration is evident in much of the company's advertising of the time with the slogan 'See Britain First on Shell' being used in conjunction with images of picturesque locations. Overlooking the fact that these areas had been populated for millennia and had been seen many times before, not least by the people who lived in them, the idea of being the first, creates an idea of personal triumph but also social cachet in being the first of one's peers to 'do' a particular sight.

This practice of 'finding' the country through motor tourism was popularised and chronicled by H.V. Morton in the enormously popular *In Search of England* (1927).[30] Implicit in his title is the idea that England has somehow become lost, a handy phrasing which at once conjures up ideas of a real or authentic England, as opposed to the one in which most people carry out their daily lives. Furthermore, that this 'real' England is either temporally missing, in that it belongs to another time, or another place – namely the countryside. For Morton, England is only to be found in fleeting glimpses of a landscape in which history, topography and antiquity can be read. Morton characterises this hide and seek approach to tourism as a national pastime that is new, exciting and patriotic:

Never before have so many people been searching for England … The popularity
of the cheap motor-car is also greatly responsible for this long overdue interest
in English history, antiquities and topography. More people than in any previous
generation are seeing the real country for the first time … the roads of England,
eclipsed for a century by the railway, have come to life again; the Kings Highway
is once more a place for adventures and explorations (Morton 1927: pp. vii–viii).

In addition to the slogan, the images used in Shell campaigns tie the brand to both speed and the countryside in quite an incongruous way. As a trader in motor oil and petrol the company evidently would want to closely align themselves with speed, efficiency and technological development. The unexpected element here is that given this alignment, Shell should also want to associate itself with the countryside, rather than for example the burgeoning metropolis. This decision is clearly linked with Shell's desire to build on its image as a British brand (Mellor 1987: p. 11), a result of which was to also shape the national idea of what constituted Britain in the imagination.

A particularly striking poster image from this time was designed by Edward McKnight Kauffer (Plate 1). It seems to demonstrate this heady mixture of futuristic technological development with an ancient and mystical English landscape. The stylised image of Stonehenge at night time is exciting, the starry sky perhaps hints at the stones' connection to another world. The stones are condensed into a tight circle. This is an essence of Stonehenge, one that gives the necessary amount of monumentality but is not overly concerned with accurate representation. This is Stonehenge for the pressed for time. Writing on Kauffer's practice as a designer, Webb and Skipworth note that:

> [H]e divided the public into two sections – the fast-moving and the slow-moving. Echoing a critic of an earlier generation who had defined a poster as 'something that is read by someone who runs', Kauffer preferred to design for the fast moving, whom he considered to be far the larger section of the discerning public (Webb and Skipworth 2007: 19–20).

It was not just the audience for these adverts that were perceived as in a hurry, but the adverts themselves were also moving at speed. In order to show their support for the CPRE's campaign against advertising signage in the countryside, Shell pledged to remove all its promotional material from rural petrol stations and other countryside locations. Instead a scheme was devised using the sides of the company's lorries as moving billboards (Hewitt 1998: p. vi).

Kauffer's image represents a moment when the countryside could be associated with speed, indeed a moment when the speed of new technology needed to be cut with the beauty, and ancientness of the landscape. The rhetorics of speed and newness were in the first decades of the twentieth century – the decades which coincided with the development of the personal automobile – adopted by artistic and political movements of the Futurists in Italy and the Vorticists in England. The *Manifesto of Futurism* authored by the central figure of the group Filippo Tommaso Marinetti, used the automobile as a powerful symbol of a new world in which dynamism, speed and simultaneity were the defining conditions of modernity:

> We affirm that the world's magnificence has been enriched by a new beauty: the beauty of speed. A racing car whose hood is adorned with great pipes, like serpents of explosive breath – a roaring car that seems to ride on grapeshot is more beautiful than the Victory of Samothrace (Marinetti 1996 [1909]: p. 147).

The reference to the *Victory of Samothrace* refers to the ancient Greek rendering of the winged Goddess Nike as messenger of victory. The futurists declared it was now time for this classical emblem of triumphant action to be supplanted by a figure representing the new beauty of the industrially produced object – the automobile becomes the high-speed, noisy herald of modernity. Partly in response to the Futurist manifesto, which appeared in English to coincide with the Futurists exhibition in London in 1912, Percy Wyndham Lewis produced *Our Vortex* (1914), a de-facto manifesto for the Vorticist faction of the English avant-garde. Like the Futurists, Wyndham Lewis advocated a violent rejection of the past. However, he also saw the future as an equally sentimental notion. For the Vorticists 'the Present is the only active thing' (Wyndham Lewis 1996 [1914]: p. 155). An interesting counterpoint to the Futurists obsession with speed and forward motion, the Vorticists saw themselves as the still point of the present at the centre of the whirling vortex, producing enigmatic statements mixing speed and stillness: 'This is a great Vorticist age, a great still age of artists … Our Vortex desires the immobile rhythm of its swiftness … Our Vortex is white and abstract with its red-hot swiftness' (Wyndam Lewis 1996 [1914]: p. 156). Kauffer himself maintained a practice as a painter as well as a poster designer, and was a founder member of *Group X*, a Vorticist group which included Wyndham Lewis.

The mechanised trauma of the First World War impacted considerably on the Vorticists' philosophy. The untempered valorisation of the mechanical was no longer tenable, and the need for a return to more classical appreciation of the values of order, and a re-connection with tradition was voiced (Harrison and Wood 1996: p. 218). Although coming a decade behind the thoughts projected by the foremost avant-garde figures (Wyndham Lewis published his treatise on the need for a new generation of artists 'The Children of the New Epoch' in 1921), the Shell posters of the 1930s could be seen as reflecting this turn. Although essentially aiming to sell oil and petrol through the increase in personal motoring, few adverts in this decade portray cars, instead through the employment of artists and designers concerned with developing new forms of modernism, the adverts create a hybrid of the established order and comfort of the English countryside, with a speedy modernist edge.

The close relationship with the landscape courted by Shell in its advertising campaigns and guides display dialectical stances on development and preservation. The company's involvement with the increase in personal motoring, leading to road building and expansion, pull in the direction of change and development. As does the guide's promotion of motor tourism, which spawned many of the elements the guides protest so vehemently about: roadside shacks offering tea, a proliferation of signs, and hastily erected holiday chalets. Added to this is the oil extraction and processing industry which is responsible for many defilements of the landscape and environment more generally. Yet the use of neo-romantic re-imaginings of the countryside in the lorry bills, the valorisation of old things and rugged landscapes in the *Shell Guides* and the alliance with groups like the CPRE pull in the other direction.

Shell has consistently attempted to create a position for itself as simultaneously signifying both of these perceived oppositions. Patrick Wright comments that in the Shell advertising campaigns 'those two constructed neutralities 'nature' and 'technology' walk hand in hand through this progressive, if slightly bizarre, modern world' (Wright 1985: p. 60). Wright sees nature as being connected to cyclical time, while technology is aligned with the uni-directional onward movement of linear time, and argues that a clear example of Shell seeking to combine both of these models can be found in the campaigns that centred on the need for different oils in different seasons (Wright 1985: p. 62). An occurrence of this is shown in Plate 2, also designed by Edward McKnight Kauffer, advertising the exhilarating, if slightly spooky, possibilities for cold weather exploration of the New Forest using winter Shell oil. Like the lorry bills and much of the company's advertising material the *Shell Guides* are multivalent, complex and contradictory. As we have seen they align themselves with both the ancient and the modern, the romantic and the avant garde, preservation and development, and nature and technology.

Finally I would also like to explore how the themes of speed and stillness (or slowness) are manifested in these publications. Many aspects of the guides effectively slow down the tourist experience. This is done by attention to detail, in direct contrast to the motorway 'landscape of speed' in which the detail contributed

ORDINARY THINGS are often well worth looking at. Up to one hundred years ago craftsmanship in England was rarely skimped. This ironwork support for the sign of the Bull Inn, STONY STRATFORD (with modern accretions) is a fine bit of blacksmith's ironwork of the late 18th century. On the right is a pretty, early 19th century shop-front in the same town.

by variegated leaves and flowering trees was deemed so inappropriate. The pages of the *Shell Guides* bristle like a gothic cathedral, with an excess of detail. The features of an apparently uninteresting village, town or landscape are transformed into clusters of minutiae which could keep a willing visitor occupied for weeks. The reader's attention is constantly drawn to the particularities of a place, such as stained glass windows, strangely shaped door knockers, shop signs and frontages. Everyday features which in one's own town would not warrant a second glance are valorised by the *Shell Guide* authors, often taken as evidence of an ancient arcadia, where skilled craftsmen would devote endless time and energy to even the most mundane projects. In his guide to Buckinghamshire, underneath a photograph of an elaborately worked wrought iron pub sign, which also bears modern pendants from the AA and RAC motoring clubs (Figure 2.10), John Nash writes in praise of everyday detail:

> Ordinary things are often well worth looking at. Up to one hundred years ago craftsmanship in England was rarely skimped. This iron work support for the sign of the Bull Inn, STONY STRATFORD (with modern accretions) is a fine bit of blacksmith's iron work of the late eighteenth century (Nash 1937: p. 35).

Such an attunement to the importance of vernacular detail, creates an impression of England as a palimpsest of undiscovered intricacy, the negotiation and proper appreciation of which required an investment of time.

Excess of detail can impede the passage of time, slowing down the progress of the visitor by encouraging them to attend to this shop sign or that chimney breast before moving on; however an accumulation of detail can, in some cases, work to speed up experience. A deluge of apparently unconnected detail can work to create

2.10 'Ordinary Things' image of pub sign and text below it, *Bucks Shell Guide*, 1937. © Shell Brands International AG. Courtesy the Shell Art Collection.

2.11   Front and back covers of the *Wiltshire Shell Guide*, 1935. © Shell Brands International AG. Courtesy the Shell Art Collection.

a disorientating fragmentation in which the eye flits from image to image, fact to fact, consuming a place, without synthesis of its disconnected elements. Such a fragmentation of place is played out to spectacular effect on the front cover of the Wiltshire guide (Figure 2.11) which features an intensely detailed photo-montage by the aristocratic artist Lord Berners.[31] It features images of the many notable characteristics of the county such as its pigs, sheep, Stonehenge, and Salisbury Cathedral, mixed together with stony faced Victorian women, crazed golfers, performing dogs and men with guns, all blissfully out of scale. This is an image of Wiltshire, indeed an image of England which communicates a combination of national eccentricity, pride and irreverence. It contributes to the *Shell Guide's* image of England as a mystic arcadia. There are no elements of modernity featured in this montage, all the people are dressed in Victorian garb and all the architecture is eighteenth century or older. This is an image which accesses the idea of the countryside as belonging to the past, a sort of deep non-specific past in which it should be preserved, positing the idea that travelling into the countryside was in fact to travel back in time. As Matless notes, at this time 'Motoring became styled as a modern practice in pursuit of an older England ... The petrol engine allowed a passage into an old country' (1998: p. 64).

While the content of this collage may have its origins in an earlier time its form is fully contemporary. Montage as a process of combining miscellaneous elements, was being widely used as a Surrealist methodology at this time. As mentioned above, montage is also a medium which Benjamin aligned with modernity (particularly with regard to film), for its specific ability to record and communicate disorientation, speed and shocks (Benjamin 1970 [1934]: p. 171).

It is in this capacity that the use of montage here can be thought of as an example of how the *Shell Guides* perform the complex manoeuvre of associating speed and modernity, not with the city but with the countryside and more than this, simultaneously articulating ideas of an ancient past.

The overcrowding of fragments within the collage articulates the compression of the tourist experience. The speed of which is also articulated most effectively by John Rayner in the Hampshire guide, when he urges the motorist to visit the astonishing paintings by Stanley Spencer which adorn the walls of the Sandham Memorial Chapel, in Burghclere (incidentally also just off the A34), 'When you have spent six minutes looking at them' he advises you should immediately get back on the road and head for the next attraction (Rayner 1937: p. 16).

Through an examination of the experiences, histories and visual cultures of driving in the countryside, this chapter has exposed rural modernity to be underpinned by a web of tensions pulled taut by divergent tendencies. Our starting point was the uncomfortable montage of tarmac and grassy burial mound, an image that seems redolent of the rural as a landscape of both speed and stillness. Further investigation reveals this notion to be augmented with many other oppositional currents: the ancient and modern, preservation and development, place and non-place, nature and technology, and neo-romantic and avant-garde aesthetics.

The next chapter is also textured by some of these oppositions, it too centres on an everyday practice in the countryside, that of littering. Like roads, litter is often seen as being a product of modernity which spreads out of the city and into the countryside. In a similar way it is also associated with pollution and environmental damage. Most interestingly however, litter is seen as being particularly 'out of place' in the countryside, and investigation of this reaction is productive in both revealing and complicating our assumptions about what (or who) belongs in a modern rural landscape.

NOTES

1   Subsequently republished as a book (Nairn 1955).

2   The M1 motorway did not open until 1959 and then did not fully connect the South of England to Scotland, see Moran (2009: pp. 23–6).

3   The 'Things in Fields' referred to here are remnants of war time structures, hastily erected and still present 10 years after the end of hostilities.

4   Subtopia could be linked to Mumford's (1940) notion of Megalopolis which he identifies as the emergence of the big city from the multitude of regional cities, he asks 'Will urban life come to mean the further concentration of power in a few metropolises whose ramifying suburban dormitories will finally swallow the rural hinterland?' (Mumford 1940: p. 223). This term is also used by Gottmann (1961) to describe the concentrated urbanisation over the massive area that is America's Northeastern Seaboard.

5   The term subtopia finds purchase in *Architectural Review* where its use continues into the 1960s, it also features in Chaney (1990) in his article on the MetroCentre in Gateshead.

6   There is also a connection here to the idea of the non-place, the transition between subtopia as no-place and the more contemporary notion of the non-place as a product of super-modernity is made in the next section with an examination of Cross' *3 hours from here*.

7   Moran points out that to align this sinister creeping force with housing developments, rather than the very real threat of fascism at this time is somewhat ironic (Moran 2009: p. 136).

8   Lefebvre refers to societies of bureaucratically controlled consumption in relation to the network of controls that constitute the everyday enforced by the state through increased organisation of public and private life, and by state capitalism, which through advertising controls supposedly free areas of life such as hopes and desires, see Lefebvre (2008 [1958], 2009 [1971]).

9   Designers of the blue and white motorway signage Kinneir and Calvert were tasked with designing non-motorway road signage to be rolled out nationwide in the early 1960s, see Moran (2009: pp. 66–75).

10   The exhibition in which *3 Hours from Here* was shown was called *An English Journey*, as was the resulting publication (Bode 2004).

11   This quote is not entirely representative of Priestley's account which is generally positive, commenting on the relative prosperity of the city and the neatness of its streets and its inhabitants (Priestley [1934]1977: pp. 27–8). Southampton's history of urban development is also a feature of Owen Hatherley's *Militant Modernism* (2009) and Jonathan Meads' *An Encyclopaedia of Myself* (2014).

12   The history of the 'Big Shed' warehouse and distribution centre is detailed in Moran (2009: pp. 148–50). Architecture critic Martin Pawley has also written on the subject with regard to out of town shopping centres, see Pawley (1988).

13   Patrick Keiller's films are also important sources in any such lineage, taking the form of journeys they map the often mundane spaces, rhythms and architecture of non-metropolitan England, in a post-Thatcher era in *Robinson in Space* (1997) and more recently after the banking crisis of 2008 in *Robinson in Ruins* (2010).

14   As Merriman (2004: p. 146) points out this state has also been theorised as 'placeless', 'abstract', and 'ageographical'.

15   Their ahistoricity is of course an illusion, and many road and supermarket developments are vehemently challenged by local residents, the timelessness of the non-place could almost be designed as answer to these protests, which are discussed more fully later.

16   Moran (2009: pp. 91–5) identifies this term as originating in Florida in 1988 as a derivation from 'roid rage', the aggressive behaviour of steroid users, and maps its use in the British tabloid press. Lupton (1999) places its origins in Los Angeles in the same time frame, and explores the matrix of symbolic meanings of cars and driving which may have contributed to this phenomenon. Sinclair in his psychogeographic account of the M25, *London Orbital* (2002) sees road rage in terms of the rhythms and energies created by hyper-modern modes of experience, he writes of an incident that ends in a death as one of the 'gates that act as circuit-breakers, disturbing the energy generator that hums continually around the undisciplined body mass of London' (2002: p. 12).

17   It should be noted that those involved in primarily childcare and household duties may not be able to make these distinctions so easily.

18   This piece of road is significant in both Nairn and Cross' journeys, in 1955 Nairn used the old A33 route from Southampton to Winchester en route to the A34, which

circumnavigated St Catherine's Hill on the outskirts of Winchester, whereas as in 2004 Cross takes the new M3 extension which is effectively built through the middle of the Down.

19   The anti M3 campaign was begun by local residents in March 1985, it gathered pace and became of national significance from 1987 onwards (Bryant 1996), the Donga Tribe set up camp directly on the building site in 1992, where a number of battles with security firms took place, most notably the Bailey Bridge battle in 1993 resulting in many arrests and the Mass Trespass in 1994.

20   *Country Life* was founded in 1897 and continues to be produced as a weekly glossy magazine aimed at the wealthy country elite (Hewison 1987: p. 57).

21   There is also a *Shell Guide* to the *West Coast of Scotland and Oban* (Bone 1938), and in the 1960s and 1970s guides were published to Mid Wales and North Wales (Mawson 2010).

22   However, they continued to maintain a distinctive design aesthetic particularly in terms of the use of photographic images under the long editorship of artist John Piper. Piper became joint editor with Betjeman in 1959 and after Betjeman left in 1967, Piper took over as sole editor and continued until the publication of the final *Shell Guide* in 1985 (Mawson 2010).

23   Notably in his guide to *Oxon* (1938) John Piper chose to leave out the city of Oxford.

24   The *Shell Guides* and *Outrage* are also connected by *Architectural Review*, as noted above *Outrage* was first published as an edition of *Architectural Review*, and John Betjeman was working for Architectural Review when he began editing on the *Shell Guides*, Architectural Press, who published *Architectual Review*, also published the *Shell Guides* between 1934–36.

25   Betjeman's love of Victoriana is particularly evident in many of the typefaces and setting used which are reminiscent of Victorian newspapers and journals. Heathcote points out that this was a subversive interest at the time (2011: p. 21), however, in a contemporary reading of the guides it adds an additional texture of archaism.

26   Nash was also involved in the functionalist/modernist movement as a founder member of Unit One (the English modernist group which included Barbara Hepworth and Ben Nicholson as members) and as Montagu goes on to note 'found himself in the cross-fire of these two opposing tendencies (Montagu 2003: p. 13).

27   Nash's object personages are similar to the Surrealists' objet trouvé, however for Nash they had an innate mysticism 'To attain personal distinction, an object must show in its lineaments a veritable personality of its own … it must be a thing which is an embodiment and most surely possess power' (Nash quoted in Montagu 2003: p. 93).

28   First published in 1838 by Koblenz based (later Leipzig) Karl Baedeker A Baedecker guide to the Rhineland was published earlier in 1832, but the later 1838 version was much revised and took what became the classic form for the Baedecker guides (Koshar 1998).

29   Shell Guides did not provide itineraries in the same way as the Baedekers, rather they featured a selection of sites of interest, particularly in their Gazetteer sections, leaving the driver, in the spirit of individual exploration, to devise his own tours.

30   In *Search of England* was so popular that it had achieved its twenty-sixth edition just 12 years after its publication (Matless 1998: p. 65). It also spawned numerous spin offs for the author including *The Call of England* (1928), then perhaps predictably throughout the 1930s published: *In Search of Scotland, In Search of Scotland Again, In Search of Wales, In Search of Ireland*, and later *I Saw Two Englands* (1942).

31   In addition to producing pieces of visual art Berners was also a well known composer and writer (Dickinson 2008). His country residence was Faringdon House in Oxfordshire, and his painting of Faringdon Folly was used on a Shell Lorry Bill in 1936 (Hewitt 1998: p. 75). He famously used to dye white pigeons a selection of pastel shades to enliven his estate and appeared as the extravagant Lord Merlin in Nancy Mitford's *In Pursuit of Love* (1945).

3

Keeping Britain Tidy: Litter and Anxiety

3.1 Abandoned shoe amongst fly tipping in Micheldever Wood, Hampshire.

The creation and disposal of waste is an everyday experience, and litter belongs to this quotidian realm. It is part of the visual landscape of the everyday in both country and city, and it is made up of everyday things: cigarette butts, tissues, drink cans, sandwich cartons, chocolate wrappers, fast food packaging, flyers. These items are products of modernity, they are the flotsam and jetsam of mass consumerism. They bear testament to the routines that shape the daily maintenance of the body: eating drinking, expelling, and servicing addictions. Their presence also marks the regular routines and transitions which constitute the everyday: work, meal times, commutes and dog walks.

Sometimes litter also contains things that are out of the ordinary, where it is difficult to understand how they have come to be discarded and their presence cannot easily be tied in to an everyday narrative. The ubiquitous single shoe is an instance of this (Figure 3.1). It has a disconcerting effect, it is an everyday object but it is not in its everyday place, it has become inserted into a different sequence of events with possibly disturbing undertones. It could be evidence of an attack, or perhaps it has been dumped as part of a whole load of other things and has become separated from its pair. Perhaps this has happened in the course of its owner's intriguing albeit chaotic lifestyle and has been dumped because of its singleton status. The presence of litter in the countryside, whether it is the common or unusual forms, is not benign. It creates a range of emotional responses from slight annoyance to outrage, from nervous curiosity to actual fear. Litter in the countryside feels out of place, uncomfortable, anxious – feelings that result from its power to inflame a set of deeply ingrained binary relationships that define the non-metropolitan: litter is man-made in comparison to the landscape which is seen as 'natural', litter is a product of modernity, whereas the rural is timeless or outside of modernity, litter is urban and when it appears in the countryside it is evidence of the urban invading the rural.

This chapter is structured around three instances of litter-induced anxiety. First it examines the case of litter trails that were recorded in the Cambridgeshire countryside during the Second World War. These trails were thought to be laid by fifth columnists leaving signals in preparation for an enemy invasion. Here litter is an agent in revealing the countryside to be an unstable and potentially dangerous place. It also reveals an illicit league of traitorous insiders and a threat of invasion from outsiders. The reports on the trails form part of the Mass-Observation Archive and add an unusually rural perspective to the archive's early holdings. They can be seen to be in dialogue with Mass-Observation's strategies of the collection of fragments as a way of accessing the everyday dreams and anxieties of the population. The second instance of litter anxiety also accesses fears of invasion, however in this instance it is not soldiers but tourists who are the focus of these fears. Through examining the histories and concerns of anti-litter campaigns from the 1930s into the 1960s, this section shows how litter can be seen as a sign of the blurring of established boundaries between the country and the city. The breaking down of such established orders is a product of mass tourism and population change in the countryside, and this section argues that reactions to these changes, such as anti-litter campaigns, can be read as designating people, as well as litter, as being out of place. The final section examines the work of artist Stephen Willats, in particular his methodology of mapping litter as a tool for revealing the uses and interrelations of everyday spaces. Willats' investigations once again access the notion of outsiders and insiders in relation to the ownership of space and show how dropping litter can be a demonstration of ownership and belonging.

First however, it is necessary to explore some ideas about litter and its relationship to the everyday and to the non-metropolitan. Items which turn up as litter, such as used condoms, used tissues, used nappies, bagged dog faeces, and half eaten or decaying food stuffs, certainly arouse disgust and could be thought of as abject. In Kristeva's (1982) formulation of this concept, powerful feelings of abjection are caused by objects which effect the breakdown between self and other, subject and object. As evidence of bodily processes, fluids and excretions these forms of litter can, according to this theory, disturbingly signal our own materiality by transgressing the psychic boundaries between the self and the world. This reading of litter designates it as a potentially phobic object, a term which does not seem so far fetched if we think about the equipment issued to litter pickers, which often includes thick gloves, long handled grabber sticks, and high visibility jackets.

This psychoanalytical approach to the analysis of waste does have its limitations. Gay Hawkins (2006) argues that this perspective does not take account of the changing cultural meanings of waste over time. Hawkins also importantly argues that rather than being a threat to the formulation of the self, our relationship with waste and the everyday habits and disciplines that this relationship produces, are a vital part of how the self is repeatedly performed. The designation of an object as waste names it as other to the self, the subsequent procedures of disposal perform that distinction. What therefore becomes psychically troubling in the case of litter is not the nature of the waste itself, but its visibility. The re-appearance of waste signals that the performance of the differentiation between self and other has been unsuccessful. An abiding image of horror is the landfill site with its abundance of waste. However, in terms of everyday contact, litter in the landscape can carry a similar charge to the landfill, what litter lacks in volume it makes up for in contrast with the surrounding landscape and physical nearness.

The effective disposal of waste is seen as a characteristic of civilised modern living. The wide range of consumer products designed to facilitate processes of instant and hygienic disposal, such as spotlessly white bathroom suites and in sink waste disposal units, stand testament to this (Lupton and Miller 1992: p. 26). So when waste turns up again, as litter for example, it causes anxiety. Referencing Simmel's *Philosophy of Money* (2004 [1900]) Hawkins asserts that for modernity to appear to be effective it is important that things circulate, that they remain in motion: goods, money, people. When objects re-surface as litter they are essentially out of circulation, they are stuck. In this instance the all important consumer cycles are brought to a halt, and in this moment shown to be malfunctioning, allowing the spectre of unsustainability to rear its ugly head. For the effective disposal of waste fuels the fiction of its disappearance, disposal is a euphemism for another cycle reliant on the power relations of capitalist society, with much of the waste generated by western countries being shipped to less economically buoyant states for 'processing'.

The modern fictions of flow and the dynamic cycles of consumption and disposal are reflected in the way litter has been aestheticised. The famous scene in the film *American Beauty* where the flight of a plastic bag is buffeted by the wind into a dance of ephemeral beauty, implicitly enacts the fleeting and the impermanent. Themes which belie the weighty burden that the plastic bag bears of impending environmental catastrophe (Hawkins 2001: p. 4). In his analysis of trash and manufactured mass-culture Julian Stallabrass says that:

> The constant flux of objects onto the streets, and their removal or disintegration, has a rhythm which is usually too slow and disjointed to grasp, although we might get

an impression of it when papers are blown about in high winds, or carrier bags lifted into the air like balloons. When snorkelling once I caught sight of something which seemed to summarize this process: swimming between two narrow rock faces, I saw that the sea bed at their foot was carpeted with garbage and unidentifiable detritus forming a thick mass which shifted in and out with each tug and push of the waves, changing its form subtly as it did so (Stallabrass 1996: p. 182).

Although on a much larger scale than the plastic bag film, both images access the sublime in the constant almost ungraspable movements of trash. However, what such interpretations of waste overlook to some extent, is its materiality rather than its symbolic nature. What happens if, instead of thinking of litter as part of an ever changing process of movement and change, we start recognising it as stuck? It is almost easier to make this move thinking about litter in the countryside rather than in the city. Litter in the countryside, is not subject to shifting patterns of movement generated by large amounts of people or traffic and it has fallen out of any institutional systems of collection and disposal. In the countryside it sits, it decays, and interestingly it sometimes becomes colonised by its new environment as in Figure 3.2.[1] In this respect one of the differences between representations of litter in the city and litter in the countryside, is that litter in the city is seen as a product of modernity, and in the countryside it is seen as a failure of modernity.[2]

It is possible to argue that litter is an historically specific phenomenon and one which saw its birth with the twentieth century. Claire Jack, in her *Short History of Litter in the Twentieth Century* (2005), situates its development as an identifiable phenomenon and simultaneously as a problem, as being a product of the coincidence of two aspects of modernity: the decline in horse drawn transport and the increase in the mass production of consumer goods. During the nineteenth century, all waste that was left on the streets, a large proportion of which was horse manure, was gathered together and passed onto farmers to use as fertilizer. In the

3.2   Trainer colonised by the environment, found at the edge of a footpath.

first decades of the twentieth century horse drawn traffic significantly declined, while at the same time new forms of consumer products and packaging came onto the market, meaning that not only did forms of litter increase, but it also became newly conspicuous for its recognisable wrapping. Without the horse manure there was no profit to be gained from collecting the refuse from the street and litter started to be regarded as a serious issue and a municipal responsibility. In their study of the aesthetics of waste, Lupton and Miller (1992) note that the model of easily recognisable branded packaging for food items, which became popular in the US in the late 1800s, had spread to most consumer items by the 1930s. They argue that the disposability of the packaging, and particularly the emphasis on streamlined forms and smooth surfaces, of both the packaging design and the goods themselves, indicated seamless flowing movement, and contributed to the notion of the disposability of goods, a mindset that was essential to the consumer cycle of purchase and disposal. They add that 'The policy of 'planned obsolescence' pictured the economy itself as a 'body', whose health depended on a continual cycle of production and waste, ingestion and excretion' (Lupton and Miller 1992: p. 5). From horse manure to metaphorical human excretion the history of litter is tied to processes of modernity and its close relationship with waste. The story told by Jack of how litter came to be defined and thought about as a problem, accesses the persistent narrative that sees litter/waste, and by extension signs of modernity, as being generated by the city and gradually moving outwards into the countryside. When litter is found in the countryside it is out of place, an insidious sign of modernity seeping out from the city in these polluting fragments.

Definitions of litter as a noun and as a verb refer to its connection with disorder. To litter is to strew with objects scattered in disorder, it refers to odds and ends, fragments and leavings lying about, to states of confusion and untidiness, and disorderly accumulations. Litter is an agent of the disruption of order, it pixelates the binary edges between city/country, modernity/anti-modern. Through this disruption assumed orders and ideologies are revealed. No matter where litter lies (except perhaps in a litter bin) it is out of place. The Keep Britain Tidy campaign's definition of litter is 'waste in the wrong place caused by human agency' (Keep Britain Tidy 2010), a description that echoes Mary Douglas' classic definition of dirt as 'matter out of place' (Douglas 1991 [1966]: p. 35), made in her famous study *Purity and Danger*.[3] Douglas argues that from an anthropological perspective, examining aspects of pollution and taboo can reveal the rules, value systems and classifications which constitute that society, summarised by the classic maxim 'Where there is dirt there is system', followed by the not so neat, but still insightful 'Dirt is the by-product of a systematic ordering and classification of matter' (Douglas 1991 [1966]: p. 35). Similarly, littering practices and reactions to them can be seen to reveal systems of order, value and assumptions about place, in England over the past hundred years.

Litter in the countryside as opposed to the city is seen as being particularly incongruous, to the point of causing outrage among many otherwise placid citizens.

The contrast between mass produced, brightly coloured packaging and the landscape in which it resides, reaffirms deeply held notions that the countryside is natural and eternal, and at risk of being corrupted by the synthetic and the throw away. Such ingrained ways of thinking about the countryside, places it outside of modernity, or at least as the helpless victim of modern developments, rather than as a legitimate space of modernity, with its own agency.

LITTER TRAILS

In 1940 strange montages of litter started to appear in fields and woods, on grass verges and village signposts. Assemblages of cigarette cartons pegged up on sticks, scraps of packaging with intricate cut outs, readymade chocolate wrappers displayed in series, and drawings chalked onto gateposts. These were not, despite their appearance, remnants of surrealist practices or the beginnings of land art interventions, they were in fact litter trails. Or rather this is the name attributed to them. Explanations for their presence ranged from the covert activities of fifth columnists to secret signals between lovers, however the origins and intentions of such unlikely material practices remain unclear to this day.

The story of the litter trails unfolds through a set of documents which has found its way in to the Mass-Observation Archive. It consists of a collection of correspondence and detailed reports generated by a group of Cambridge academics almost a year into the Second World War. These papers reveal suspicions that a fifth column of enemy agents was in operation in the Cambridgeshire countryside, and that their presence had become apparent to the sharp eyed observers through their use of carefully laid trails of litter and outdoor drawings as forms of covert communication.[4]

The reports are in themselves as carefully and as artfully put together as the phenomena they describe. In addition to detailed textual description of the found litter constructions, they also contain meticulously rendered sketches of the notable scraps and drawings which they encountered, together with hand drawn maps plotting their findings. These include a detailed drawing of a fragment of a *Craven A* cigarette packet, in which the distinctive lettering on the packaging has been diligently imitated, as has the brand's logo – a small cat. The reason for including the drawing in the report was to illustrate the presence and position of

3.3 Drawing from the Litter Trails Report, 1940. Reproduced with permission of Curtis Brown Group Ltd, London on behalf of The Trustees of the Mass-Observation Archive. © The Trustees of the Mass-Observation Archive.

a small notch that had been deliberately cut out of the packaging. The presence of unusual yet barely perceptible details like this notch, was all part of the case that this was not an ordinary piece of litter, but one that had been deliberately manipulated and thus marked as a signal. The drawing of this cigarette packet demonstrates the extreme attention to detail which characterises this report, not only with regard to the facts that were being recorded in the text, but also in the way in which these facts are supported by the act of making precise drawings. The process involved in making these drawings requires that every detail is observed and recorded. In a case like this it is never clear what will turn out to be significant. It is of note that the investigation was led by T.C. Lethbridge, who was a trained archaeologist, a discipline which places much importance on the accurate recording of finds, often fragments in themselves, through making detailed drawings.[5] It is also worth noting the importance of waste in archaeological method. The reconstruction of patterns of behaviour through the analysis of discarded fragments of material is recognised as an important archaeological procedure. In their key text book on archaeological practice Renfrew and Bahn cite numerous instances of how, what they term 'debris scatter', has led to greater understanding of ancient settlements (Renfrew and Bahn 1994: p. 168).

The litter trail drawings show that the observers were working in a heightened atmosphere of surveillance, paranoia and anxiety, where the most everyday and overlooked scraps might be of national importance. That drawings were used rather than photographs can be explained through war time shortages of film and developing materials, but I think it also points both to an obsessive trait enacted though the concentrated repetition necessary in making observational drawings, and to the amateur and somewhat outsider nature of the observers, a status which may have contributed to the fact that their findings were often not taken very seriously by the relevant authorities.

The litter trails are a fascinating example of extreme reactions to litter in the countryside. They enact and complicate a number of recurring ideas about the countryside that form the basis of this chapter. Perhaps most obviously, they introduce the idea that the presence of litter in the countryside signals some sort of invasion, or at least indicating the presence of strangers. In this case litter is seen as part of the preparations for a full scale enemy invasion in the wider context of the Second World War, and evidence of strangers or people who were not what they appeared to be, living amongst the community. While the realities of this interpretation are questionable, it is perhaps more useful to think of the litter trails as communicating something about the anxiety which the presence of litter in the countryside generates. This anxiety is born out of the idea that litter is out of place in the countryside and that in this way it is related to both outsiders and modernity, most fundamentally it creates anxiety around the anticipated change that both these things might bring.

It is also possible to see these fragments of litter as a form of spatial collage. Litter and collage both stem from over production, the excesses and disposability of mass production generate both collage and littering as cultural practices (O'Reilly 2008: p. 17). Spread out over the Cambridgeshire countryside these brightly coloured shards shine out in contrast to the greens and browns of earth and vegetation, creating a contrasting jolt that is not unlike the shocks Benjamin saw montage capable of providing as a medium for representing modernity. Benjamin said of the Dadaists' incorporation of litter in to their artworks 'the tiniest fragment of everyday life says more than painting. Just as the bloody fingerprint of a murderer on the page of a book says more than the text' (Benjamin [1934] 1970: p. 90). These fragments of a different reality have the power to disrupt a smooth rendering of any narrative, be it the illusionistic art works of which Benjamin is critical, or the illusion of the rural as being safe, stable and outside of modernity.

That the litter trail material may have come to rest in the Mass-Observation archive is perhaps somewhat of an anomaly as it did not result from the activities of the group's members or observers.[6] However, the material certainly belongs in the archive as it indirectly animates many of the methods and concerns of the organisation which are sometimes neglected. In particular engaging with Mass-Observation through these documents accesses the importance of the collage as a methodology for recording the everyday, a way of thinking which was central to the operation of the organisation. In the litter trails we see fragments of litter recorded, collated, and used as evidence of a wider national narrative. In a similar way Mass-Observation itself sought to access the mass feelings of the nation through the montage of fragments of everyday experience. As this section will detail, it is also possible to see further correspondences between the litter trails material and the concerns of Mass-Observation in their attempts to reconcile artistic and scientific methods of investigation, in their concern with coincidence, and in their attunement to symbolic anxieties.

Mass-Observation officially launched in 1937 with a letter to the *New Statesman and Nation* announcing the organisation's aims: primarily the urgent need to develop an anthropological approach to studying British society, an 'anthropology of ourselves' (Harrisson et al. 1937). The letter was signed by Charles Madge, a published poet and journalist for the *Daily Mirror*, Humphrey Jennings, an artist and poet who is most well known for his documentary films made with the GPO film unit, and Tom Harrisson a self-trained anthropologist with a background in ornithology, who had just started working as a mill hand in Bolton in order to study the working class experience.

The three parties approached the project with different concerns. Madge and Jennings were particularly interested in the possibility of using poetic and psychoanalytical methods in the service of social investigation. While Jennings' involvement with the project was short lived, he was instrumental in instigating collage as a form of investigating and presenting the everyday.[7] Whereas Tom Harrisson's approach owed more to his experience of ethnographic fieldwork in the South Pacific Islands and his interest in methods of participant observation. Such differences in intellectual position and approach makes Mass-Observation a fascinating attempt to try and fuse these two often opposing cultures together. While a geographical as well as ideological split in the organisation between Madge in London and Harrisson in Bolton is often used to characterise the workings of the organisation, it is worth remembering that both parties were to some extent engaging with the interface between art and science. Madge and Jennings were attempting to use aspects of surrealism as a form of social science, and Harrisson's more traditionally anthropological study of Bolton included contributions from the artists William Coldstream and Julian Trevelyan (Hubble 2006: p. 7). It is the early work of the organisation, particularly that carried out by Madge and Jennings that has the most interesting relationship with the litter trail material, and which is the primary focus of this section.

Prior to meeting with Harrisson, Madge and Jennings, together with a small group of artists and writers in Blackheath, had already been exploring ideas around how to capture what they called 'mass wish-situations' (Madge 1937) or the thoughts, feelings and experiences of the nation.[8] They framed their enquiry into the everyday using elements of psychoanalytic theory, stating that what they were trying to observe and record was 'so repressed that only what is admitted to be a first class upheaval brings them to the surface' (Madge 1937: p. 12). Madge and Jennings argued that poetic rather than purely scientific methods might be the key to accessing this region. Outlining the development of an anthropology which would yield meaningful results when applied to the study of the home nation Madge wrote that:

> Fieldwork, i.e. the collection of evidence of mass wish-situations has otherwise to proceed in a far more roundabout way than the anthropologist has been accustomed to in Africa or Australia. Clues to these situations may turn up in the popular phenomenon of the 'Coincidence'. In fact it is probable that in the ultra repressed condition of our society they can only materialise in this form, so mysterious in appearance (Madge 1937: p. 12).

In the context of Mass-Observation it seems the idea of coincidence can be thought of in two similar but slightly nuanced ways. Firstly, Madge refers to the influence of Freud's work in *The Psychopathology of Everyday Life* in which parapraxes (slips of the tongue or pen, misreadings, errors and forgetting things) act as evidence of repressed fears, desires or memories surfacing in everyday actions (Freud 1975 [1901]). Such errors, are not only evidence of repressed thoughts but are actually caused by their wilful re-emergence through sub-conscious behaviour. An example of how this idea fed into their investigations can be seen in their interest in newspapers as active venues for coincidence. From this changed perspective the newspaper sheet itself becomes a collaged mass of visual and symbolic imagery with numerous apparently unconnected stories presented side by side. Madge describes how the coincidence of fragments of stories which make up the front page of a newspaper could be read as a different form of text 'Humphrey Jennings and I had been noticing the way in which the items on a newspaper page, especially the front page, added up to make a kind of poem – or so we interpreted it' (Madge quoted in Marcus 2001: p. 6). This led them to look for connections, coincidences and moments where these daily forms of communication might symbolically register the temperature of the nation. One of these moments came with the Abdication of Edward VIII followed by the destruction of Crystal Palace:

> … when the papers were full of Edward and Mrs Simpson we saw them as in part an expression of mass wishes and fantasies, and were on the look out for other symbolic news-material that might be related to them. At the end of November the Crystal Palace was burned down, and the flames were visible from

6 Grotes Buildings [the headquarters of Mass-Observation in Blackheath] as a distant glow in the sky: the shock that this seemed to evoke at a symbolic level was perhaps akin to the shock that the abdication crisis bought to our stable monarchy (Madge 1937: p. 12).

Here we see the interconnection of fragments or coincidences, revealing what might be thought of as a mass subconscious. This is an example that introduces the idea that the psychological effects of a national crisis might be registered or enacted visually in other ways. In this case the fire stands in for the shock of the perceived instability of previously unquestioned national institutions that was caused by the abdication crisis. In the case of the litter trails the coincidence of pieces of litter in the landscape, begin to stand in for, to become evidence of another form of national crisis: the threat of invasion. A psychoanalytic perspective can also come into play here, with the idea that the mass anxieties of a nation at war, are manifested through the obsessive recording of fragments of litter.

The second reading of how coincidence was important for Mass-Observation is in its association with simultaneity. For Mass-Observation any form of mass consciousness needed to be alert to the heterogeneity of 'the mass'. This meant that a picture of mass desires, opinions or experiences need to be based on multiple and simultaneous voices. This approach is particularly evident in the first full scale Mass-Observation publication *May the Twelfth* (1937), in which Madge and Jennings worked to provide a picture of the events around the coronation of George VI on 12 May 1937. The book contained day surveys from the national panel of observers.[9] In addition mobile observers were sent to report their experiences on the streets of London in shifts which covered the full 24 hours around the event. Leaflets were also distributed amongst the crowds asking 'WHERE WERE YOU ON MAY 12? MASS-OBSERVATION WANTS YOUR STORY' (Jennings and Madge 1937: p. 89). The book also includes a substantial section at the beginning which performs an extensive newspaper survey in the run up to the coronation, consisting of extracts demonstrating the extensive if sometimes eccentric or controversial preparations for the day that were reported in the national and local press. The publication is endlessly quotable and full of vivid description of how the day was lived by many different people. I hesitate to single out any particular accounts for quotation as it seems this would be against the spirit of the endeavour which was indeed to evoke the multitude, each one of their fragmentary accounts building a kaleidoscopic depiction of the populous which pivots around this extraordinary set of events.

The litter trail material is unusual in the archive as it did not result from a directive issued by the organisation, nor were its authors part of the volunteer observer panel. It resides with the material on wall chalkings (graffiti) that was collected by Mass-Observation in 1940.[10] The collection of such material speaks of Mass-Observation's concern with not only the detail of the everyday but in finding ways in which public opinion might be communicated through alternative channels. The walls of the city have often been a place where the disenfranchised can express their voices, and recording slogans and messages chalked or painted onto walls could be seen as an effective way of gauging mass feeling. Given the timing of this project, much of the street graffiti was to do with war time figures and policies, including slogans such as 'End England's Shame Demand a Second Front Now!' and 'Mosely is a Rat' (TC41/1/A).[11] However, a comprehensive report on the Fulham area also notes: faces, cricket stumps, arrows, dartboards, scoreboards, hearts and swastikas amongst the wall chalkings, and goes on to detail notes and doodles found in telephone boxes and in public lavatories (many of which are carefully drawn in the report). This desire to record not only substantial pieces of graffiti but also minor doodles in phone boxes and toilet cubicles relates to the idea that a certain mass sub-conscious might come to light through the collection and examination of the fragmented textures of the city. Kathleen Raine (one of the original Blackheath group) wrote of the idea that hidden and fleeting aspects of the everyday might be captured by attending to the forgotten fabric of the city and reading it as a text:

> We hoped to discern on the surface of dingy walls, on advertisement hoardings, or written upon the worn stones of pavements, or in the play of light and shadow cast by some street-lamp upon puddles at the corner of a shabby street, traces of the beautiful, degraded, dishonoured, suffering, but still the deus absconditus (Raine quoted in Marcus 2000: p. 15).[12]

Perhaps with this approach in mind the initial pamphlet issued by Mass-Observation lists 'Litter on the streets' (Madge and Harrisson 1937: p. 49) amongst a selection of possible topics for study that had been suggested by the panel of observers. While this idea was never formed into a directive, litter has made its way into the archive in other forms. In accounts of the London streets in *May the Twelfth* litter is both metaphorically and literally an underlying presence. In describing the aftermath of the celebrations the editors add a long footnote about the many and various ways that paper has played a role in the day, from bunting to improvised shelters from the inclement weather (Madge and Jennings 1937: p. 145). They note the idea that throughout the day the rain combined with the movement of people has broken all these preparations – these paper goods, down into a mush that now litters the streets an inch deep. They even suggest that the abundance of paper everywhere affected the sale of special issues of newspapers produced with haste in order to report and commemorate the event. It was as if people were so surrounded by paper based debris that they couldn't bear to introduce more of it into the street by purchasing a newspaper. In a fascinating essay Steven Connor (2001: p. 57) sees the mush of paper underfoot as being symbolic of the mass-conscious that Madge and Jennings were trying to access, and that the figure of the periscope (a large number of which were sold on the streets to enable spectators to get a better view) can be thought of as the individual raising themselves above the crowd in order to add their personal perspective to the mix. Connor neatly points out the inter-related nature of the two figures – the paper mush and the periscope, the crowd and the individual – as the periscopes were made of cardboard (pulped paper). The image of a mass of spectators all viewing the event through fragmented shards of mirror either encased in the cardboard periscope, or as some did on small mirrors brought from home, adds a vivid enactment of the importance of fragmentation and simultaneity in Madge and Jennings' ideas about how to represent a mass-consciousness.

While a systematic study of the litter on the streets never became part of a Mass-Observation directive, it was realised with a different intention by the litter trail investigators. A letter from Mass-Observation reveals the connection between their wall chalkings project and the litter trails documents. The connection is Mr John Parker MP, General Secretary of the Fabian Society and chairman of a committee interested in the possible activities of fifth columnists. In the summer of 1940 he had a piece published in the socialist weekly newspaper the *Tribune*, in which he raised concerns about the use of wall chalkings as a form of communication between enemy agents. This was a topic which had reached a level of general concern at this time and an order from the War Office had been issued to the Local Defence Volunteers (Home Guard) to look out for markings on telegraph poles (TC41/1/A). Tom Harrisson heard about Parker's interest in this material and wrote to him:

> We regularly collect this material in Bolton and Fulham, and if you would be interested to have some sort of base line for normal activities of this sort established, we might be able to help you. It is particularly easy to confuse 'doodling' with deliberate designs? [sic] And there is an easy mysticism in random numbers (TC41/1/A).

At this point Mass-Observation under the leadership of Harrisson was now working for the Home Intelligence Department of the Ministry of Information. The techniques Mass-Observation had developed for the detailed study of public opinion were seen by government organisations to be of ideological use to the war effort, an affiliation that troubled Madge and eventually led to his departure from the group in 1940 (Highmore 2002: p. 77). Initially one of the motivating factors for Mass-Observation was a feeling that the people were denied access to what they called 'the facts' (Madge and Harrisson 1937: p. 47) by a press which neither expressed the opinions of the electorate, nor adequately communicated the debates or policies of the elected leaders. There was also concern about the ever widening gap or 'gulf of ignorance' as it was described, between the ruling and the working classes (Calder and Sheridan 1985: p. 3). Mass-Observation aimed to gather information about the everyday lives of ordinary people and their opinions and relay them back to the public in as accessible a manner as possible. Working for the Ministry of Information was contrary to these aims, and compromised its independence.

Less than two months before Harrisson's letter, John Parker had also been contacted by M.P. Charlesworth, Fellow and President of St. John's college, Cambridge and one of the academics involved in the litter trail investigations. Charlesworth had read Parker's piece in the *Tribune* and, after unfruitful attempts at attracting the attention of the authorities, hoped that he might be interested in their findings. Charlesworth sent Parker the reports compiled by Lethbridge *Observations upon Unusual Phenomena noted in the Cambridge District, June–August 1940* and *Litter Trails* (TC41/1/A). It seems Parker was interested in the material and replied by return of post, however no more correspondence on the subject is in evidence and what happened next, if anything remains a mystery. Lethbridge's reports, however, make fascinating reading and it is here that the connection between wall chalkings and litter becomes evident.

The reports disclose that when the Home Guard were ordered to look out for markings on telegraph poles, strange drawings which seemed to be working in conjunction with carefully placed bits of litter were discovered. On closer inspection, observers became increasingly concerned about the unusually large amounts of litter in locations around the Cambridgeshire countryside. The tone of Lethbridge's report, which it is worth quoting at length shows both his fixation with applying logical method to what might easily be regarded as paranoiac fantasy and reflects current feelings about littering at the time:

> Now it is of course obvious that the British are one of the filthiest races where litter is concerned; they do not hesitate to scatter paper of all kinds broadcast everywhere. From this it follows that verges of all kinds in the lowlands have a varying amount of old paper, cigarette cartons, etc. lying upon them. This litter however is proportional to the amount of traffic upon the road in question, and tends to be much more concentrated at bus stops or any place where people wait. It is perfectly easy to observe a distinction between the quantity of litter to be expected on the sides of a main road with heavy traffic upon it and that on the verges of a by-road or cart track. When the quantity upon such a by-road or cart track is far in excess of the normal amount observed on a main road some other explanation than 'love tokens' or 'Acts of God' is necessary (TC41/1/A).

It was not just the quantity of litter which aroused suspicion; it seemed that much of the litter had already been already been pierced by a litter collector's spike and redistributed. The presence of items such as bus tickets from Birmingham also indicated, as Lethbridge puts it 'that litter collected in towns has been placed in the countryside' (TC41/1/A). As has already been shown with reference to Jack (2005), the movement of litter from the town to the countryside is a recurring theme. In this case it indicates the idea that the relatively rural Cambridgeshire district would not have been capable of generating the amount of litter needed to produce the reported litter trail phenomena, it therefore being necessary to import litter from the city, where it is of course abundant. The assumption that extra litter is needed, inscribes the binary notions that I will be exploring further in the chapter, specifically that the countryside does not make its own litter, but essentially suffers the litter of others, and that litter is particularly out of place in the countryside, in this case it seemed to literally 'belong' in the metropolis of Birmingham.

In addition to the out of place-ness of this litter and its unusual quantity, strange assemblages were also reported. These included 'cigarette cartons pegged up on sticks', 'small heaps of stones and sharpened sticks' 'two gold flake packets both cut and torn', and brightly coloured cigarette cartons 'often mutilated or defaced in certain definite ways, viz. corners torn or cut off, long slits and holes roughly square or oblong, neatly cut out' (TC41/1/A). The voluntary team of observers mapped the location of each occurrence. An exercise which appeared to show that the litter was marking trails which if followed would allow access to military installations in the area avoiding local defence posts and main roads.[13]

The documents show that Lethbridge was quite clearly convinced that these instances of litter in the countryside were the work of fifth columnists preparing the way for a military invasion. He states that 'we maybe fairly confident that we are observing the handiwork of traitors' (TC41/1/A). Of course Lethbridge was well aware of the apparently fanciful nature of his theory, where scraps of throw away rubbish stand in for a full scale enemy offensive. This is obvious in his endless justifications and refutations of any idea that the appearance of these litter trails could be put down to the activities children, tramps, boy scouts or lovelorn locals. He states that, 'it should be remembered that, if we are right in thinking that these phenomena are due to enemy agents, that is precisely the effect that they are probably intending to produce. Anyone who is not on the lookout will regard it as just simply untidy litter' (TC41/1/A).

There is much to suggest that these were indeed litter trails laid for nefarious purposes, for instance, the presence of military grid points in some of the drawings found scribbled close to the litter, and reports that leaving trails of cigarette cards had been a military tactic used in Flanders (TC41/1/A). However, the trails were dismissed by the authorities. John Parker MP, in his correspondence with those investigating the litter trails wrote '[we] have found great difficulty inducing Scotland Yard to take action, as they regard the matter of little importance' (TC41/1/A) and of course no invasion took place. Although it is possible to argue that an invasion attempt was foiled by the discovery and subsequent destruction of the trails. Lethbridge concludes his report:

> We are strongly of the opinion that plans had been made to aid some kind of hostile immigration in the neighbourhood of Cambridge about the beginning of July, and that this came to nothing … It seems probable that we are still finding the arrangements which were made in preparation for an invasion which has been deferred and it may be thought there is no need to do anything further about it. To this the answer is that the people who made these arrangements are still with us, and are capable of making others at a suitable moment (TC41/1/A).

A chilling finale, which reminds us that this litter has been dropped by a dangerous form of outsider: enemy agents posing as locals, or perhaps even more disturbing, members of the community who were in fact traitors.

This is in fact a very rural narrative. All the locations in which litter trails were observed were in the countryside which in itself reveals some ideas about the different characteristics of litter in the country and in the city. The idea that perhaps litter trails as a method of communication would not have been practicable in the city shows that we think of the city as a place perhaps so replete with litter that specially laid trails would be invisible amongst the existing detritus, whereas in the countryside the trails would stand out as there is less litter, and more of a contrast in the surroundings. Perhaps conversely it also shows that there is an acceptance that there is enough litter in the countryside for the trails not to look entirely out of place. It also reveals an assumption that litter in the city might be moved or swept along either by a municipal employee or by the general flux of people, transport and the localised currents of the city. Whereas in the country there is an assumption of less movement, and fewer people meaning that that litter will remain relatively stationary, it will stay where it is dropped until it is broken down by the weather.

The figure of the 'outsider' in these debates is ever present. The geographical other, for example the figure of the urbanite sprinkling litter throughout the countryside, is a habitual image and will be discussed in the next section of this chapter, but what the litter trails bring to this story is the idea of the metaphorical 'outsider' actually being an insider, a local, who secretly stands in ideological opposition to the mainstream, whether it be in terms of the morality and meanings of dropping litter or in their foundational political principles (i.e. wartime traitors). Lethbridge surmises that the litter trails must have been left by 'not only aliens or naturalized aliens, but also natives, who for any reason are discontented with their position or prospects or who may be honestly convinced that our country needs purging and a different form of government' (TC41/1/A). In this story we see litter as evidence of illicit activities taking place, enacted by residents of the countryside. Litter becomes evidence of a parallel world with different values.

Andrew Biswell (2009) has written that the litter trail investigations could be seen in the context of the popular enthusiasm for detective and spy stories of the time, citing many examples of tales of infiltration and treachery. Particularly relevant is Graham Greene's short story *The Lieutenant Died Last*, which was made into the film *Went the Day Well?* (1942). It tells the chilling tale of the vanguard of a German invasion team, infiltrating an English village by impersonating British troops, an operation which is facilitated by the village squire who is revealed to be a German spy. Biswell argues that 'What might look at first glance like a paranoid over-interpretation turns out to have its roots in the common belief, largely created by novelists and poets, that a vast network of foreign agents were everywhere' (2009: p. 27). While feelings of anxiety were obviously heightened at this point in time and were undoubtedly both fuelled and reflected by cultural production, it is also necessary to situate this reaction to litter trails as part of a wider story of anxiety about the disruption of order, which has been enacted through reactions to litter in the countryside from the early years of the twentieth century.

This anxiety around disruption or change in what is assumed as an eternal English countryside can be seen by adding another film to the set of references proposed by Biswell: Powell and Pressburger's *A Canterbury Tale* (1944). A parable of the ancient and modern in the English countryside which combines the trope of unnerving hidden activities with almost surreal events, set against a bucolically patriotic image of England, signified by the ancient landscape of Kent and Canterbury Cathedral. Made and set during the war, it is the story of two soldiers and a land girl who arrive in the small Kent town of Chillingbourne late one night. As they make their way from the station to the town hall in the black-out darkness the land girl becomes the latest victim of the 'Glue Man', whose trademark is to pour the sticky substance into the hair of girls who have come to work in the area. The trio involve themselves in attempting to uncover the identity of the 'Glue Man' who is finally revealed to be the local magistrate and erstwhile head of the town. His actions are motivated by a hostility to one of the most recent changes brought about by the war: women performing the roles traditionally occupied by men.

In addition to revealing evidence of a parallel world of activities and beliefs taking place in the countryside and their role in revealing anxieties around change, the litter trails also demonstrate a synecdochical structuring that runs throughout these discussions of litter, where a specific countryside location – in this case the Cambridgeshire countryside – stands in for the nation as a whole, and the litter fragment stands in for something much bigger and more important, on this occasion an enemy invasion. Fundamentally the story shows that narratives around litter and by extension other overlooked aspects of the everyday, are often denigrated and thought of as unimportant, however the habits, reactions and relationships which they engender point to a much wider significance.

The next area I want to examine, is how anxieties about litter reflect worries about the relationship between town and country. It explores how objects (litter) and people become designated as being in the wrong place and how maintaining the disorder has been conceptualised in terms of national identity.

ANTI-LITTER CAMPAIGNS

One of the first campaigns against litter in the countryside was initiated by the Campaign for the Protection of Rural England (CPRE) in 1928. The campaign can be seen as a response to the opening up of the countryside at this time as a space of leisure. Significant developments in transport such as the construction of railway branch lines and the increasing use of automobiles and charabancs (early motorised buses) made it much more appealing for urban dwellers to travel to the countryside at the weekend. In fact access to countryside at this time not only became desirable but was seen by many as a right, one that was fervently exercised by the often politically aligned walking clubs that were a feature of this time. In the same year that the CPRE's anti-litter campaign began, the British Workers' Sports Federation (BWSF) was established as a nationwide organisation with an emphasis on walking. It joined the already multiple regional hiking groups, and in 1930 the Youth Hostel Association was formed to provide low cost accommodation for hikers (Solnit 2002: p. 164). In 1932 this new found right to the countryside was tested when the famous mass trespass, organised by the BWSF, took place on the Kinder Scout peak in Derbyshire, as a part of a campaign to open up access to footpaths fenced off by landowners. The trespass resulted in violence and arrests, but succeeded in strengthening the cause for free access to the countryside.[14]

The *Shell Guides*, as detailed in Chapter 2, were a product of this enthusiasm for exploration of the countryside. Here the Derbyshire guide describes a typical weekend in the Peak District:

> *The Peak in summer is extremely popular with young men and women of the industrial towns; it is positively yellow with their nether garments. If you dislike these people you had better spend your week-end in the mud-bath at Smedley's than on Kinder Scout. Aesthetically, the Peak is grand enough to stand any number of them and any amount of their litter (Hobhouse 1935: p. 46).*

This vivid image presents the walkers not only as bringers of litter as but as human litter themselves, with their yellow nether garments adorning the countryside like a mass produced version of Wordsworth's daffodils. This is striking in contrast to the private motorist who might opt for the spa treatment at Smedley's as a more luxurious and fittingly private health giving leisure pursuit.[15]

The CPRE's campaign was not only directed towards walkers and motorists, but those seen as more of a scourge: the picnicker. Often arriving en masse from nearby cities, charabanc parties are represented as the urban working class at their worst. In *Landscape and Englishness*, David Matless frames the presence of working class city dwellers in the countryside as a kind of 'cultural trespass' (Matless 1998: p. 67), and that in this tension the city dweller was often cast 'as a cultural grotesque, signifying a commercial rather than industrial working class whose leisure is centred around consumption and display' (Matless 1998: p. 68). These visitors were seen as uneducated or disrespectful in their treatment of the countryside and were blamed for a significant increase in littering. CPRE commentator C.E.M. Joad wrote that they leave the land 'so covered with paper after the last of the charabanc parties have left that those ignorant of the tastes and habits of Englishmen on holiday would have imagined a convolution of nature in the shape of a summer snowstorm' (Joad 1937: p. 72). This statement aligns the visitors with something that is against the natural order – 'a convolution of nature'.

This hostile position is, however, complicated by Joad's insistence on the countryside as a right. His negative comments about city dwelling tourists' use of the countryside come from an essay entitled 'The People's Claim' in which he asserts that 'the people' have a right to access the countryside and that littering along with other countryside faux pas such as leaving gates open and picking wild flowers should be tackled through education rather than exclusion. In the tone of a benevolent patriarch he argues that the bad behaviour of the "common man" must be tolerated in the hope that through time, education, and exposure to the supposed civilizing properties of thecountryside, it will right itself: 'the only way to create good taste and good manners is to provide occasions for their exercise and to persist in providing them despite their abuse' (Joad 1937: p. 75).

In some cases, such as the Women's Institute (WI) campaigns detailed below, it was the countryside residents who were expressing concern, but in many cases those who lived in popular countryside destinations were able to take full economic advantage of the increasing number of visitors to the regions - this does not of course mean that they welcomed the litter these visitors brought. However, many of the most vocal commentators at this time were metropolitan intellectuals or activists, who saw themselves as custodians rather than residents of the countryside.

The anxieties about litter and by extension about the new leisure class should also be seen in the context of other technological and cultural changes which were recasting the rural as a site of modernity. At this time the CPRE were also protesting against new housing developments, electricity pylons and advertising hoardings which were appearing throughout the countryside. The 1930s recorded the greatest annual losses of land to urban use. Local council legislation was not sufficiently effective at this time at preventing development, meaning that agricultural land could be bought cheaply and built upon. At the same time growing transport links meant that, urban dwellers were not just able to visit the countryside at the weekends, but increasingly they were choosing to live outside major conurbations and commute (Rogers 1989: p. 97).

Anti-litter campaigns have continued to the present day through the activities of the Keep Britain Tidy organisation.[16] Initiated in 1954 by the Women's Institute (a social and campaigning organisation for rural women), The Keep Britain Tidy Group was originally a reaction against litter in the countryside, although as the group developed it began to include members with more urban interests. The passion with which the WI expressed themselves on the matter speaks of the outrage that litter in the countryside can provoke. At the WI's 1954 AGM a motion was passed to create the Keep Britain Tidy Group:

> That this meeting requests the National Federation of Women's Institutes Executive Committee to inaugurate a campaign to preserve the countryside against desecration by litter of all kinds, and urges every member of the WI to make it a personal matter to mitigate this evil (NFWI Archive 1954b: p. 123).

The idea that the countryside could be 'desecrated' by the 'evil' of litter is one that reveals the connection between the British landscape, and national and religious identity. An association which was at the heart of the WI organisation, perhaps most vividly demonstrated by the adoption of the hymn *Jerusalem* as their anthem, in which landscape, Christianity and nation are tied together in its lyrics:

> And did those feet in ancient time
> Walk upon England's mountains green
> And was the holy lamb of God
> On England's pleasant pastures seen? (Blake 1804: p. 2).[17]

The KBT group sought to access feelings of patriotism through both its linguistic and visual rhetorics. Its early posters made use of national emblems seemingly indicating that action against litter was every citizen's duty. Plates 3 and 4 show Britannia on her chariot and the English lion, both transformed into litter pickers. The lion squashes a piece of collaged newspaper into a litter bin whilst flying the union flag from his tail, while Britannia is transmuted into a male street sweeper armed with broom rather than trident. The thrust of such images would seem to be that litter bugs are in essence traitors, a visual echo of the relationship between litter and patriotism developed through the litter trail documents.

The use of the word 'tidy' in the campaign's name is perhaps a strange choice. It is more of an indoor word, a domestic word, the idea of tidying your living room is more apposite than the idea of tidying the street or the footpath. It has the effect of domesticating the outdoors, turning the countryside into a living room and encouraging the application of the same feelings of ownership to the communal space of the country as you might feel towards the private space of the domestic. The privileging of tidiness as the preferred aesthetic relates to Lowenthal's (1994) emphasis on the importance of order in conceptualisations of the countryside (detailed in Chapter 1). This is a notion of order that is played out not only in terms of stewardship of the countryside but also with regard to maintaining social order: everybody as well as everything should be in its place. Edensor interestingly points out that this aesthetic has also been rigorously adopted by the National Trust in the organisation's quest to represent an essence of the English countryside as neat and tidy (Edensor 2002: p. 41).

This idea of domestication may also relate to gender. Much of the documentation shows those involved in the co-ordination and the hard graft of litter picking to be women and children. Of course the Women's Institute members played a large role in the efforts of the KBT organisation, but earlier examples also bear out these gendered roles, for instance a newspaper article from 1930, covering a litter pick in the New Forest in Hampshire, reports that it was girl guides mobilised by female members of local gentry (Lady Montagu of Beaulieu and Lady Frankfort) who were responsible for recovering 'some 70 sacks, bulging with scraps of paper and the relics of careless picnic parties' (*The Times* 1930). There are a number of significant things to draw from this, firstly and most obviously that tidying and keeping things clean fits into the traditional spectrum of women's work, and the vocabulary used in the campaigns situates this activity in the domestic realm. Related to this is the idea that women have a different relationship with the abject, their traditional role as mothers and carers, is often characterised by a closer relationship with bodily materials, blood, vomit, excreta. Essentially they are aligned with an aptitude for dealing with abject and contaminated material. The high proportion of involvement of women in these activities has also placed the removal of litter from the countryside in the voluntary realm, rather than in the public/paid sphere which to some extent it inhabits in urban locations with the paid role of the municipal street sweeper, characterised in Plate 3.

It is therefore interesting to view this subject in relation to Gillian Rose's arguments that the landscape has been consistently gendered as female in the discipline of geography and in representations throughout art history (Rose 1993: pp. 86–112). Many writers have also made the argument that while nature is gendered as female, culture – that which invades the landscape – is gendered as male (for extensive bibliography see Taylor 1994: p. 207). The development of this binary opposition covers everything from the male gaze of knowledge and ownership, to the forces of capitalism exploiting and despoiling a feminised and therefore subservient space. It is interesting to see a form of visual re-enactment of these symbolic repetitions in an archival photograph from the KBT campaign, showing members of the WI forming a defensive (albeit smiling) barricade, literally barring the way into the landscape beyond (Figure 3.4).

So far this chapter has explored the relationship between litter, order and ownership. Litter is synonymous with disorder and therefore runs contrary to the narrative of order that is a necessary part of the conceptualisation of the countryside. The anxieties around litter can be related to anxieties about disruption of order in the countryside, be that in terms of different people accessing the space (tourists, new residents, or even enemy invaders), or new things, signs of modernity (new housing, roads, power stations, advertisements). Essentially these anxieties could be characterised as a fear of pollution. Edensor has shown how idealised portrayals of the countryside (such as the magazine *This England*, detailed in Chapter 1) attempt

3.4   Image from Women's Institute Keep Britain Tidy Campaign, c.1955. Courtesy of Keep Britain Tidy.

to communicate rural England as a space of purity, uncomplicated by things that don't fit in with an easy rendering of the rural scene, such as agribusiness, housing estates, television aerials and parked cars. In this purified national space 'anything 'out of place' stands out as un-English' (Edensor 2002: p. 43). We have seen that litter in the landscape has been equated with un-English activities in the litter trail documents and in the nationalistic images used by the KBT campaign. Being out of place, or standing out as un-English, also relates to the experiences of many Black and Asian residents of, or visitors to the countryside. This is an aspect of perceived change or disorder in the countryside that can also be related to attitudes towards litter.

A competition was run by the WI to encourage its members to send in inventive ideas in response to the problem of 'How to cure litter'. One of the favourite ideas was the suggestion that a poster should be made showing 'A large sow leading her litter into a sty, with the caption: "Please follow the example of this good animal and TAKE YOUR LITTER HOME!"' (NFWI Archive 1954a: p. 149). Although I can find no evidence of the piggy poster ever having come to fruition, the slogan became central to the WI's campaign, although in the slightly amended form 'Please Take Litter Home' as seen in Figure 3.4. This phrasing has since become widely used in the anti-litter lexicon, and the 'your' is not always omitted as in recent example in Figure 3.5.

This statement works from the assumption that your home is elsewhere – that you are not at home in the countryside. The apparently polite request, barely conceals its undertones of hostility. When considered in conjunction with the WI respondent's conflation of the two meanings of litter as brood or off-spring as well as rubbish, then the idea of taking your litter home, becomes newly connected to the idea of people and their families being 'invited' to return home, a dimension that opens up questions about access to the countryside not only in terms of class, which as we have seen was the concern of C.E.M. Joad and campaigns in the 1920s and 1930s, but also ethnicity.

3.5 Litter sign in Avebury, Wiltshire, 2010.

This could be seen in the context of Britain as undergoing radical changes in terms of immigration during the 1950s.[18] However, exclusion of black and Asian people from the countryside is still very much a current area of debate. Sarah Neal and Julian Agyeman's collection of essays subtitled *Ethnicity, Nation and Exclusion in Contemporary Rural Britain* (2006), explores racism in the countryside and extends the idea of what constitutes the ethnic outsider with an examination of New Age Traveller and Gypsy communities' experiences in rural Britain. The work of photographer Ingrid Pollard is a key visual mapping of outsider subjectivity in the British landscape. For over 20 years she has used the conventions of landscape and portrait photography, to articulate the complex experiences of belonging and un-belonging as a black British woman. Her most cited work *Pastoral Interlude* (1987) was made in the Lake District and is comprised of self portraits in the landscape overlayed with stream of consciousness statements which reveal her feelings of conspicuous discomfort and trepidation. In the same year as Pollard was walking and photographing in the Lakes, V.S. Naipaul published *The Enigma of Arrival* (2002 [1987]), a novel which in part enacts the author's immigration from Trinidad and Tobago and the process of re-constructing a home and identity through the landscape and stories of a rural Wiltshire village. In 2004 a report by the Commission for Racial Equality showed that although ethnic minorities make up 8 per cent of the UK population they represented just 1 per cent of visitors to the countryside. Then chairman of the Commission, Trevor Phillips, suggested that a form of 'passive apartheid' existed in the British countryside (BBC 2004). The report, perhaps predictably, sparked a wave of protest from rural residents with many newspapers interviewing black and Asian residents of rural communities for their views on the subject, most often recounting positive experiences (Smith 2004; Carlin 2004). The subject seems to return on an annual basis, being re-visited in Sunday magazine features each summer, just as city dwellers begin to hanker after the wide green spaces of the countryside. For example the *Sunday Times* profiled a mixed race family's move to the small town of Lewes in Sussex, and the instances of racism the encountered there (James Smith 2010). In the previous year the same publication ran a headline 'Is the Countryside Racist' on the cover of the magazine linked to an article by Sathnam Sanghera, on efforts by the National Parks to encourage visitors from ethnic minorities (Sanghera 2009).

The visual rhetorics of the anti-litter campaigns made it possible to make the connection between inorganic 'rubbish' and unwanted others in the countryside. They also demonstrate that maintaining order 'keeping things tidy' is a mark of belonging and ownership of a space. The next section complicates this idea by re-thinking litter in the countryside not as being brought in by visitors but as being the product of activities of residents. Furthermore that it is the leaving of litter that asserts ownership rather than the act of tidying it up. I want to make this shift through an examination of the work of British artist Stephen Willats.

STEPHEN WILLATS: LURKY PLACES AND DANGEROUS PATHWAYS

Stephen Willats is an artist who uses the everyday as his material. Since the early 1960s he has made work which investigates and documents societal structures, codes of communication, and relationships between people and the places in which they live. His practice is framed by urban experience and is often the result of collaboration with the residents of inner city housing estates and tower blocks.

My reading of his work as it contributes to this chapter on litter, focuses on Willats' projects on pieces of waste ground and footpaths and their use by residents of the surrounding area. Specifically his work *Dangerous Pathway* (1999), which unusually for Willats takes a semi-rural/semi-urban footpath as its location. This work is important for thinking about the non-metropolitan everyday because in line with Willats' other projects it shows this non-metropolitan space as an everyday site of codes of control and strategies of resistance. What it contributes to this chapter is a disruption of the persistent association of litter with outsiders or visitors that was explored in the previous sections, and complicates the relationship between feelings of ownership and littering.

Stephen Willats is part of a generation of young artists who in the 1950s and 1960s rejected the traditional modes of art making with which they were presented in favour of developing an art practice concerned with mapping processes and behaviours. At this time traditional modes of artistic approach were still very much focused on the idea of the artist as a sole producer and that the production of art was essentially a personal journey, relatively unconcerned with the role of the audience. Willats and his contemporaries – artists and teachers such as Roy Ascot, Brian Eno and Gustav Metzer, founded an approach that was grounded in interaction with audiences. For Willats the primary audience of the work was simultaneously involved in its creation. This is particularly true of the work conducted with residents of housing estates in which the results of questionnaires and other forms of research collected by the artist would be displayed and the residents responses would inform and become part of the next stage of the work.

Willats was a student on the Groundcourse at Ealing College of Art, which was a form of foundation course developed by Roy Ascott in the early 1960s. Ascott was particularly interested in the science of cybernetics and its emphasis on process and mapping informed his structuring of the course (Mason 2008: p. 56). The influential writer on cybernetics W. Ross Ashby, drawing on the formulation put forward in a seminal text by Norbert Weiner, characterised cybernetics as 'the science of control and communication' (Ashby 1964: p. 1). It is the study of behaviours and processes rather than things or objects, which means it can be used across disciplines to map processes involved in complex systems. Ashby states that what is most important about cybernetics is its ability to conceive of complex systems with simultaneous multiple variables. Such thinking mirrored the turn away from objects and towards processes or concepts taking place in the development of conceptual art practices at this time. Cybernetics provided a framework for thinking about society as an infinitely variable machine operating within certain structures of control and methods of communication.

The Groundcourse became an experimental form of art education in which the emphasis was put on developing theoretical frameworks using mapping systems and drawings, rather than traditional standalone art objects. There was a collaborative approach between staff and students, disrupting the notion of art as a singular process of personal exploration. The focus throughout was on relationships and networks. Subsequently continuing this collaboration into multi-disciplinary practice, Willats formed working relationships with scientists, mathematicians, architects and advertising creatives (Obrist 2009). Ascott, with whom Willats later worked at Ipswich Civic College, emphasised the idea that 'art could become a powerful force for change in society and believed that the artist should be conscious of the didactic and social role of art' (Mason 2008: p. 58).

This notion of combining scientific and artistic methods for experimental social investigation echoes the early experiments of Mass-Observation discussed earlier in this chapter. Willats' work continues to reflect this foundational training in thinking about society as a set of systems, and his interest in investigating how people and communities work within or react against such systems, is key to his practice, as is a multi-disciplinary approach which draws on cybernetics, information theory, sociology and anthropology.

An example of how societal systems and structures inform Willats's practice can been seen in his attention to how local systems and practices are formed by the physical architecture in which communities are contained. It is significant that his training and early practice as an artist took place against the backdrop of the grand social planning initiatives of the 1960s which famously changed the non-metropolitan landscape with the development of the large New Town projects, and smaller scale housing developments on the edges of many towns and villages. The ubiquitous concrete tower block was a manifestation of these plans in inner city areas. For many these projects significantly improved housing conditions and there was a utopian feel to them. In its early years the tower block became synonymous with a brighter post war future:

> If you've been to Notting Hill Gate you'll know that right outside the station there is a huge tower block and this tower block was a very important cultural symbol in London; it was one of the first and became quite famous. I'd come from the wastelands of west London and for me this building was a fantastic phenomenon and it seemed a sort of signpost to the future in an optimistic way. The building for me at that point was an iconic symbol of a way forward, affecting all different kinds of realms of culture and life and society (Obrist 2009).

Even in this initial atmosphere of optimism Willats began to see the restrictions imposed upon the residents through this new form of architecture:

> I noticed that the structure was very segmented. Here was a uniform façade, which was monumental, but on the other side of this monumental façade there was a complex segmented structure containing people's lives (Obrist 2009).

This attunement to the impositions of modernist architecture has resulted in a body of work over the last 40 years which closely documents the restrictions, interactions and strategies for self organisation and resistance, experienced by individuals and communities in the UK and Continental Europe. Over this time Willats has developed a distinctive aesthetic which, perhaps unsurprisingly given his continued interest in cybernetics and information theory, is characterised by diagrams, flow charts, arrows, maps, photographs, films, essays and interviews. Rather than artworks as such they are the visible products of process-led research developed through interaction with residents.

The work of Stephen Willats may seem to be a strange choice for a study in to the non-metropolitan as so much of what he is known for centres on urban communities and their patterns of living. However, I want to focus on a part of Willats' practice that reoccurs in many of his pieces, namely his treatment of litter as evidence. Litter has featured in pieces such as *The Lurky Place* (1978), *Pat Purdy and* the Glue Sniffers Camp (1981), Dangerous Pathway (1999) Person to Person, People to People (2007), and Starting Afresh with a Blank Canvas (2007–2008), in which it variously acts as a marker of disenfranchisement, use, resistance and ownership of space. These works are not all strictly studies of urban spaces, but include projects undertaken amongst the New Town architecture of Milton Keynes (Person to Person, People to People) and, as mentioned above, Dangerous Pathway (1999) is a study of a semi-rural footpath. Willats' work ties litter to structure, and ways of resisting this structure. In this way it reaffirms the statements made at the beginning of this chapter by Douglas (1991[1966]) who identified that the designation of certain materials as dirt reveals fundamental societal structures, and Hawkins (2006) who shows how the practices of identification and disposal of waste repeatedly perform the relationship between the self and the rest of the world. Willats' approach to litter also develops the themes implicit in the anti-litter campaigns which see litter as a signifier of the disruption of order regarding who inhabits certain spaces.

In the rural anti-litter campaigns detailed in the previous section, litter was always regarded as being dropped by visitors. What is interesting in Willats' work is that litter is seen as being dropped by residents, a factor which complicates these assumptions around litter in the countryside. To begin with it is useful to think about one of Willats' more urban surveys of litter The Lurky Place which attempts to map the meanings of litter found on waste ground, close to a housing estate. It is significant that in order to find a discussion of litter dropped by residents rather than visitors it is necessary to turn to an urban practitioner, however the places described by Willats are not exclusively urban and their non-metropolitan equivalents are easy to bring to mind. The Lurky Place centred on a piece of waste ground on the outskirts of West London which was bordered by residential areas and industrial sites. Using the visual methodology that has become a distinctive characteristic of his work, double images linked by a thick black line, Willats pairs an image of a piece of litter with one of the surrounding cityscape, creating a connection between this overlooked material, the land, and by extension the people who use or inhabit it. The litter documented in the piece includes, a squashed aerosol can, a paper target with shot holes in it and a piece of dress material.

Willats sees the litter he found in The Lurky Place as evidence of how the place is used by local residents almost as a zone of resistance. He contends that this place is an unofficial place, and acts as a realm of relative freedom for the inhabitants of this area, where activities and fantasies which are outside work and everyday chores can be exercised. He states that:

> The way people's destinies are largely determined by the dulling routines of their daily lives is contrasted with the freedom of pursuits and interests carried out within 'The Lurky Place' (Willats 1978: p. 1).

Perhaps we can all identify a Lurky Place of our own, most likely from childhood or adolescence, and non-metropolitan Lurky Places certainly abound in spaces such as woodland, unused railway lines, abandoned structures and farm land. The Lurky Place becomes an alternative space to everyday life and as Willats sees it, a place to assert individual identity. But what sort of pursuits does this litter signify? Essentially we are talking about drug taking, lighting fires, shooting air rifles, drinking and having sex – Willats also notes that activities as diverse as track bike racing and horse riding are also taking place (Willats 1996: p. 29). One could question if such activities can really be seen as forms of creative resistance? However, Willats argues that it is necessary to shift our perceptions of what might be thought of as anti-social behaviour: 'the destruction of the environment is not destruction at all, but it is creative; people are simply registering their mark to show they exist. Acts of so-called vandalism as counter-consciousness are no more than anarchistic exhibitions of people's energies and individualism' (Willats 1996: p. 28).

The materiality of litter in Lurky places is also interesting. Willats argues that the meaning of objects changes as they pass from the everyday world into this place of festive disorder. In line with the idea that this place provides a space which is counter to dominant mainstream culture, objects brought into the space undergo transformation into an alternative realm. An example of this is glue, a substance which in the everyday world is used for construction and repair, in the *Lurky Place* is transformed into a drug – a means of communal exuberance and escape (Willats 1996: p. 30). A similar transformation can also be seen happening in places where the results of fly tipping or joy riding are evident, car seats, builder's rubble and discarded white goods all become components in homemade camps.

In the previous section we saw that anti-litter campaigns aligned the idea of keeping a place tidy i.e. not littering, with taking ownership of that place. This was specifically conducted through advertising campaigns which aligned the countryside with both the nation and the domestic space of the living room, a double construction of ownership. The majority of rural campaigning was directed towards tourists, and it was implied that dropping litter was an act carried out by those who were not residents of the countryside such as urban visitors, or 'outsiders' more generally. Willats' work however complicates this notion by allowing us to think more broadly about litter in the countryside not only being the product of visitors but also of residents. Willats shows that litter can indicate a hidden everyday, a parallel world of perhaps illicit activities which spaces such as this enable to exist; a parallel world where litter can signal ownership, of certain spaces, including rural Lurky places, it is evidence of practices that assert identities and communities that are counter to the mainstream, if only in very temporary ways.

In 1999 Willats employed a similar methodology to examine ideas of litter and ownership in a more rural location. In his piece *Dangerous Pathway* which consists of a super 8 film and a series of paired photographs, Willats examines a footpath bordered by trees and hedges, a ubiquitous space of the non-metropolitan. This is an in between space which is neither entirely rural nor urban. What it represents is the ordinary everyday bits of countryside, which are usually surprisingly easy to access from many built up areas and speaks of the undecided nature of the non-metropolitan. These bits of countryside are essentially unremarkable and for that reason are frequented by locals, rather than day trippers meaning that the litter found along the footpath can be thought of as being left by residents rather than visitors.

The film is made with a hand held super 8 camera and takes the form of a walk along the footpath, pausing to zoom in on things found along the way, these include bits of litter, but also barbed wire fences, padlocked gates and keep out signs. In the accompanying photographs each aspect that has been focused on in the film is reproduced and paired with an image of various parts of the footpath, presumably the location where the bit of litter or other item of interest was found, although there is no definite indication of this. The pieces of litter Willats came across were a mixture of the usual – crisp packets, junk mail, drinks cans – and the unusual – bits of rope and rubber tubing.

So what makes this pathway dangerous? We've seen from the litter trail documents that litter has been recognised as a signal of a very real danger – the threat of invasion. Through the anti-litter campaigns we have also seen how the presence of litter gave an implicit signal of the danger of disrupting established structures of who inhabits the countryside. In this piece there are a number of reasons that the pathway and specifically the presence of litter along it becomes dangerous. The title of the piece may refer to the uncomfortable feeling that the presence of litter can create, this is different from the outraged feeling already discussed in relation to the anti-litter campaigns. This discomfort is more like a form of anxiety as if the presence of the litter evokes some hidden forms of elicit behaviour, giving the pathway an uncertain charge, marking it as having another life removed from the ordinary everyday uses. This anxiety is also tied up with the idea that perhaps you might come upon such dubious activities taking place should you continue along the path. In an unlikely parallel with the activities of the litter trail fifth columnists, anxiety is also caused by the realisation that while this litter has been dropped by residents, the very act of dropping litter marks them as 'outsiders' in some way – outsiders who reside within the community, littering might represent a momentary lapse into outsiderness, or a concerted attempt to resist everyday societal norms.

The connection between litter and danger is made explicit in the 'clean and safe' policies investigated by Anna Minton in *Ground Control* (2009). The conflation of the words 'clean and safe' creates an opposing phrase in which dirt – and therefore litter, is aligned with danger. Minton's study demonstrates that urban planners and managers of commercial districts place a high level of importance and significant economic investment on keeping streets, together with shopping and business areas free from litter, in the belief that people/consumers associate litter with crime and therefore feel threatened in places where litter is evident. Encouraging a 'non-threatening' experience of place has obvious benefits for both the feel and economic success of residential and commercial districts. However, Minton shows that a high level of litter management often enforced by private firms of security guards, has the subsidiary effect of functioning as a way of managing who uses these spaces. In a similar way that anti-litter campaigns in the countryside were directed at certain groups of visitors, so anti-litter strategies in urban areas are used to control who occupies certain spaces, once again creating human litter. Minton states that:

> Clean and Safe is really about far more than safety, its about creating places that
> are for certain types of people and certain activities and not others. Exclusion
> is either covert, by making people feel uncomfortable, or overt, by banning
> them, with the list of undesirables spanning far more than the usual suspects of
> beggars and the homeless to include groups of young people, old people, political

protestors, photographers [and] really anyone who is not there to go shopping (Minton 2009: pp. 45–6).

Enforcing a clean and safe policy allows a space to be kept clear of unwanted people by seeing them as potential creators of litter or other undesirable pollutions.

In terms of its ability to signal enemy invasions, or alternative illicit activities or cultural transgression, litter can be associated with danger. The phrase 'dangerous pathway' is more usually associated with coastal paths which are being undermined by erosion and it could be argued that a different form of erosion is taking place here, the erosion of accepted forms of ownership. By depicting barbed wire, fences, padlocks and no trespassing signs, alongside the litter, the pathway becomes an interface between different forms of ownership, the barbed wire of economic ownership and the litter signalling a parallel world of unofficial ownership.

As the litter trails, the Keep Britain Tidy campaigns and the work of Stephen Willats have shown, litter is an agent of disruption. The presence of litter physically and symbolically disorders rural space, and in so doing reveals those assumed orders to be constructions. In World War II, the montage of litter in the countryside punctured idealised notions of the English landscape and revealed a potentially dangerous parallel world of treacherous activity. The vehement reactions against litter perceived to be brought in by visitors to the countryside, as articulated in the anti-litter campaigns, points to constructions of the rural as a pure space, which is outside the various 'pollutions' of modernity. Ideas of belonging and un-belonging in this space creates forms of human litter – people perceived to be 'out of place'. Here ownership of the landscape is exercised through an attitude of defence – tidying is patriotic, littering is once again treacherous.

Just as the litter trails revealed a parallel world of subversive activity, Willats' projects show how litter can evidence the creation of alternative zones, spaces in which practices take place which run counter to the mainstream and the everyday. In these scenarios it is the leaving of litter, rather than the clearing of it, that signals a conceptual ownership of space.

I referred at the start of this chapter to litter's ability to pixilate the binary edges between the city and the country, and between the modern and the anti-modern. The idea of pixilation seems appropriate here as it is often seen as a kind of corruption or degradation of an image (much as litter is seen as a corrupting force), but pixilation also makes the boundaries between objects and places less clear. Litter complicates the boundaries between what characterises urban and rural space, and who belongs where.

Modernity is figured in the changes in population and use of the countryside, with which litter has been associated. While the modernising rhetoric of development and preservation is perhaps less overtly evident in this chapter, in comparison to the last, it is possible to see the shadow of these tensions in debates around litter. The preservation of the countryside (and indeed the country as a whole) was enacted by the anti-litter campaigners and litter trail academics. While the changes in use and ownership of rural places which generated much of the anxiety around litter could be seen as a product of development.

So far this book has examined the everyday practices of driving and littering. Through their alignments with modernity, both of these practices are more usually associated with the urban. However, through an examination of visual and archival materials, different stories have emerged which allow them to be re-thought from a rural perspective, in turn showing how the non-metropolitan can be recast as a complex site of modernity. The following chapters focus on practices that are more traditionally embedded in the non-metropolitan, Chapter 4 centres on the activities of Women's Institute and Chapter 5 examines calendar customs and folk art. These sections perform a slightly different manoeuvre in that rather than re-situating urban practices in a rural narrative (as in Chapters 2 and 3), they think about how these traditionally rural practices might be re-situated in discourses of modernity.

NOTES

1   Aesthetically this difference can also be seen as belonging to the register of the picturesque rather the sublime. The definition of the picturesque has always incorporated 'strange sights, and signs of ageing and decay' with picturesque subjects including old mills, gnarled oaks, well worn paths through fields, sluices covered with moss, backyards filled with junk and ramshackle cabins'(Taylor 1994: p. 265). While Stallabrass' reef of litter might be sublime, the abandoned shoe in Figure 3.2 could be considered picturesque.

2   This is also the case for other perceived forms of littering in the countryside such as the visual littering of advertising signs detailed with reference to the *Shell Guides* in Chapter 2.

3   Steven Connor notes that while this definition is widely attributed to Mary Douglas, she did not formulate it, rather she referred to it as an 'old idea of matter out of place' (Connor 2011).

4   Litter trail documents show that reports were also being made of litter trails being found in different part of the country, specifically records are made of similar occurrences in Salisbury.

5   T.C. Lethbridge, was a somewhat infamous archaeologist whose many projects include the discovery of ancient hill figures in Wandlebury, Cambridgeshire (Lethbridge 1957), and went on to develop controversial occultist archaeological methods involving using a pendulum to douse for objects (Lethbridge 1976).

6   The documents came to the archive through a connection made by Tom Harrisson with John Parker MP who was concerned with litter trails as a threat to national security at the time.

7   Jennings left Mass-Observation in late 1937 (Hubble 2006: p. 7). His interest in collage as methodology is evident in his later projects such as his posthumously published *Pandemonium* (1985) which builds a picture of modernity through the collation of fragments of texts. Jennings film *Listen to Britain* (1942) also employs montages to map the nation.

8   This group included Kathleen Raine a poet and married to Madge; David Gascoyne a poet and writer with an interest in French surrealism; and Stuart Legg who was working with Jennings on the GPO film unit (Highmore 2002: p. 76).

9   Several international examples were also included, which the authors asserted were to provide a 'control' measure – a vocabulary more often associated with quantitative

scientific methodology, and one that reveals their seriousness in experimenting with collage as a mode of investigation.

10   This is because on some occasions it was believed that the litter trails were being used in conjunction with messages written on walls and gates.

11   TC41/1/A refers to the Mass-Observation Archive Topic Collection: Wall Chalkings (41), Box no.1, File A, which contains the litter trails documents.

12   'deus absconditus' refers to the idea of a hidden God.

13   Artist Tim Brennan remade these maps, for the exhibition *English Anxieties* (John Hansard Gallery Southampton and Ffottogallery, Chapter, Cardiff, 2009). Brennan used the Isotype visual system developed by Otto Neurath and the Isotype Institute in the 1940s, which was utilised in the Mass-Observation publication *Exmore Village* (Turner 1947). Brennan's exhibition and subsequent catalogue also included a fascinating selection of photographs of archival material, which visually enacts the methodology of fragmented and simultaneous accounts used by Madge and Jennings in *May the Twelfth* (1937).

14   The activism which started with the mass trespasses eventually resulted in the successful passing of The National Parks and Access to the Countryside Act of 1949, which required every council in England to publish maps detailing all the rights of way over the land in its constituency (Solnit 2002: p. 166).

15   Smedley's Hydro was a famous water spa in Matlock, it closed in 1955 and is now used by Derbyshire county council as County Hall (Peakland Heritage 2011).

16   The KBTG received government funding in the years after its initiation by the WI and eventually became independent from the organisation. In recent years the organisation has been re-branded several times, in 1984 it became the 'Tidy Britain Group', in 2001 it became ENCAMS, which was short for Environmental Campaigns and was intended to reflect the group's concerns with the environment on a wider scale than just litter. In 2009 it returned to Keep Britain Tidy, its most widely recognised branding, but one which does not reflect the fact that the organisation only works in England. Its most recent campaigns have targeted chewing gum, coastal litter, graffiti, drug litter, fly-tipping and dog fouling (Keep Britain Tidy 2010).

17   It is interesting to note that in recent times this hymn has been subject to a ban at Southwark Cathedral by the Dean who stated that the lyrics are too nationalistic (Borland 2008).

18   Between 1948 and 1962 Britain experienced a large amount of immigration from Commonwealth and colonial countries. Government rhetoric centred on the colonial right to migrate to the 'Mother Country', however many accounts show that British society at large was riddled with overt and covert racism at this time (Marr 2007: pp. 192–201).

1   Lorry Bill 298: Edward McKnight Kauffer, *Stonehenge*, 1931. Courtesy the Shell Art
     Collection and Estate of Edward McKnight Kauffer.

2   Lorry Bill 308: Edward McKnight Kauffer, *The New Forest*, 1931. Courtesy the Shell Art
     Collection and Estate of Edward McKnight Kauffer.

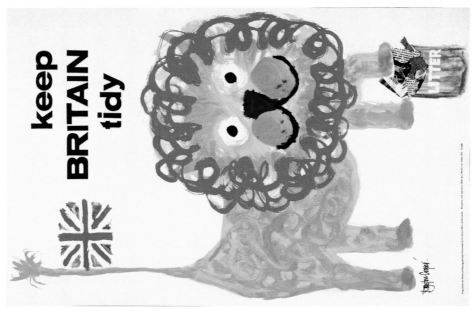

4 Keep Britain Tidy poster designed Royston Cooper circa 1963.

3 Keep Britain Tidy poster designed by Abram Games, 1963. ©
Estate of Abram Games

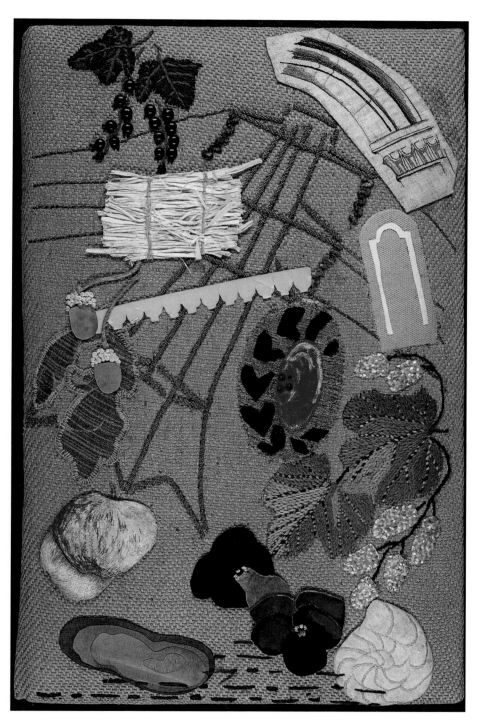

5   A collage to suggest Binsted, front cover, Binsted Women's Institute Golden Jubilee Scrapbook, 1965. Hampshire Record Office: Binsted Women's Institute: 153M85/2.

Binsted has no resident policeman. The beat is covered from either Buck's Horn Oak or Bentley.

Hampshire County Travelling Library

Stops at many points in the village once a fortnight and is used by many local residents who appreciate the service.

Welfare Clinic is held once a month in the Youth Club hut, for mothers with children under school age. Although the organisation is a voluntary one, with Mrs West as secretary, the welfare nurse is in attendance. An enjoyable Christmas party is held in January, and a garden meeting at Bunches, during the summer.

Three doctors have surgeries in the village.
Dr. W. P. N. MOORE,
BENTLEY, HANTS.
Cedars Inn, Tuesday afternoons
Drs MEYER & GOODING
Rowledge, Surrey
use the Wickham Institute on Wednesday afternoons.

PLEASE RETURN

HOSPITAL

Dentist visits the school periodically to attend the children, but others have to visit Alton or Farnham for this service.
Hospitals Treloar's Hospital and the General in Alton, The County Hospital in Farnham, are the nearest, with many others, in both Hants and Surrey available for special cases.
Ambulance is available for out-patients needing treatment, and for stretcher cases.
District Nurse although not resident in the village, visits when necessary.

A Sub-Post Office is situated in a private house in the centre of the village.

Open from 12-6p.m. weekdays and 9-12 p.m. Saturdays.

Mail is collected and delivered twice daily excepting Saturday and Sundays. There is one each on Saturday and one collection only on Sunday.

Telephones Bentley exchange serves most of this area, Alton and Bordon carrying a few subscribers on the perimeter. Use of the telephone has increased considerably, and would do so much faster if the Post Office could meet the demand. This they try to do in some part, with the unpopular "party line". Binsted itself has one public call box and there are two or three more in the hamlets.

Electricity is supplied by the Southern Electricity Board and covers the whole village. Binsted differs little from any other village today in its wide use of electricity. It has made possible the mechinisation of hop-picking and hop-drying. There is no street lighting, but it is a pleasure to know that underground cables have been used in the vicinity of the Church, the beauty of whose surroundings is preserved.

Hampshire County Council Roads. Situated at the top of a hill, with narrow hollow lanes, Binsted is particularly vulnerable to drifting snow, and it is a comfort to know that a snow plough is kept at Roxfords Farm by Mr. W.W. Stephens and his son. The employees there soon get into action to keep the roads open.

Water is provided by the Wey Valley Water Co. whose wells are situated in Tilford in Surrey. In this as in previous years we have suffered failures in supply. Whatever the causes, frost, old pipes, greatly increased demands, electrical pumping failure, or other reasons this causes inconvenience and annoyance in the village, particularly in the smaller houses where there are no storage tanks.

THE WEY NEAR BENTLEY

A Refuse Collection is made once a week and emptied in to the Hill Court Lane tip. Bins and other containers must be put for collection on the roadside.

6   Public Services page, Binsted Women's Institute Golden Jubilee Scrapbook, 1965. Hampshire Record Office: Binsted Women's Institute: 153M85/2.

7   Anna Fox, *Country Girls*, 1996–2001. Courtesy Anna Fox and James Hyman Photography, London.

8   Anna Fox, *The Village*, 1991–1993. Courtesy Anna Fox and James Hyman Photography, London.

9   Anna Fox, *Hampshire Village Pram Race*, 2006, from the series *Back to the Village*, 1999–2008.
Courtesy Anna Fox and James Hyman Photography, London.

10   *The Midnight Barrel*, part of Folk Archive by Jeremy Deller and Alan Kane. Photo: Jessica Mallock.

11   Delaine Le Bas, *Witch Hunt*, mixed media installation at Aspex Gallery, 2009. Photo: Tara Darby. Courtesy of Galerie Kai Dikhas Berlin.

4

The Networked Village: Women's Institute Golden Jubilee Scrapbooks

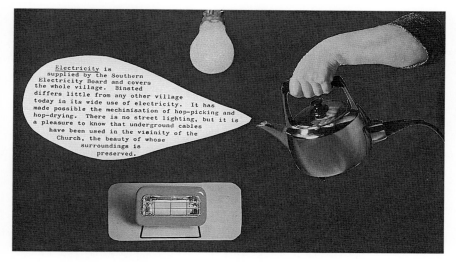

4.1　Detail from Public Services page, Binsted Women's Institute Golden Jubilee Scrapbook, 1965. Hampshire Record Office: Binsted Women's Institute: 153M85/2.

In the previous chapter we saw the role that the Women's Institute (WI) played in initiating the Keep Britain Tidy campaign and waging war in very practical ways to maintain established orders in the countryside. This chapter looks more closely at this rural women's organisation and how a set of scrapbooks produced by the group document further changes in the countryside, from the influx of members from the new middle class residents of the village, to the appearance of pylons in the landscape. Factors that situate the rural as an active site of modernity and reveal fascinating aspects of what constitutes the non-metropolitan everyday at this time.

The scrapbooks were produced to celebrate the Golden Jubilee of the WI in 1965, and were intended to provide a snap shot of village life at that moment in time. Now held in county archives or by the institutes themselves, the books reveal something of the complexity in how modernity has been felt in non-metropolitan places, evidencing dramatic yet uneven changes in the landscape, in consumption and in the home. Part of the importance of these documents is that they articulate both a non-metropolitan everyday and a female everyday.

The scrapbooks are of course collages, indeed they are perhaps the most literal appearance of collage in this book. The productivity of collage in the case of these scrapbooks is that the technique opens up possibilities for alternative, marginal and unofficial stories of the everyday to be told. Here it is the unorthodox methodology of collage as a way of registering the everyday that allows a rural, female everyday to be communicated. As I will go on to discuss, the materiality of the scrapbook collage is also particularly productive. In the *Shell Guides* for example, collage became a visual representation of an uneasy, fragmented countryside. The surrealist nature of the collages portrayed a place that is old and strange, but is also textured by the tensions of preservation and development. In the scrapbooks these tensions are also made evident through the juxtapositions of different yet simultaneous realities that collage enables. However, these realities are most powerfully communicated through the disparate materialities of the found objects which populate this non-metropolitan arena and find their way into the scrapbooks. These collages were not made with the intention of disrupting traditional views of the countryside (as in the case of the *Shell Guides*), rather they were made with the aim of representing everyday village life, and utilised the materials that were to hand. Nevertheless, as explored in detail below, the presence of some of these materials – pop art inspired stamps for example – confound expectations and present an aesthetic of the lived experience of rural modernity.

In the course of this research I have viewed scrapbooks from villages in Hampshire, East Sussex and Essex, and read about the contents of many more, however many of the themes explored in this chapter are seen through the lens of the scrapbook made by Binsted WI. This scrapbook was the most visually fascinating that I viewed. In a study which attempts to move between the fragment and the wider narrative, it seemed appropriate to focus my sustained attention on one example of the many possible scrapbooks and see how the stories it tells might relate to the overarching themes of this study. By attending to these scrapbooks as both visual and textual objects, this chapter works towards re-situating the rural, the female and the domestic everyday as existing as part of wider networks of modernity. It is divided into seven sections. First, it begins by focusing on the visual elements of the scrapbooks, specifically the use of collage as a medium and its potential for revealing the lived experience of different yet intertwined realities. The second section centres on the public and private aspects of the scrapbooks, exploring the relationship between the personal and seemingly trivial aspects of the everyday and the larger, narratives of modernity which they also express. The third and fourth sections draw on material from the archives of the National Federation of Women's Institutes (NFWI), in order to reconstruct the history and intentions around the creation of the scrapbooks. They examine subsequent projects generated around the scrapbooks and the interconnected picture of village life that they represent. The fifth section then explores how this notion of interconnectedness is also activated through the WI as an organisation that worked to connect rurally based women not only with each other in strong friendship networks but also to mainstream political systems. The sixth section focuses on how demographic changes in the countryside were reflected in the WI as an organisation and how this effected the notion of what it means to be rural. The final part of the chapter draws together these local and national women's networks by thinking through the idea of the network as embodied by another rural network: the national grid. The rural use of electricity and the presence of pylons in the landscape are both described in the scrapbooks, providing an interesting lens through which to develop this study's discussions of the interconnectedness of the country and the city, and the tensions between ancient and modern played out in rural locations.

CUTTING AND STICKING

The scrapbooks are intimately involved in the detail of non-metropolitan everyday life, covering everything from the geographical position of the village, to the daily school dinner menu. The scrapbooks include sections on: houses in the village, work, school, church, pastimes, nature, village organisations, amenities (Plate 6), shopping (Figure 4.2), transport, food and drink, seasonal celebrations, and fashions. Not only do they record the everyday, but the recording process involved in the making of these documents was ingrained into the everyday life of the contributors. One of the ways in which this is evident is in sections such as the weather statistics which were often a feature in the scrapbooks. Details of the weather were kept daily, and monthly summaries and statistics on temperature and rainfall were often recorded. Perhaps more importantly though for many members at this time, their involvement with the WI fundamentally shaped their everyday routines, activities, and relationships. Membership (or non-membership) effected friendship groups and integration into the village community, attending meetings would necessitate particular domestic arrangements e.g. changes in meal times so that the woman could get to the meeting on time, and monthly crafting tasks, contributions to WI markets and involvement in WI campaigns, meant that for many women the WI was embedded in their everyday.

Accelerated processes of modernity and technological developments characterised the 1960s and this is evident in the scrapbooks, not only in what was written by the contributors but also in the way the scrapbooks look. It is their visual qualities that make them a unique resource and a contribution to a specific figuration of the modern rural. The WI chose to create scrapbooks rather than a straight forward written account of their villages, a recording technique which is aligned with the traditionally female occupations of crafting, and informal custodianship of everyday histories.

The latter role finds its most common expression in the position that female family members, most notably the mother, take in compiling and maintaining the family photo album, a gendered activity which continues to apply in many families even now when the photo album might take a virtual socially networked form rather than a construction of paper and card. The WI scrapbooks, like photo

4.2 Shopping page, Public Services page, Binsted Women's Institute Golden Jubilee Scrapbook, 1965. Hampshire Record Office: Binsted Women's Institute: 153M85/2.

albums, can be seen as part of a valuable heritage of informal, amateur and personal history recording by women, where the material form mirrors the unconventional content.[1] Artist Jo Spence and curator Patricia Holland argue that:

> Women have pioneered forms of writing about the past which explore areas tangential to the mainstream of political and economic change. As with other marginalised groups, forms which are themselves marginal, impure, apparently trivial have offered ways of seeing the past which insist on linking the personal with the political, the mundane with the great event, the trivial with the important. Blurring the boundaries between personal reminiscence, cultural comment and social history … these exploratory styles fit easily with the bricolage and loose ends of the family album (Spence and Holland 1991: p. 9).

Bricolage is often used to describe the practice of constructing artworks from a collection of found images or objects. It is from the French verb *bricolet* the meaning of which is to 'fiddle or tinker', which given the above sentiments would seem to be a suitably trivial activity. It can however also be used to mean making ingenious creations with whatever is close at hand.[2] de Certeau sees this definition as central to the practice of everyday life, as the individual makes, adapts and improvises with the products that populate the daily terrain (de Certeau 1984: p. xviii). Significantly, de Certeau frames the practice of bricolage as a tactic of the weak against the strong, a position which supports Spence and Holland in their account of the marginalised activities of the amateur family archivist. This position is also echoed in the WI scrapbooks which, as detailed later in this chapter, have been passed over as trivial accounts of rural modernity.

In true bricolage style (or even simply collage), the scrapbooks include paintings and embroidery, swatches of fabric from clothes and furnishings, samples of wallpaper from contributors' homes, hand drawn maps, black and white and colour photographs, everyday ephemera such as bus time tables, leaflets, stamps, programmes, menu cards, and collaged elements cut from women's magazines and colour supplements. This unorthodox approach to documentary, means that information about the time becomes available on a visual level – the collected ephemera tells its own story of the mundane and the great event. In addition to the written content, the visual material also articulates the progress of printing technologies, design innovations, lifestyle aspirations, mass availability of colour magazines and personal colour photography, together with the continued practice of traditional skills like embroidery and dress making. The scrapbooks communicate how the world was represented to the women of the WI at this time, through media and consumer products and how they chose to represent their world to future generations.

Collage is particularly effective at interweaving the apparently trivial with the grand narrative. Its ability as a medium to facilitate the emergence of two different but simultaneous realities is commented on by art critic Lucy Lippard as a strategy that allows alternative stories to be told:

> Obviously I mean collage in its broadest sense, not just pasted papers or any particular technique but the 'juxtaposition of unlike realities to create a new reality'. Collage as dialectic. Collage as Revolution (Lippard 1981: p. 16).

4.3   Martha Rosler, *Cleaning the Drapes*, from the series *House Beautiful: Bringing the War Home* (1966–1972). Courtesy of the artist and Galerie Nagel, Berlin/Cologne.

The possibilities of the dialectic of collage are explored in a long running series of photomontages by Martha Rosler titled *House Beautiful: Bringing the War Home* (c.1966–72; new series 2004–2008). In the original set of works in this project, Rosler combined news photos of the Vietnam war – images of which were in fact part of every American living room each evening as they were broadcast on national television news – with idealised interior scenes taken from women's magazines showing perfect kitchens, bedrooms and living rooms. The effect is immediate and intense. Although not dealing with such shocking subject matter the collaged pages of the WI scrapbooks also access something of different but simultaneous realities, this time orientated towards their appearance in the non-metropolitan everyday. These differences register most effectively in terms of the unevenness between the representations of modernity which these women were exposed to and their own day to day realities. This becomes particularly apparent in one of the most extensively collaged spreads in the Binsted scrapbook dealing with Public Services available in the village (Plate 6).

These pages make use of details cut out of magazines and pamphlets as well as personal photographs, actual everyday objects such as stamps and an envelope, as well as elements made of cut out coloured paper. There are some visual echoes of distinctive photomontage techniques developed by artists working in the medium, for example the disembodied arms at the top corners of the pages and the floating mouth – presumably making reference to dental services – such

fragmented body parts are a recurring motif in the work of Hannah Hoch. The appearance of so many modern, desirable consumer objects such as the latest electric cooker and the matching bathroom suit (newly available in pastel shades), also makes a visual connection to Richard Hamilton's iconic image from 1956 *Just what is it that makes todays homes so different, so appealing?* (Figure 4.4). Obviously an homage to the great moments of photomontage history was not the primary intention for this scrapbook, rather its focus was to represent what it was like to live in an English village in 1965. However, the use of collage both in terms of the inclusion of elements directly gleaned from everyday life and its mechanism of putting one thing against another, brings to light a series of juxtapositions that generate fascinating jolts of unevenness in the processes of modernity.

4.4   Richard Hamilton, *Just what is it that makes todays homes so different, so appealing?*, 1956. © R. Hamilton. All Rights Reserved, DACS 2014.

This is evident in the section representing the post office (Plate 6) – which at this time was also responsible for the telephone service. The makers of this page have included an envelope embellished with two of the new stamps issued in 1965. One of the stamps celebrates the centenary of the Salvation Army, and the other commemorates the death of Winston Churchill. Both images are redolent of the fashionable metropolitan aesthetics of that decade. They both draw heavily on Pop Art images of the time, it is easy to make parallels with Warhol's celebrity screen prints in circulation at this time. It is the Churchill stamp however that presents an extra element of modern radicality. In 1964 Tony Benn was appointed Post Master General, a role in which he took the opportunity to drastically change the criteria for stamp design. In 1965 he commissioned an album of stamp designs from David Gentleman which were ground breaking in the breadth of subjects portrayed, in their new landscape format, and perhaps most radically, in Gentleman's suggestion that the Queen's head no longer need be a compulsory element of the postage stamp format (Muir 2009: pp. 2–6). The Churchill stamp was produced experimentally without the Queen's head but was never sanctioned for production by the Stamp Advisory Committee.

The seemingly republican impulse to replace the image of the head of the Monarch with the words 'Great Britain' or 'UK Postage', as proposed by Gentleman, together with the accepted proposal that a greater range of secular subjects should be portrayed on British postage stamps, fundamentally changed the way this everyday object looked.[3] Furthermore these changes could be seen as evidencing a shift in feeling more generally towards a less reverential attitude in modern British society.

While the new Post Master General was busy commissioning stamps that reflected cutting edge design and radical new thinking, the scrapbooks reveal the unevenness of modernity in rural areas. The text on the envelope describes the village post office as being run essentially in someone's front room: 'A Sub-Post Office is situated in a private house in the centre of the village' (BWIS 1965).[4] That these stamps form part of these pages demonstrates the collage of old and new that continues to texture the non-metropolitan everyday.

PUBLIC AND PRIVATE

The perspective on the everyday that these scrapbooks offer is particularly interesting because it is primarily female, centred on the home and situated within the rural. The scrapbooks make us think differently about the way that everyday life has been theorised. They raise important questions such as: whose everyday life is written about and significantly, given the non-metropolitan lens of this project: *where* does this everyday life take place?

As detailed in Chapter 1, Naomi Schor opens up some of these questions for debate in her study of how everyday life in 1900s Paris has been represented. Schor articulates the divisions which exist in the way that everyday life has been written about. These oppositions bisect the male and female everyday, the street and the home, the public and the private and the heroic and the mundane. She argues that it is the everyday that is gendered female, that is situated in the private sphere of the home, and is characterised by its mundanity, that is least often explored by theorists. Through an examination of her personal archive of postcards from this period, with their scenes of the city street on one side, and their domestic notes about remembering to pick up cheese on the other, her study disrupts these binaries showing that the two forms of everyday life are intricately woven together and lived simultaneously. The WI jubilee scrapbooks play out Schor's theory in the context of the English village in the 1960s, where the major technological, cultural and social developments of the decade are registered indirectly and surface through the accumulation of everyday details of home and village life.

It is significant that when talking about the established locations of the everyday, Schor identifies the home and the street as the two sites set up in opposition. This spatial pairing is also used by Rita Felski (also detailed in Chapter 1) as way of challenging how everyday life is articulated as a concept by cultural theorists, historians and feminists. For Felski the notion of 'the home' used by Schor to refer essentially to the indoor world of the house, changes subtly to an idea of 'home', that not only indicates a physical structure but also a feeling of familiarity and habit which can be associated with a geographic area. Felski argues that 'home' – in contrast to 'the street' for example, should be considered as the defining space for the everyday:

> Like everyday life itself, home constitutes a base, a taken-for granted grounding, which allows us to make forays into other worlds. It is central to the anthromorphic organisation of space in everyday life; we experience space not according to the distanced gaze of the cartographer, but in circles of increasing proximity or distance from the experiencing self. Home lies at the centre of these circles (Felski 1999: p. 22).

A real sense of the idea of home, of an articulation of a specific place at a specific time is played out in these scrapbooks. They are about the place in which the makers live, it is where their everyday lives take place. As part of the process of gathering material the makers have re-examined what is most often taken for granted, and in this reclamation of the familiar new perspectives on 'home' are generated. Importantly the idea of home, and specifically the rural home, rather than being continuous and isolated is, indeed, networked and involved in processes of change. In the archiving of their homes, village and everyday life these documents move between the public and the private, the apparently trivial details and the grand narrative. Again we can turn to the Binsted scrapbook to demonstrate this interplay.

Binsted is a small village, essentially composed of nine scattered hamlets, it is described in the scrapbook as:

> one of the largest parishes in England covering 7,799 acres, with a sparse population of 1,709. Its rich upper green sand soil so valuable for agriculture has protected the village from urbanisation, despite the distance to London being only 45 miles (BWIS 1965).[5]

Situated in north Hampshire, its closest town, Alton is four miles away and its closest railway station is in the neighbouring village of Bentley. As its description indicates the village has a long history of agriculture primarily in the cultivation of hops and soft fruit.

In many respects Binsted in 1965 had experienced a great many of the changes that have characterised the nature of rural England since the 1930s. With regard to employment and population changes the scrapbook tells us that:

> *Many people today earn their living outside the village using their own transport to go to work. New-comers are attracted to Binsted because it is still a country village and yet they can use Bentley Station, two and a half miles away downhill to go to London – and elsewhere (BWIS 1965).*

In terms of changes to the physical infrastructure of the village, before and after photographs in the scrapbook show that relatively recently a small crescent of council houses (rather than the ribbon developments so maligned by Nairn and Clough-Williams in Chapter 2) has been built on a site which formally held two run down half timbered cottages, and the building of new houses and bungalows is reported by contributors from each of the hamlets. Photos also show road works to widen and straighten the main street in the village, an indication of increasing car use. An early portent of the car's dominance in contemporary society comes on a page of the scrapbook which is given over to Dick Hampton's Earth Moving Ltd. Its prominence in the scrapbook indicates its place as a significant employer within the village. The company supplies workers and machinery primarily for road building projects, and tellingly Dick himself is described as 'one of the busiest men in Hampshire' (BWIS 1965). In 1965 Hamptons were involved in contracts on the M5, the M1, new power stations, a reservoir, several by-pass roads and the Severn bridge approach road, and listed over 700 employees working around the country, a picture that vividly illustrates the dramatic expansion in road building and municipal energy and infra structure projects at this time.

The involvement of a small Hampshire village, from the very beginning, in such a fundamental shift in how contemporary Britain looks and functions is evidence of the perhaps unexpected ways in which processes of modernity have been experienced in rural places.

THE MAKING OF THE VILLAGE SCRAPBOOKS

In 1965 the NFWI celebrated its golden jubilee with a plethora of gatherings, activities and merchandise. It produced a specially designed tea towel, diary, golden goblet, commemorative publication and recipe book for members to buy, it had a pink rose named 'WI Jubilee', and Cecil Day Lewis wrote a special poem. Drawing on the organisation's reputation for high quality baking, preserving and produce, they staged a very profitable *Golden Market* at the 1965 Ideal Home Show, which saw members from all over the country driving their produce into London where each day it sold out. They also mounted a slightly less popular exhibition showcasing the work of the organisation entitled *The Country Woman Today*. The Queen, a WI member herself, hosted a garden party at Buckingham Palace to which one member from each WI was invited. For those not lucky enough to attend, dinners and celebration parties were hosted by institutes all over the country. In Binsted the scrapbook records that a cheese and wine party was the focus of their celebration:

> A very happy party was arranged to celebrate the Golden Jubilee. Over 80 guests were present ... Wonderful food and drink was arranged on a very festive board. A large cake was made and iced by two of our members, and won in the raffle ... An exhibition of W.I. Activity was staged. Altogether a very successful event (BWIS 1965).

The creation of the village scrap books was a significant part of the celebrations. In 1964 *Home and Country* carried a report from the organisation's AGM where the chairman Mrs Gabrielle Pike declared that:

> Each W.I. should enter the 'Village Scrapbook Today' competition, which could well result in an 'historic contribution towards the social history of this country'.

Since it was to be a scrapbook of today and not the past, she urged members to '*think* 1965 – what you're wearing – what you're thinking – what you like and what you don't like, and without fail see that YOUR village is a link in this huge picture we hope to paint' (Harrison 1964: p. 227).[6] During that year individual WIs were sent the scrapbook brief written by the national scrapbook committee which stated that:

> We hope that all your members will want to help in someway, but at least six members should contribute to the book, with drawings, plans, photographs, lettering, research, written descriptions, printed matter and other material; and do make the book as appealing to the eye as possible ... We would like to emphasise again that what we want is not a history, but a picture of your village and its life in 1965, which you can hand down to future generations (NFWI Archive Golden Jubilee General 1965).[7]

The brief instructed that the book should broadly cover four subject areas: 'the place, the people, what they do and the future' (NFWI Archive Golden Jubilee General 1965). The intention was that the scrapbook be actually compiled throughout the jubilee year of 1965 and then entered into the national competition early in 1966. The idea of being part of this national patchwork of scrapbooks, tasked with making a real contribution to the social history for generations to come, clearly captured the imaginations of many of the members and 2,500 scrapbooks were created.

The judging of the scrapbook competition took place in three stages, beginning with each WI sending its scrapbook to its county office where the three best entries were decided and sent to the national office. Here one book from each county was selected to go forward into the final stage. Judging of the national competition was undertaken by a panel consisting of: the artist and professor at the Royal College of Art Edward Bawden (whose wife was a member), Miss Lloyd Thomas, a retired headmistress of Channing High School, in Highgate, London who served on the NFWI General Education, Sub Committee and Lionel Munby, editor of the Amateur Historian magazine. In traditional WI fashion for order and fairness five winners were eventually selected; one from each of the four regions (North, South, East and West) together with a special prize for the best entry in Welsh.[8] The winning institute members received a bursary to attend a course at Denman College. An exhibition entitled *Scrapbooks of the Countryside Today*, featuring the winning scrapbooks together with the best one from each county, totalling 61 scrapbooks in all, was mounted at the Ceylon Tea Centre in Regent Street, to coincide with the NFWI 1966 AGM.[9]

The exhibition was very well attended with all expectations of visitor numbers being exceeded; the scrapbook correspondence file contains records of many complaints of overcrowding and overheating inside the exhibition space. The exhibition was predominantly aimed at WI members rather than the general public, and there is little evidence that the scrapbooks made a great deal of impact on a wider national scale. There is very little newspaper coverage of the exhibition or of the scrapbook project during this time, a notable exception being the reproduction of six facsimile pages from the winning scrapbook from the East of England category: Radwinter in Essex, in *The Observer* colour supplement magazine. The inclusion of the project in the pages of a Sunday supplement is particularly interesting. First of all Paul Jennings, the author of *The Living Village* (1968), a book which draws on material from the scrapbooks (discussed below), had written for *The Observer* for around 17 years, so it is possible that he alerted the editors of the supplement to the scrapbooks project in the hope that a feature in the magazine would raise the profile of the project and subsequently generate interest in his forthcoming book, although no direct mention of the book is made in the article. Colour supplements were a relatively new phenomenon in 1966; *The Observer* launched its colour supplement in 1964, just two years after *The Times* brought out their ground breaking *Sunday Times Colour Section* in 1962. Then, as today, these publications carried an effective if contradictory, mixture of 'hard hitting' photojournalism and aspirational lifestyle material. This form of colour documentary photography seemed to speak of the now, the present, the important. They articulate significant developments in transportation and communication of the time with their apparent ability to bring to the reader at home, exotic places and people – even if the exoticism was sometimes generated more by the class difference between those featured in the pages and those reading about them, rather than in any real geographical sense. The decision to feature pages from the scrapbook would, it seems, tick both the exotic documentary and the aspirational lifestyle boxes, as the piece represents the village and its inhabitants as belonging to a different time and place. The village is presented as a picturesque, self-sufficient community, isolated from the modern (urban) world, a perspective to inspire dreams of an 'escape to the country' for any urban Sunday morning newspaper reader. The cover shows an idyllic image of freshly picked garden peas and flowers left on a doorstep, the door is ajar – there are no security worries here.

The supplement's introduction insists that the pages are reproduced to create an 'authentic flavour of the original' (*The Observer* 1966: p. 3), however many of the photographs featured do not appear in the original scrapbook, leading me to believe that the newspaper sent their own photographer to the village to gather images more aligned with the Sunday supplement perspective. The rural is portrayed as distant both geographically and chronologically. The images made for reproduction situates the village in the past with elderly residents in black and white photographs. On one page Miss Katie Newell a village spinster in her cardigan, apron and hat, cleans the church brasses, and flat capped pensioners Clem Mynott and Joe Taylor play dominoes every Friday at The Lion. Meanwhile on the opposite page in a full colour advert, a couple stare out at the reader, the woman with the latest Vidal Sassoon bob and weighty false eyelashes, the man – a rugged James Bond action type, brandishing an aqualung in which, the advertisers (Crawfords whisky), would have us believe he has smuggled a bottle of their prized liquor. As with Sunday supplement magazines today, parallel worlds both equally constructed, are paraded in front of the reader as fodder for their fantasies and ultimately their consumption. The complexity of non-metropolitan living is ironed out, with the aspects of modernity that were very much present in the scrapbooks essentially erased for the Sunday supplement audience.

THE LIVING VILLAGE

After the competition and exhibition the scrapbooks were returned to their institutes and the majority were filed away in local institute's archival cupboards, village halls or in member's attics, with a handful being deposited in county archives. In this way the scrapbooks became part of the history of the individual institute rather than the contribution to a wider social history as they had been originally intended. In some ways this situation was addressed by the publication *The Living Village* (1968) by Paul Jennings. Jennings worked with publishers Hodder and Stoughton to use the scrapbooks as material for a book about the contemporary countryside. Jennings was reasonably well known at the time for his humorous column on the vagaries of everyday life called 'Oddly ...' in *The Observer* and as a children's author. He was to some extent seen as a voice from the countryside, often drawing on inspiration from his family life in rural Suffolk for his columns, which were popular enough to be collected into a series of slim volumes.[10] It is symptomatic of the way that these scrapbooks have been overlooked as important contributions to social history that Jennings, known for his light hearted humorous approach was to be their chronicler rather than an author with a background in rural social history, for instance W.G. Hoskins.[11]

It is clear that the 2,500 scrapbooks were in need of some sort of synthesis in order to draw out their value beyond the local, but the form that Jennings' project eventually took is significant and in many ways problematic. Firstly the choice of Jennings as the author of the book which was to bring the project to wider public attention signals the NFWI's dependence on a mainstream, male dominated authorship, which seemed to miss certain opportunities to act in an more independent way. Secondly, it seems to exhibit an imbalance between Jennings' role as author and the role of the scrapbook contributors. Jennings quotes extensively from the scrapbooks and most (but not all) of the quotes are followed by the village and county from which the scrapbook originates, however the contributors are unidentified. The tone of the book reflects Jennings' irreverent and at times opinionated character, this style is entertaining in his newspaper column, however in this context it means that effectively the voices and labour of the thousands of women who took part in the project are to some extent subjugated by the single voice of 'the author'. A review of *The Living Village* in *The Times Literary Supplement* makes this imbalance clear 'Mr Jennings and his *anonymous* helpers have made a valuable report' [my italics] (NFWI Archive *Golden Jubilee and Scrapbook Competition* 1964–69). Perhaps a more satisfactory editorial approach would have been to draw on the structure of Mass-Observation's *May the Twelfth* (1937), that favoured the collaging of fragments as a way of archiving the multiple experiences of the everyday (see Chapter 3). This approach may have come closer to a more meaningful rendering of the network of village voices that was originally intended. In addition the book seems somewhat reluctant to declare its WI connections, there is no mention of the organisation and its connection to the project anywhere on the cover of the book, there is, however, a large photograph of the author and his family sitting in a meadow.

Significantly *The Living Village* does not value the scrapbooks as visual artefacts, the book is entirely text based with no images. Given the visually stunning nature of many of these works this is a strange choice. This fact is interesting because it says something about what is valued as a proper contribution to history. The choice to produce scrapbooks rather than traditional textual histories is one that speaks of the WI's connection with craft activities and the pleasure and prestige associated with the processes of making. It is this methodology, as Spence and Holland (1991: p. 9) have pointed out, that situate the books as marginal archives, and it is their connection with the female, the amateur and the visual which has led to their neglect as historical documents. Scrapbooks are associated with found artefacts and the contingent rather than thoroughness or rigour. While the ephemera they archive speaks of the everyday, such as bus timetables, tickets and leaflets, it can also be considered as throw-away or effectively as rubbish. The scrapbook genre is also highly personal, the members used material from their own lives: their own photographs, scraps of material and wallpaper from their own homes and hand drawn maps, all of which compromises any notions of seriousness or objectivity which is associated with professional histories. However, as this chapter has demonstrated, the importance of these scrapbooks lies in their visual nature revealing the subjective, the personal, the inside of rural everyday life and how it is intertwined with wider processes of modernity taking place all over the country.

Scrapbooks had previously been used by individual WIs to mark anniversaries and special events in their own histories but this was the first time it had been coordinated as a national venture. From the initial stages of the project it was clear that they were conceived as visual artefacts. Margery Fisher wrote an article in *Home and Country* to encourage Institutes to take up the scrapbook challenge:

> *A great deal will depend on what the finished book looks like.*

> *This is a scrapbook, and illustrations will be as important as text … The pages should look good, with a pleasing combination of words and illustrations. The most accomplished paintings would be wasted if they were not well placed on the page, and conversely newspaper cuttings, unattractive in themselves, could look very striking if they were helped by lettering or formal patterns. Besides*

photographs and pictures, there are all kinds of objects we can use – wallpaper, pressed flowers, material, even bills imaginatively arranged. Ingenuity is going to matter much more in these books than expenditure (Fisher 1964: pp. 294–5).

A document setting out notes for the scrapbook judges suggested they should look out for:

Use of Materials

Imaginative use of every possible kind of material, e.g. plans, drawings and paintings, photographs, lettering, printed matter, samples of fabrics and wallpapers, etc.

Presentation

General appearance of the book and the individual pages, layout, etc. Whether the book attracts the eye and arrests the attention (NFWI Archive Golden Jubilee and Scrapbook Competition 1964–69).

Given this emphasis on the visual it is interesting to read correspondence between Jennings and the NFWI which demonstrates his privileging of text over visuals. In response to Hodder and Stoughton's suggestion of including a map in the book showing where the scrapbook extracts came from Jennings complains that people are more concerned with the visual these days and are not content to simply read, a situation, which he blames on television. This perhaps points to an attitude that places the visual on the level of the popular and frivolous in contrast to the serious and worthy textual account. The omission of images from the final publication was, it seems, more to do with this opinion on Jennings' part than any economic considerations by the publishers, who seemed keen to include some visual material.[12] A letter from Hodder and Stoughton encapsulates the two main complaints about the book: that there is no list of all those who contributed to the scrapbooks and that there are no pictures.

So far we have seen that the use of scrapbooks is a primarily visual medium and one that works through collage as a channel for effectively archiving the multiple realities that constitute the everyday. Trivialised as lacking the rigour or objectiveness of more academic renderings of village life, it has been demonstrated that these scrapbooks allow different stories about the rural to come to light. Through these documents it is possible to see the English village in the 1960s as a place of change rather than continuity, playing an intrinsic role in wider narratives of modernity, and networked through national organisations like the WI.

THE WI AS RURAL NETWORK

As an organisation the WI has a firm place in the contemporary imagination as middle-class, white, conservative and predominantly for women over the age of 60. Popular representations of the organisation fluctuate between portraying it affectionately as a well-loved national institution, and as an outdated, inflexible seat of prejudice. Recent examples include the BBC sit-com *Jam and Jerusalem* (2006) written by and featuring comedienne Jennifer Saunders, and Nigel Cole's feature film *Calendar Girls* (2003), which presented a mild challenge to the WI stereotype by telling the 'real life' story of the members of Rylestone WI in Yorkshire, who earned international notoriety by posing nude for a charity calendar.[13]

Some challenges are being made to this stereotyping, WI groups with younger memberships have been featured in the media, but these are predominantly in fashionable metropolitan enclaves such as Islington or as an alternative to the usual university societies (Hewitson 2010; Pidd 2009). These groups do not necessarily present a challenge to the stereotype, rather they thrive on it, generating membership through the current retro-chic of home baking, knitting and gardening. Where actual rather than fictionalised members of the WI have been represented in mainstream media, it has been in lifestyle programmes which tap into the well established association between the organisation and excellence in cookery, crafting and domestic skills.

Lifestyle television has been a popular genre since the 1950s (Brunsdon 2004). The fashionable pursuit of modernity in the home was first articulated through the multiple series of shows featuring DIY personality Barry Bucknell, and his series *Bucknell's House* (1962–63), is contemporary with the scrapbooks project. Each week he would renovate a different aspect of a Victorian house, his approach typified the ideas of the time about modernity and progress. He is well known for his practice of hiding or removing Victorian period features such as panelled doors, moulding and fireplaces. They signalled the old, attracted dirt and were difficult to clean. The taste of this post festival of Britain generation, was for clean lines and surfaces, ease of cleaning and the multiple forms of technology which claimed to bring convenience, amongst them the electric fire (a feature of Figure 4.1). This orientation towards modern design is reflected in the scrapbooks, one example includes a photograph of a members home titled *A Modern Sitting Room* in which an electric fire, television set, and un-panelled door are visible (CSJWIS 1965).[14]

During the 1990s and early 2000s there was a dramatic expansion of lifestyle programming with shows about interior design, home management, cookery and home entertaining, all taking prime time slots in the main television station schedules. While these areas represent the established territory of the WI, the reinvigorated interest has not been reflected in a return to the once high membership figures for the organisation. When WI members appear on these shows it is as judges of cake and preserve competitions, they have exacting standards and promote strict adherence to traditional methods, often portrayed as a stuffy point of contrast to the more relaxed and contemporary style of the presenters.[15]

Efforts are being made by today's WI to negotiate this ambivalent public image. Its website and publicity material emphasise the involvement of younger members using the phrase 'all kinds of opportunities for all kinds of women' on leaflets and posters, emphasising the inclusiveness of the organisation (Women's Institute 2009). Recent popular history books such as *Jambusters* (Summers 2013) and *A Force to be Reckoned With* (Robinson 2011), also work to re-frame the organisation's image. However, the WI finds itself navigating a difficult path between trying to attract the diverse new membership necessary to reinvigorate the organisation, while at the same time ensuring that they do not alienate their stalwart supporters, many of whom have been members throughout their adult lives. These long term supporters may have become members as young women during the 1960s and have adapted the activities of their local WIs to match their own changing concerns and interests, a factor which in turn has contributed to a marked decrease in membership figures signifying a disinterest in the organisation among younger generations of women. The dominant demographic of the WI is reflected in the structure of many of the local Institutes, for example, many WIs meets on a weekday afternoon, a time which excludes women in full time employment, or indeed women with small children.

Many WI meetings take a similar form today as they did 50 years ago, consisting of a formal meeting where organisational issues are discussed together with any local or national campaigns taking place. This is followed by a talk or demonstration given by a member or more usually an external speaker. Examples from my local WI programme includes a talk from the deputy mayor called 'A year in Office', another called 'The History of Underwear' and one on the interpretation of dreams. Next comes the more social element of tea and conversation, with many meetings still including some form of member's competition such as the best arrangement of flowers in an egg cup, or best homemade Christmas decoration. Such activities may seem like trivial re-enactments of a more innocent age, however it is important not to discount the vital role of the WI in the lives of many of its members. Its place in the public imaginary makes it an easy target for stereotypical characterisation which belies the complex individual experiences of its members. In their study of WI members Sarah Neal and Sue Walters (2008) found that while the National Federation of Women's Institutes might emphasise the organisation's political aims and activities, its members at a local level value most the opportunity it offers to meet friends and create social support networks. This is evident in the statements of Neal and Water's interviewees:

> *Shelia: It's a lovely afternoon where you go and meet your friends, have an interesting lecture and then a nice cup of tea and cake and then you go home again.*

> *Rosemary: I just love the WI and it plays an enormous part in my life. If I took WI in its entirety out of my life, well I'd just be reduced to dusting (Neal and Waters 2008: p. 287).*

It is equally important to realise that in addition to providing much needed support networks in the countryside, the WI also has a rich history of campaigning to improve the social and economic condition of rural women both in Britain and abroad. The WI movement originated in Canada where it had been used as a social and economic tool to activate extremely isolated rural communities (McCall 1943: p. 10). It was adopted in Britain in 1915 as part of the war time government's Agricultural Organisation Society, with its aim being to educate rurally based women in elements of agriculture, horticulture and the raising of livestock, encouraging them particularly to grow and preserve their own food, and to keep bees, goats and pigs. The first British WI was formed in Llanfair P.G. in Anglesey, and the movement soon became extremely popular with many rural locations starting their own institutions. By 1918 the organisation had become independent from the government and by 1925 membership numbers had reached a quarter of a million (Andrews 1997: p. xiv).

In its first incarnations the WI was considered to be quite radical in approach, one of the reasons for this was because they operated under a democratic structure of equally weighted votes. This was seen as reaction against the still feudalistic systems which infiltrated everyday life in the countryside at this time, where the 'lady of the manor' would be in control of any organisations or events. While this democratic element was structurally built into the organisation, in day to day practice more ingrained class differences were often reproduced in the hierarchy of the individual institutes with the most prestigious positions often being occupied by wealthier residents of the village. Another aspect of the organisation's perceived radicalism was its insistence on non-sectarianism opening it up to accusations of irreligion (Pugh 2000: p. 227). This radicalism was also reflected in many of its founder members who were deeply involved in the suffrage movement and instigated many of the WI's political campaigns to materially improve the lives of rural women. Over the organisation's history these have included campaigns for improved water supply in rural areas and the installation of indoor plumbing to prevent pipes freezing, the building of new state aided housing in the countryside, improved bus links and telephone services, and effective access to midwifery services and infant welfare centres for rural women. These important political activities of the WI are often forgotten and the organisation is trivialised. In her study of the first 45 years of the organisation Maggie Andrews argues that 'To many women in the NFWI between 1915 and 1960 the organisation was a hugely important part of their lives. It was very significantly a space with women's values and norms and many women never missed a meeting except literally for the birth of a child or the death of their mother. To trivialise the Women's Institute movement as 'Jam and Jerusalem' is therefore to trivialise them' (Andrews 1997: p. xii).

In his history of women's political movements in Britain, Martin Pugh creates an image of the organisation as being divided between its national 'political' activities and its local 'social or practical' activities, a split that is still evident in Neal and Walter's (2008) study of the present day institution. For Pugh while the national organisation politely and in his opinion ineffectively, chivvied politicians, the local membership were much more concerned with the practicalities of home making, centring on handicrafts, cookery skills and gardening, together with a secondary emphasis on music, drama and dancing.[16] Pugh argues that 'WIs owed their success to concentration on the home-making and entertainment; their political dimension was a burden which could be carried only if it excluded feminist and other controversial items' (Pugh 2000: p. 230). This argument devalues the work of the WI on a number of levels: firstly it casts the organisation's political successes as insignificant because of their basis in the domestic realm by focussing on the material conditions of rural women's lives; secondly it underestimates the value of learning home-making skills; and thirdly it neglects the fact that the gathering of large groups of rural women on a formal basis was a political act in itself, enabling the creation of social support networks and the potential feelings of empowerment that such group belonging generates.

In recent years work has taken place to re-evaluate the contribution of women in the 1950s and 1960s to forms of pre-second wave feminism. Studies such as Lesley Johnson and Justine Lloyd's *Sentenced to Everyday Life* (2004) work to re-historicise the troubled figure of the housewife. Like many of the members of the WI, a large number of women at this time who were considered or indeed considered themselves to be housewives, were also engaging in various forms of full and part time work in addition to their unpaid household duties. In the scrapbooks WI members are employed and self-employed, running the village shop and post office, as dress makers, and as dinner ladies at the village school. However, the WI as an organisation placed a great deal of emphasis on the realm of the home and the sphere of domestic work in its activities, it can certainly be seen at this time as an organisation for the housewife. Johnson and Lloyd's re-evaluation of this role provides a perspective which can be used to re-cast the political and social work of the WI in a more significant light. They show that the emphasis of second wave feminists on the need for women to move out of the low status domestic realm and into the higher status public sphere of the labour market, where they should compete equally with men, demonised the figure of the housewife, with its abolition becoming key to the second wave project.

Simone de Beauvoir in *The Second Sex* (1953 [1949]) saw the repetitious and mundane activities of the housewife as preventing the self-realisation of women. Stuck in a cycle of the daily maintenance of the household de Beauvoir argued that women are trapped in a suspended moment of immanence by repeating the same tasks everyday, unable to move forward or enact any meaningful development of their own lives. Betty Friedan in *The Feminine Mystique* ([1963] 1992) chronicles the dissatisfaction felt by a generation of American women in their role as housewives and mothers. Friedan's text is testament to the very real psychological and physical manifestations of their desperation in living with a problem that society did not acknowledge:

> Sometimes a woman would say 'I feel empty somehow ... incomplete'. Or she would say, 'I feel as if I don't exist'. Sometimes she blotted out the feeling with a tranquillizer. Sometimes she thought the problem was with her husband, or her children, or that what she really needed was to redecorate her house, or move to another neighbourhood, or have an affair, or another baby. Sometimes she went to the doctor with symptoms she could hardly describe: 'A tired feeling ... I get so angry with the children it scares me ... I feel like crying without any reason'. ... A number of women told me about great bleeding blisters that break out on their hands and arms. 'I call it the housewife's blight', said a family doctor in Pennsylvania. 'I see it so often lately in these young women with four, five, six children, who bury themselves in dishpans. But it isn't caused by detergent and it isn't cured by cortisone' (Friedan [1963] 1992: p. 18).

Friedan built on de Beauvoir's ideas of self-actualisation by asserting that rather than following the role model of housewife as celebrated career choice for women set out in post war popular culture, women should view their lives as a project, and devise life plans which enable them to develop identities which were independent from the home. Later second wave texts such as Germaine Greer's *The Female Eunuch* (1970) and Anne Oakley's *Housewife* (1974) reinvigorated the denunciation of housewifery as a fundamental tool in the oppression of women.

Johnson and Lloyd argue that a more complex analysis of the pre-second wave history of feminism is necessary. Through their re-historicisation of the housewife it is possible to see that the negative attitude towards the housewife established by second wave feminists devalued any political activities that such housewives were involved in, primarily because they centred on the domestic realm. The dismissal of the housewife as an apolitical victim of servitude disavows the history that created the conditions for second wave feminism to emerge, and in so doing removes the possibility for the work of organisations like the NFWI to be seen as progressive or radical.

This imbalance is re-addressed to some extent by Andrews' work on the organisation. She notes that while women, during her period of study (1915–60), were consistently placed in the low status realm of the domestic, rather than the high status worlds of the public or the political, it was by working within and at the same time, trying to change these parameters, that they found their political voice:

> *Women while accepting a primarily domestic sphere are, due to external circumstance, forced to become political, strident even, in order to carry out their socially defined tasks. Thus the women's domestic base was used to justify their demands for social reforms. In so doing rather than challenging women's association with domesticity, the meaning of domesticity was challenged, its boundaries were redefined. Domesticity became not passive but assertive (Andrews 1997: p. 152).*

Andrews works to re-evaluate the role of the domestic activities which were de-valued by Pugh, asking: 'Can flower arranging be feminist?' (Andrews 1997: p. 146). She finds that this much trivialised activity, the preserve of this much trivialised group of people – housewives and spinsters – can indeed signify a creative use and ownership of space. 'Women in patriarchal and capitalist society carve out their own spaces, their own alternative culture, but in that space allowed them by the dominant culture' (Andrews 1997: pp. 153–4). At the time the scrapbooks were made this space was certainly the home, but it was also the everyday. This was the territory of the scrapbooks, and this WI competition designated a space and a method for these rural women to operate within, a space where they could creatively represent their everyday experiences and contribute their own histories.

THE JET-AGE WI

In the decade which saw the 50 year anniversary of the organisation, and the making of the scrapbooks, fundamental shifts in the WI's membership took place. The 1950s and 1960s saw the increasing relocation of middle class households from cities and suburbs into the countryside. A home in the country became aspirational

Pilot's family gets jet-age heating

When Ann and Peter (he's a jet airliner captain) saw this converted oast house for sale, they knew they'd found the home they were looking for. It wasn't perfect—yet. That 'old world' look was fine—outside—but inside they wanted slap-up-to-date comfort. First on their list was modern central heating.

The perfect system. It was a foregone conclusion that Ann and Peter would choose gas central heating. They had seen and admired it in so many of their friends' homes. Now they have one of those spotless, white gas boilers. Neither of them has to lift a finger to it—even think about it—it's *completely automatic*.

Let it freeze! *Inside they're cosy and warm!* The boys think it's super-snug now they've got gas central heating. But they're not so sure it's a good thing to have all that hot water on tap—for baths and washing behind the ears.

Never a chill-spot anywhere. Hall, living room, bedrooms, kitchen—wherever you go at Ann's and Peter's, warmth welcomes you in. And it's all done with neat, un-obtrusive radiators and 'small bore' pipes . . . *and a boiler that looks after itself.*

Perfect—that's the only word for gas central heating. *Perfect, because it gives you all the warmth, all the hot water, all the luxury you've ever dreamed of. Perfect, because it looks after itself. It's today's truly automatic system. Easiest to run, because there are no fuel deliveries to worry about and an occasional servicing keeps it in A1 condition: cheaper to install, because there are no costly storage facilities to pay for. And it can be yours, without deposit, on the most generous of easy terms.*

ONLY GAS CAN GIVE YOU PERFECT CENTRAL HEATING

ISSUED BY THE GAS COUNCIL

4.5   Gas Council advert, 1961. Courtesy National Grid Archives.

marker of success, as evidenced in advertising campaigns of the time. Figure 4.5 shows an advert issued by the Gas Council for *Woman's Realm* magazine, it tells the story of just such a move:

> When Ann and Peter (he's a jet airliner captain) saw this converted oast house for sale, they knew they'd found the home they were looking for. It wasn't perfect – yet. That 'old world' look was fine – outside – but inside they wanted slap-up-to-date comfort. First on their list was modern central heating (Gas Council 1961).

This advert seems to typify so much about social and economic conditions and attitudes of the time: the oast house has been converted from a working agricultural resource into a residential property symptomatic of post-war technological changes in agricultural production, such a period property with its 'old world look' is seen as highly desirable and this upper middle class family are keen to move in.[17] The husband's occupation as a jet airliner pilot is also significant, not only does this suggest affluence, it also indicates membership of a glamorous modern world, a world which demands the most up to date technology in central heating. This couple are modernisers, the willingness to move into an old property and renovate it could also be seen as a reflection of the new popularity of DIY and the ethos of Barry Bucknell as discussed above. What also becomes evident in this advert is an overlapping of old and new, the new existing within the old, without conflict: 'unobtrusive radiators' warm this aged building fired by 'a boiler that looks after itself'. In this domestic paradise the tensions between the ancient and the modern have been resolved through the installation of the latest technology. In this scenario from the early sixties one of the first things the airline pilot's wife might do would be to join her local WI.

Andrews argues that this influx of relatively affluent former town dwellers led to a decrease in the organisation's political activism and its relevance in the lives of rural women. I want to complicate this picture somewhat and argue that while the demographic of the WI certainly shifted during this time, membership figures were increasing significantly. In 1951 there were 446,000 members in 7,700 institutes (Pugh 2000: p. 227) and by 1965 there were 450,583 members of the WI, in 8,784 institutes. This represents the creation of 1,084 new institutes. In the jubilee year alone there was an overall increase of 8,600 members (NFWI Archive 1966). At the 1964 national AGM Chairman Mrs Gabrielle Pike proposed that as a focus for the coming jubilee year 'I charge every institute with a waiting list, or a local area bye-law, to try and start a twin institute – it is wrong and selfish that there are lots of potential members being kept out' (Harrison 1964: p. 227). This statement shows that demand to join the WI was still at very healthy levels. In addition to the new middle class members who had relocated to the countryside, a significant proportion of this demand may have been generated by the new housing estates that were increasingly being built by both local councils and private developers on the edge of villages at this time. The occupants of these houses may also have been new comers to the country; however they were more likely to be working class and lower middle class families. In the mean time older members continued to attend, meaning that the membership demographic simply reflected the changed nature of village residents at this time. Andrews states that the time frame of her study ends in 1960 as the change in demographic of the membership meant that the organisation 'lost its primacy in the lives of rural women and began to take on more of the middle-aged and middle class focus that it is known for today' (Andrews 1997: p. xiv). However, I would hesitate to dismiss the subsequent years of the WI as academically uninteresting or politically irrelevant. It is perhaps not the primacy of the organisation in rural women's lives that changed but more importantly for this study in terms of re-thinking the rural, it was the idea of what constituted a rural woman that underwent a transformation. The WI in the 1960s is certainly worthy of study with this shift in demographic representing a manifestation of significant changes in how everyday life in the countryside was subject to change.

We have seen how the WI was an important network for rural women both locally and nationally. It has been instrumental in affecting change in the conditions of everyday life for women in the countryside through its campaigns to improve services and provision. It has also been demonstrated how as an organisation it registered significant changes in the rural population. The final section of this chapter explores the non-metropolitan as a site of modernity, and further develops the notion of the rural network by examining how the national grid is portrayed in the scrapbooks.

PYLONS AND BIRDSEYE

The front cover of the Binsted scrapbook (Plate 5) has a design worked in appliqué and embroidery, consisting of pictorial elements which relate to the village, its title is *A Collage to Suggest Binsted*. It includes things you might expect to find characterising a rural English village such as representations of agricultural crops like blackcurrants, hops, apple orchards and potato fields, together with notable village buildings such as the church. However, more surprisingly running through the centre of the design is a striking representation of an electricity pylon. There is a strangeness here, even an absurdity in seeing an electricity pylon, an arguably unaesthetic and utilitarian item, so carefully rendered in silver thread. The juxtaposition here once again articulates different but simultaneous realities. However, the surprising element here is that there is no jolt of contrast between the pylon and the more classically rural motifs. The design is balanced and interweaves the old and the new. The ubiquity of the pylon in today's landscapes means that in most cases they are a taken for granted element of the countryside, seldom raising comment and certainly not seen as an aspect that would be central to representing a village in this way.

Pylons could be seen as something that was very much associated with the everyday life of the women of the village, it might be something that is part of the daily view from a window, or encountered on a regular walking routes, it could also represent (even if it did not necessarily bring) the village's connection to a regular electricity supply, something that had transformed the lives of a generation of women. The inclusion of the pylon so centrally in the design perhaps points to the members' desire to show that they did not wish to shy away from the less picturesque elements of life in the countryside, and that theirs would be an honest representation of Binsted as it was in 1965, which included a mixture of the ancient and the modern. The presence of the pylon could also indicate its perceived newness to the village, it reminds us that at this point in time pylons were still something to be remarked upon, noticed and debated. While the presence of existing pylons is now taken for granted as a feature of the landscape, contemporary public outrage inspired by plans to construct new systems of 'super pylons' across the Scottish Highlands, is a reminder of how disturbing the installation of the original pylons must have been.[18]

The presence of systems of pylons in the landscape provides an example of how modernity could be thought of as being experienced differently in rural places. Rather than the overwhelming feeling of fragmentation and confusion that often characterises the portrayal of the experience of modernity in the city (Williams 1993 [1972, Simmel 1997 [1902], Benjamin 1999 [1955]), in the countryside it could be thought of as being experienced as moments of contrast. Pylons contrast completely with the landscape which surrounds them, they are much taller than the tallest trees or even, as one article points out, utilising the habitual measure of scale for large things in the countryside, 'far higher than many church steeples' (Sykes 1964: p. 236). Pylons are often thought about in the context of a 'view' of the landscape, something that belongs to a visual rather than a physical realm of sensation. A prime example of this orientation can be found in Nairn's *Outrage* (1955) (as detailed in Chapter 2), his project to identify and condemn all elements of what he called subtopia, in which he reserves some of his most venomous comments for the pylons and their accompanying strings of wire. He uses photographs of pylons throughout the book to illustrate what he sees as the ill considered corruption of open spaces 'Wire obliterates the pattern of the countryside just as surely as though it were a blanket of semi-detached housing. The view becomes wire and pylon first and site second. In some cases it becomes wire and pylon everywhere and site nowhere' (Nairn 1955: p. 379) (Figure 4.6). Nairn makes a clear distinction between wire and site, the wire is not part of the site or landscape, like all signs of modernity it is an aberration rather than a significant part of what rural modernity looks like. Importantly the wire is not simply something which is obscuring the view, it is something which is disrupting long held ideas about what constitutes the countryside, and disrupting the clear division between town and country. The wire physically and symbolically connects the rural to the urban.

Embodied experience of the countryside that is related to routine and habit (Felski 1999), rather than an appreciation of the countryside as the 'view' from a car window, generates more striking contrasts; on walking up as close as you can get to a pylon the physical scale of the structure as compared to the human scale is overwhelming, while the actual size of the structure is perhaps no greater than an average city building, because it is surrounded by fields and open space rather than other buildings the impact is huge.[19] The other element is the noise, the electric fizz which accompanies power lines and feels tangible in the air, there is something chemical here that permeates the atmosphere, making it feel radically different from the windblown open air of pylon-free spaces.

In a brief conversation in Chris Petit's filmic tribute to the urban and rural landscapes of England *Radio On* (1979), a German character, pointing to a line

of pylons enquires what the word is for them in English, 'Pylon' says the main protagonist, and then struggling to place the word into a sentence for his German companion he falls back on the old adage '*Pylons* spoil the countryside, that's what everyone says, [but] by themselves they are beautiful'. When rendered in silver thread are they beautiful? Perhaps this transformation does not make them beautiful, but what it does appear to do is to domesticate them, bring them under control in some way, incorporate them into a balanced design where their enormous scale can be tamed and their hard, mass-produced structures can be individually, hand stitched. This is an effect of the scrapbooking process.

Pylons are an archetypal form of modern industrial architecture: metallic construction, hard angles and inorganic lines. In part to placate protestors to the initial installation of pylons in the 1920s, the Central Electricity Board made much of their design credentials repeatedly linking them with the prominent architect Reginald Blomfield. However, the pylon structure was based on a design by the American Miliken Brothers with modifications by Blomfield (Bristow 2009). In a letter to *The Times* Blomfield felt it necessary to set the record straight stating that his main input was on the colour of the pylons, for which he recommended green (Blomfield quoted in Weightman 2011: p. 156); a choice which he presumably thought would add some element of camouflage, toning down the contrast

4.6   Ian Nairn, 'Wirescape', from *Outrage*, 1955.

between the stark modernist forms and the surrounding landscape. However, the fact that we feel this contrast at all brings to the surface ingrained assumptions about the countryside, namely that it is not a place of technological development and that it is shaped by nature rather than man-made interventions. The presence of these starkly modern structures 'Quick perspectives on the future' as Stephen Spender called them in his poem *Pylons* (1933), could instead be viewed as giving a new perspective on what the countryside is, a complex arena of overlay, an active site of intertwining binaries, a visual articulation of different but simultaneous realities.

It is not only their form which marks them out as a product of modernity but also the function which they both provide and symbolise. The connection of the country in a National Grid is a modern idea. The concept that all parts of the country would maintain a connection through this web of wires, could be seen as a predecessor of the idea of the networked society. What they actually enabled was the transportation of power from the stations where it was produced to the sub-stations in the conurbations where it was required. However, what they symbolised for many in the countryside was the availability of electricity and therefore entry into the modern world of electrical consumer goods.

In 1965 the issue of pylons in the countryside was hardly new. The national grid had been a familiar concept for almost 40 years, however domestic and industrial electricity consumption was increasing exponentially, and the existing system of supply was undergoing some radical changes. Some of these changes were explained to the WI in an article which appeared in *Home and Country*, shortly before the scrapbook project began. The article was called 'The Wirescape' and in it the author explained that 'The demand for electricity for factories, for public services like lighting and for use on the farm and in the home *now doubles in about seven years*. That means twice the amount of power plant every seven years, and twice the growth of the wirescape octopus' (Sykes 1964: p. 235). Clearly drawing on the familiar metaphor of the octopus as some insidious menace, used by Clough Williams-Ellis (1928) some 30 years earlier, the article also accesses the image of invasion that played a key role in conceptualising the increase of roads and litter in countryside:

> *Don't look out the window. There may be a hideous monster creeping up on you (if you live in the country). Men, dwarfed by the structures on which they work, may be bringing steel latticework, pylons, later to be festooned with wires, right across the view from your windows. Before now, actual violence, including threats of shooting, has been offered to the unfortunate contractors who have to run overhead power lines, even recently, in the most peaceable parts of this country (Sykes 1964: p. 235).*

However, after this initial outburst Sykes changes to a well informed avuncular tone and explains that to meet this new demand more rurally based power stations were being built, and that the rural locations were being chosen out of pragmatism not victimisation. This was primarily because they were sited within easy reach of the coalfields which provided the fuel they needed, and of the sea or rivers which provided the large amounts of water necessary for the cooling towers. The idea being that it is more efficient to transport the coal a short distance, and the electricity generated a long distance through the system of wire and pylons. This is an ideology which sees the rural spaces of the country as simply empty and ripe for utilisation. A position that also taps into a more ancient system of the country feeding the city (Williams 1993 [1973]), with farmers transporting their livestock and produce along ancient drove roads, and later railway lines.[20] The new rural power stations that Sykes was referring to were presented as a source of national pride in an advert which featured in the festival of Britain programme, featuring specially commissioned paintings showing the power stations in their picturesque locations. An attitude that continued into the 1960s with local and national news programmes profiling new power stations as symbols of Britain's technological advancement (*The Secret Life of the National Grid* 2010).

David Matless notes that the preservationist rhetoric was somewhat ambivalent when it came to the idea of pylons, some factions were pro-standardisation and saw the steel lattice work towers as aesthetically pleasing modernist objects which were far more preferable than the ill matched and badly designed collection of wooden posts which in some cases they replaced (Matless 1998: p. 52). Matless' analysis also complicates the preservationists' position by showing that in some cases the preservation of rural villages was seen in their ability to become economically active, and that the picturesque-ness of a village was in fact evidence of the economic hardships which were being faced by the community. In this context pylons and the power generation they represented were seen as a way of making the countryside once again economically productive (Matless 1998: p. 44).

The Binsted scrapbook shows the day to day negotiations of the forces of development and preservation:

> Binsted differs little from any other village today in its wide use of electricity. It
> has made possible the mechanisation of hop picking and hop-drying. There is no
> street lighting, but it is a pleasure to know that underground cables have been
> used in the vicinity of the Church, the beauty of whose surroundings is preserved
> (BWIS 1965: p. 43).

This text from the pages detailing the village public services (Plate 6) makes this clear: old agricultural processes are being modernised through electrification, anxieties about the visible consequences of the village's electricity supply are communicated in the relief that the electric cable will not mar the old part of the village by the church. The post war nationalisation of the national grid meant that rural places which were not profitable to supply with electricity were included in this network. However, the central role that rural areas were playing in the generation and transportation of electricity meant that, a farmer for example, may have several pylons on his land but be without mains electricity in his house (Weightman 2011: p. 159). However, once connected many rural places found themselves ahead of the curve in the adoption of one of the aspects made possible by electrification: frozen food.

There is a mania for frozen food evident in the scrapbooks, it is perhaps made more prominent by its unexpectedness. The WI is synonymous with the highest standards in home cooking, however frozen food is often mentioned as the marker of something new, modern, necessary and up to date. This is in contrast to today's attitudes to frozen products which are usually regarded as a lower class form of food, inferior to its fresh counterparts and often highly processed and unhealthy – associated with products like frozen pizza and ready meals. In the scrapbooks however frozen food carries little of this stigma. On the page concerned with 'Shopping' (Figure 4.2), the Binsted scrapbook notes that 'Frozen and pre-cooked food has considerably widened the choice of food in the country districts' (BWIS 1965). The scrapbook from the village of St. Johns in East Sussex, tells of how Mrs Edge, a WI member has changed the fortunes of the shop stating that profit has increased by 300 per cent; among the introductions to the shop which she seems very proud of is frozen food cabinet stocking a wide range of goods. Also from East Sussex the Burwash scrapbook notes that the village has three grocers all of whom sell frozen foods. In the scrapbook made by Sheet village near Petersfield in Hampshire the Birdseye logo can be seen proudly displayed in the window of the local shop, indicating that the Birdseye range of frozen foods could be purchased there.

The arrival of frozen food in rural places had a significant effect on the average WI member. It meant that the village shop could now stock a whole range of food that otherwise would be unavailable, it also meant that women did not have to make the trip into a larger village or town to buy fresh food so regularly. At this point in time most WI members would probably have had a refrigerator with a freezer compartment. Nationally 48 per cent of the population had a refrigerator in 1965 (Weightman 2011: p. 190). That the effective use of the refrigerator was a subject of interest for the WI members is evident in an article that appeared in the organisation's magazine that year called 'You and Your Refrigerator' (*Home and Country* 1965: p. 243).

A smaller proportion of WI members may have been early adopters of the chest freezer. This piece of equipment was slower to arrive in Britain than in America. Christina Hardyment in her history of domestic gadgetry, relates the tale of American frozen food magnet Clarence Birdseye who, while wintering in Labrador in the early 1920s was inspired by the Inuit practice of storing food in the arctic conditions where they were able to preserve it for many months. Birdseye patented his own method of freezing food rapidly between metal plates as early as 1925. The take up of domestic freezer ownership and the popularity of frozen food rose rapidly in the US during the 1930s and by the mid-1940s the deep freeze was appearing as a feature of all the most desirable kitchens (Hardyment 1988: p. 144). Britain was however some way behind in its wide spread adoption of the deep freeze:

> *Frigidaire records that Britain was regarded as something of a challenge. 'The hard sell was probably essential in a Britain which regarded ice as only an inconvenience of winter-time and cold drinks as an American mistake' (Hardyment 1988: p. 142).*

In their study of the deep freeze Shove and Southerton (2000) show that in pre 1970 Britain the freezer was thought of as essentially appealing as a novelty item, the latest technology to be transferred from industry to home. The imagined consumers of these early freezers were a niche market of housewives/families with a lot of home produce. It was seen as a way of 'beating the seasons' and transforming a seasonal glut of fruit and vegetables into a resource which would be available all year round (or throughout the winter at least). In this way the origin of the deep freeze was not as a labour saving device, as the amount of work involved in preparing the fruit, vegetables and meat before freezing was considerable. At this point the freezer was seen as a way to beat the seasons rather than the clock. In this way the early incarnation of the deep freezer was primarily conceived for a rural market. Evidence of this can be seen from an advert in *Country Life* from the same year as the scrapbooks, which advertised the chest freezer with the strap line 'There are no seasons in the year with Helifrost'.

The connection between the preservation of food and the freezer places it directly into the territory of the WI, which had its origins in promoting the effective preservation of fresh produce (see note 13). Shove and Southerton add that 'The freezer was first marketed to the housewife who could freeze her home baking, her home grown crops of fruit and vegetables, and perhaps her own pig' (2000: p. 306). This seems to describe the archetypal WI member, with her interest in effective home management, access to home grown produce and quite possibly the space and know how to keep a pig.

Here we see an example of how the WI, and rural women generally, are quite possibly early adopters of this new technology, placing them at the cutting edge of modernity. Shove and Southerton link the take up of the domestic freezer with the availability of frozen food in shops, specifically supermarkets 'the really critical development was superstores and with them an extensive and reliable commercial infrastructure for frozen food' (Shove and Southerton 2000: p. 307). *Iceland* the first specialist frozen food store opened in 1970, a decade which saw the domestic ownership of freezers rise by 50 per cent. This is interesting because this history ties the significant development of frozen food to supermarkets and to specialist shops like *Iceland* that were situated in large conurbations, however the scrapbooks show the important role that frozen food was playing even earlier than this in 1965 and in rural rather than urban locations. Shove and Southerton note that:

> To stand any chance of success, freezer manufacturers had to persuade people
> to adopt new methods of food preservation in place of established techniques
> like salting, bottling, curing, drying and tinning. More challenging still, they had
> to convince potential users that freezing, which modifies the structure of the
> food itself, was safe. What sort of preservational magic did the new white box
> represent? One positive strategy was to announce the freezer as a symbol of
> technological progress (Shove and Southerton 2000: p. 305).

Frozen food had a two pronged approach to advertising in the 1960s. The first, particularly adopted by Birdseye, revolved around the taste and appearance of the food, chiefly emphasising the freshness, quality and value of frozen food. An advert for *Woman's Realm* in 1966 has the text appearing amongst a plethora of healthy looking green vegetables 'Never a single bad vegetable! Never any old ones! Never any waste! Always young and tender. When you buy Birds Eye you *know* they're going to be good'. The second, adopted by the ice cream company Lyons Maid ties

4.7　Lyons Maid ice cream advert, 1968.

the new possibilities opened up by frozen food to the glamour and technological progress represented by more accessible, if still largely aspirational, foreign travel; advertising Italian *style* Cassata and American *style* ice cream accompanied by colour photos of New York City, and the Golden Gate Bridge (Figure 4.7).

These adverts add to the picture of the non-metropolitan everyday provided by the scrapbooks. Drawing on this bricolage of textual and visual information it is possible to complicate received ideas about the countryside as isolated and outside of modernity. The scrapbooks tell a different story of an arena that is networked and active in local and national change. They conjure an image of a WI member in her newly built council house, converted oast house, or tied cottage, with an electric fire and modern fixtures and fittings but no access to mains sewage and with occasional failures in water supply (see Figure 4.2). She might be eating American style ice cream or a home-made apple pie made with fruit from her garden preserved in the deep freeze.

The scrapbooks provide alternative stories about the rural from the perspective of the female and the everyday. Their use of collage as a methodology reveals the different but simultaneous realities that texture the daily rhythms and routines of non-metropolitan places. Far from the idealised notion of the rural as a place of continuity, they reveal it to be involved in a state of flux, particularly with regard to demographic shifts and technological advancements that changed the physical appearance of the countryside (road building and pylons) and the lived experience (access to frozen food for example). However, these documents do not illustrate a picture of the village as a place that was enduring change imposed from elsewhere, but rather as an important agent in implementing change (think of Dick Hampton's Earth Moving Ltd), and as enthusiastic early adopters of technology reliant consumer goods such as deep freezers, with the WI playing an important role in connecting its members in local and national networks and documenting the lived experience of rural modernity.

As we have seen, the scrapbooks are fascinating archives of village life at this time. The next chapter focuses on more contemporary ways of archiving the village, particularly in relation to festivals and folk art. It looks at how the practice of certain traditions can serve an archival function in maintaining a link to the past, and it also explores how some artists have approached the task of creating visual archives of traditional practices and folk art objects.

NOTES

1   It is interesting to note that the WI's educational institution Denman College, in Oxford, now offers a course called 'The Amateur Archivist' (Women's Institute 2011a).

2   In France *bricolage* is also used in the same way as the English phrase *do it yourself*, a process which depending on individual aptitude can mean amateurish fiddling about or ingenious creation.

3   Gentleman eventually succeeded in his quest to stop the requirement for the three quarter photographic profile of the Queen to appear on all stamps, going on to design the stylised cameo profile which is still used on stamps today (Muir 2009: p. 2).

4   BWIS 1965 refers to Hampshire County Archives (1965) Binsted Village Scrapbook.

5   Notably it was the home of H.V. Morton, author of the *In Search of England* books referred to in Chapter 2.

6   *Home and Country* was a monthly magazine produced by the NFWI, and subscribed to by members. It ceased production in 2007 to be replaced by *WI Life* which is published eight times a year and is sent to all members (Women's Institute 2011b).

7   Archive material from the National Federation of Women's Institutes Archive, held at the Women's Library, London School of Economics, is referenced as NFWI Archive, date and name where necessary, in the bibliography full document reference numbers are listed.

8   The winners were: West of England and Wales: Llanilar, Cardiganshire, South of England and Channel Islands: Toddington, Bedfordshire, North of England and Isle of Man: Outgate, Westmorland, East of England: Radwinter, Essex. It is interesting to note that the Isle of Man and the Channel Islands are identified individually in the categories, perhaps showing a sensitivity to the differing senses of national identity.

9   The V&A, The Commonwealth Institute, The Trades Union Congresss, and Baden Powell House were also approached as possible exhibition venues but all declined (NFWI Archive Golden Jubilee General 1965).

10 *Oddly Enough* (1950), *Oddly Bodlikins* (1953), *Model Oddlies* (1956), *Gladly Oddly* (1958), *Idly Oddly* (1959), *I said Oddly, Diddle I?* (1961), *Oddly ad lib* (1965) all published by Reinhardt.

11 Hoskins is quoted on the cover of the *Living Village* giving his approval to the book: 'It is a first class book'.

12 Correspondence shows that the publishers proposed that a second book be published which would focus primarily on the visual elements of the scrapbooks in the form of a high quality coffee table type book. I can find no evidence of this book ever being produced.

13 The reference to 'Jam and Jerusalem' originates from the WI's role in the Second World War, where they were tasked with running preserving stations which regulated the precious reserves of rationed sugar in order to turn the home front fruit harvest into jam. Whereas the hymn, William Blake's 'Jerusalem' has been sung at every meeting since 1923. Andrews (1997: p. vi) notes that it is thought that this hymn was selected because it had been used by the National Union of Suffrage Societies, and therefore signifies a link between the WI and the wider network of the women's movement.

14 CSJWIS 1965 refers to the Jubilee scrapbook made by members of the Crowborough St. Johns WI, in East Sussex, held by East Sussex County Archive, The Keep.

15 An example of this can be seen in an episode of *The Hairy Bakers* (2008) where the two presenters who are big hairy bikers go to Denman College and learn how to make the perfect sponge cake. They then attempt to beat the WI at their own game and make a cake using their own special ingredients, the WI judges do not know what to make of this cake, saying things like 'its very nice but its not a sponge cake' meaning that they cannot judge it in the subsequent sponge cake competition as essentially by using unorthodox ingredients the Hairy Bikers have broken the rules and the cake is declared 'not a cake'.

16 Significantly Pugh cites the adaptation of 'Jerusalem' as evidence of this interest in music rather than as a symbol of solidarity with the wider women's movement as suggested by Andrews (see note 13). The continued emphasis of these three areas of

crafts, cookery, and the performing arts, for the present day organisation can be seen in the courses offered by Denman College, where the majority of the courses offered to members fall into one of these categories (Women's Institute 2011). It should be noted that while these areas of study fall into the category of leisure pursuits, during the first five decades of the WI many of the home-making skills taught were directly related to women's everyday experience and working roles as housewives.

17   Interestingly the oast house in Binsted is still in use at this time, Figure 4.1 indicates that it had just been modernised with electric hop drying equipment, however it has subsequently been converted into a domestic residence.

18   See *The Guardian* (2009) and Davis (2009).

19   The Super Grid Pylons used post Second World War were 136 feet 6 inches tall, or approximately five times as tall as a house (Weightman 2011: p. 197).

20   An example of one of these routes is the preserved railway line from Southampton to London nicknamed the Watercress Line as it called at Alresford, a great producer of watercress which was transported fresh into London each day (Butcher 1996: p. 26).

5

Performing the Village: Festivals and Folk Art

Festivals and folk art are aspects of the countryside that one might expect to feature in a traditional or historic examination of rural visual culture. They are also aspects that have become part of the rural imaginary. The village fete for example,

5.1   Flour being distributed at the Tichborne Dole.

is used widely as an aesthetic short hand signalling a generic (better) past. It evokes community and sunshine or sometimes, the 'home front' spirit needed to pull together and grin through the ubiquitous summer rain storm. Even when these events are adopted by metropolitan communities or organisations they are done so to signal these things, and are enthusiastically embraced with a certain amount of nostalgia and kitsch.[1] Traditional celebrations of the season, from which village fetes originate, also play a role on the darker side of the rural imaginary, signalling misrule, archaic beliefs and deviant sexual behaviour as typified by the film *The Wickerman* (1973) or *Robin Redbreast* (1970), where an isolated communities incorporate human sacrifice into its seasonal festivities.

This chapter re-examines these clichés of non-metropolitan living through an exploration of three examples of contemporary engagement with festivals and folk art. It reveals that these practices can be viewed as a product of both an anxious relationship with the past and the nature of the modern globalised village. The first section centre's on my own experience of attending a local annual custom: the Tichborne Dole and how contemporary practice of this ancient festival might be related to Hobsbawm's notion of invented tradition. It then goes on to examine the relationship between the festival and everyday life and introduces the notion of festivals as events that 'perform the village'. This performance is evident in the photographic work of Anna Fox who has made a study of festive performances in her home village. Her work is discussed in relation to the photographic archives of Tony Ray-Jones and Homer Sykes. The final sections broaden the focus from festivals to folk art more widely, through an investigation of Jeremy Deller and Alan Kane's *Folk Archive*, exploring the idea that these practices are not simply grounded in a nostalgic rendering of the past but are fluid, creative responses to the contemporary village.

GALLON BUCKETS AND CARRIER BAGS

The hedgerows have bloomed with four by fours. Perched at precarious angles on the high verge, they line the narrow approach to Tichborne Manor. Today is the 25 March, the feast of the Annunciation or Lady's Day in the Christian calendar, it is close to the vernal equinox, and in this small Hampshire parish it is the day of the Tichborne Dole.

The Tichborne Dole is a calendar custom dating back to the thirteenth century, when Lady Mabella Tichborne made a deathbed plea to her parsimonious husband, Sir Roger, to ensure that the poor of the parish were considered after she died.[2] In an eccentric and cruel move, the legend has it that Sir Roger pledged to make an annual donation to the poor of the produce from the land which the dying Lady Mabella could crawl around while holding a lighted torch. Miraculously his wife managed to drag herself around a 23 acre field (still called 'The Crawls' today) before the torch burned out, and consolidated her spousal bargain with a curse should it ever fail to be honoured.[3]

We negotiate the muddy drive on foot and become part of the crowd at the back of the house. The local vicar, elevated on the stone steps of the neo-classical portico, shouts a list of surnames into the cold, grey morning. A literal roll call of each resident of the parish; when your name is called you join a queue to collect the dole. At various points in history the dole has been transmuted from wheat to bread to flour, and now each adult is entitled to one gallon of flour while a child gets half a gallon. The atmosphere in the queue is jolly, it seems the traditional thing to do is to bring a pillow case in which to carry your flour, but the less picturesque minded have brought their Tesco bags for life. The flour is cheerfully distributed by men in white baker's overalls, using archaic looking gallon buckets. As we approach the front of the queue the air is thick with flour and a film of it settles on our glasses and coats.

The connection between the tradition and the Tichborne family is no longer stable, the house is now rented out to whoever can afford it, with a proviso in the lease that the dole should continue. The charitable link with the poor of the parish is also weakened to the point of parody – this crowd is dominated by an affluent country set, evidenced not only by the four by fours in the lane but also the beyond clichéd prevalence of wax jackets and green Wellingtons, and perhaps most telling – the fact that none of them were needed elsewhere on a Thursday morning. There was also a sprinkling of pensioners, mums with young children and the long term unemployed. However, there was no pretence that a gallon of flour was going to materially affect anyone's food bill that month. The link with the land has also been lost, the flour has no connection to the original 23 acres of the Tichborne Estate; it is purchased by the tenants of Tichborne Manor and doled out until it is all gone. So what remains of this custom in its contemporary manifestation? The residue is what could be termed 'the performance of the village' articulating as it does, something of the self consciously constructed nature of contemporary village living. A construction that thrives on re-enactments of a remembered or imagined past, that requires an intricate negotiation of the ancient and the modern, yet is nonetheless imbued with the exuberance of any good performance.

In the case of the Tichborne Dole the real, symbolic and imaginary structures of the village are performed to itself in a number of ways: the alliance between the authority of the church and the economic power of the estate is demonstrated by the involvement of the parish priest as administrator of the dole; the class relations of the village are enacted with the lowly parishioners lining up to receive charity

5.2   Vicar reads out names at the Tichborne Dole.

5.3   Villagers
queue up at the
flour trough.

from the 'Lord of the Manor'; the boundaries of the community are demonstrated as only the residents of three villages are entitled to the dole, and the community is literally named as the priest reads from the electoral role. Community building and re-inscribing the relations of power are traditional functions of calendar customs and are enacted through a wide range of fascinating practices.[4] However, with the diminishing authority of the church and the estate (certainly in the case of Tichborne) taking part in a custom like this feels as if an alternative performance of the village is overlaying these traditional functions of the custom.

In this alternative performance the re-inscription of class and power still takes place but in different ways, for example the Range Rovers of the wealthy residents, imposing themselves along the lane making it impossible for the uninitiated to park or even drive towards the estate, demonstrate different sets of economic relations. Prestige here is also derived from longevity in residence with cliques of 'old' families seeming to take over the grounds of the house, assuming an ownership and authority over even the current tenants of the manor who are hosting the event. Perhaps most importantly however this is a performance of the village which shows that it is old, that it maintains a connection to the past and in so doing, claims its place in the national imaginary of the old, strange, rural.

This is an example of tradition becoming *traditional*, a process which is explored in Hobsbawm and Ranger's classic collection *The Invention of Tradition*

(2000 [1983]). Invented tradition refers to the idea that many traditions which have become embedded into society are relatively new and have been invented to reinforce certain norms and values. Examples given by the authors include the traditions purposefully constructed by institutions such as the royal Christmas speech, which was inaugurated in 1932, or more organically formed traditions such as practices that take place around football matches (Hobsbawm 2000 [1983]: p. 1). Significantly, such traditions, even when comparatively recent derive much of their power from establishing a link to a suitable notion of the past, often through the adoption of traditional forms borrowed from religious ceremonies, royal pomp and folkloric practices.

Invented traditions are a response to processes of modernity that have shaped the past 200 years, leading to the development of intense and anxious societal relationships to tradition. The constant change and flux which is often thought to characterise modernity, creates a double impact on the use and practice of tradition. Firstly creating a need for the establishment of a semblance of continuity with the past, and secondly generating a fear that 'old' knowledge and practices are being lost or dying out. Both these factors mean that tradition becomes consciously performed as such, that its primary meanings are changed from any 'original' intentions (such as charity in the case of the Tichborne Dole) towards an explicit linkage of place with past. Hobsbawm notes that while the invention of tradition has always taken place 'we should expect it to occur more frequently when a rapid transformation of society weakens or destroys the social patterns for which 'old' traditions had been designed' (Hobsbawm 2000 [1983]: p. 4). The changes in population, employment patterns and economic power which have occurred in non-metropolitan places, particularly in the post war period, have meant that even where traditional practices have been established for many hundreds of years and retain much of their customary form, their meanings have been re-invented.

Lefebvre, in his essay 'Notes Written One Sunday in the French Countryside' laments what he sees as a change in the festive exuberance of rural customs:

> *Every time spring arrives, processions intended to confirm the regularity of the season and the fertility of the fields go round the village, winding drearily along through the paths between the fields. Drearily, plunged into an immense boredom which is like an ultimate sacrifice: people 'give up' the time, put up with the inconvenience. All the Dionysiac joy has gone out of this ritual, which is known arrogantly as 'Rogation Days'. It is a request for fine weather and a rich harvest. Actually, nobody believes that prayers can be really effective, but many still believe that not to attend or to stop the ritual completely would be bad luck (Lefebvre 2008 [1958]: p. 211).*

For Lefebvre, writing of a small peasant town in pre-war France, the meaning of the custom has changed over time from a riotous pagan welcoming of the fecundity of spring, to a solemn request to the Christian God for a productive farming year, finally becoming a practice whose meaning lies in its relation to the past, in the fact that it has always been done, creating a vague and uneasy superstition about its abandonment. Perhaps if the same village were to be visited today at Rogation Tide one might find a reinvigorated festival. Not in the sense that residents have developed more devout beliefs, or that they feel a stronger connection to the land, in fact both of these elements will certainly have moved in the opposite direction. It is instead their relationship to the past which may have changed, reflected in an anxious enthusiasm to be associated with such traditions and a desire that they should not die out.

This does not imply that such reinvented traditions are in some way inauthentic. Discourses around inauthenticity rely on an imagined point of authenticity, which in the case of calendar customs, given their often uncertain origins and evolving forms is very difficult to establish. Rather the 'Range Rover-isation' of non-metropolitan traditions evidences a continuation of the modern contradiction of tradition: that as connections to the past become increasingly unstable the more fervently they are enacted. If modern life is simultaneously the death of tradition, or at least its disruption, it is also characterised by an attempt to hold on to it, through the modern impulse to create folk collections and museums. However, it could be argued that this contradiction is lived more vividly in non-metropolitan locations, as rather than taking place in the confines of a museum it is instead embedded in everyday practices such as calendar customs and village fetes.

FESTIVALS AND THE EVERYDAY

It may seem contradictory to think of these once a year occurrences as being part of the everyday. However, their influence spreads out into the everyday through the rhythms of preparation, anticipation and gossip. In addition, rural traditions like calendar customs, can be seen as belonging to the register of the festival – a phenomenon that has been accessed by anthropologists, sociologists and cultural theorists as a key critique of the everyday. Its usefulness lies in the festival's position as separate from the everyday but as structurally related to it. Festivals perform an intensified version of the everyday, a performance which reveals the community to itself. Lefebvre notes that:

> Certainly right from the start, festivals contrasted violently with everyday life, but they were not separate from it. They were like everyday life but more intense; and the moments of that life – the practical community, food, the relation with nature – in other words, work – were reunited, amplified, magnified in the festival (Lefebvre 2008 [1958]: p. 207).

In his study *Popular Culture in Early Modern Europe* (1978) historian Peter Burke identifies the ways in which the elements of the everyday become exaggerated during festive celebrations of the past. For example the everyday necessity of food is transformed into excessive feasting; the familial and sexual relationships that are part of everyday life are transformed by mass-marriages, suspension of usual moral codes around sex, and ritualised performances with phallic objects; elements of communal life are staged as ritualised performances and processions (Burke 1978: pp. 186–7). The boundary of the community or village is also often performed in exaggerated ways involving violence or sporting competitions with neighbouring communities. These elements can be found in many of the calendar customs practised today in the UK, even if only in highly ritualised forms. For example the calendar custom of Hare Pie Scrambling and Bottle Kicking at Hallerton in Leicestershire takes place on Easter Monday, a time traditionally associated with carnival as a celebration of the end of the abstinence of Lent.[5] It starts with a procession of villagers carrying a pie at its head, the pie is then thrown into the crowd with everyone scrambling to get a bit. The bottle kicking then commences, which is a lawless and rowdy mixture of rugby and football, played with three small barrels instead of a ball. The game is played by teams from Hallerton and the neighbouring village of Medbourne, with the aim being for each team to kick the bottle over the streams that form the village boundaries into their opponent's village. The victors then drink the beer from the barrels and climb the Hallerton cross, where much more drinking and feasting ensues (Hogg 1971: p. 54).

Festive forms can also invoke an inversion of the everyday which works to reveal structures of social status and moral behaviour by turning them upside down. Tropes that play upon inversion include men dressing as women, priests and other high status individuals becoming fools for the day and vice versa. Burke comments that:

> Carnival was a time of comedies, which often enacted situations of reversal in which the judge was put in the stocks or the wife triumphed over her husband, Carnival costumes allowed men and women to reverse roles. The relations of master and servant might be inverted; in England, 'Shrove Tuesday's liberty of servants' was traditional. The everyday repression of sexual and aggressive impulses were replaced by encouragements. Carnival was, in short, a time of institutionalised disorder, a set of rituals of reversal (Burke 1978: p. 190).

Even the mildest of village fetes today are the scenes of similar inversions, providing the opportunity to throw wet sponges at the local vicar or head teacher and encouraging otherwise respectable members of the community to dress up in silly costumes, under the guise of raising money for charity. Such forms of institutionalised disorder only function within the strict boundaries of control which characterise even the most raucous festivals. The disorder is time limited – everything will return to normal after the festive day. In addition rather than representing true chaos, the disorder is firmly organized around inversions of the ordinary, thereby implicitly demonstrating the existing societal structure. Through inversion and exaggeration there is room for critique of the everyday, but as many commentators have pointed out (Hill 1984; Humphrey 2001), rather than representing a potential vehicle for change or revolution, festive forms more often have the function of a safety valve – allowing citizens to let off steam in controlled ways followed by a return to business as usual.

Attending to the above studies of carnival it becomes apparent that calendar customs and other festive forms can be seen as establishing a structural relationship to the everyday, in that they make visible everyday practices through presenting an intensified and ritualised performance of the norms, values and patterns of behaviour that characterise the community. However, moving from the pre-industrial period evoked by Lefebvre and Burke, towards the contemporary enactment of festive forms raises the question: what form of everyday life is reflected in the contemporary festive practices – to today's hare pie scramblers, Tichborne dolers or vicar soakers? It is difficult to see the strange intricacies of the hare pie festival as even an inverted reflection of the modern non-metropolitan everyday. In this context a re-evaluation of the meanings of contemporary practices of calendar customs is required, a perspective that recognises the multi-layered quality of such performances of the village. In this way it is more generative to see these festivals as reflexive critical performances of a community's relationship with the past, a relationship which can be felt and enacted on an everyday level.

This is a position taken by anthropologist Victor Turner, who emphasises the reflexive nature of what he terms cultural performance. Turner uses the term cultural performance to refer to theatrical, dance, and musical performances, together with those based around religion or ritual, given their use of ritual and theatrical elements his work can also be usefully employed in thinking about calendar customs. On the relationship between cultural performance and everyday life Turner argues that:

> This relationship is not unidirectional and 'positive' – in the sense that the performative genre merely 'reflects' or 'expresses' the social system, or that cultural configuration, or at any rate their key relationships – but that it is reciprocal and reflexive – in the sense that the performance is often a critique, direct or veiled, of the social life it grows out of, an evaluation (with lively possibilities of rejection) of the way society handles history (Turner 1987: p. 22).

The final words of this quote echo Hobsbawm's invented tradition, revealing the modern condition of an anxious relationship with history. Accordingly, when thought through the frame of the non-metropolitan, one of the things that is reflected in cultural performances such as calendar customs is the everyday navigation between the ancient and the modern. Small scale daily negotiations of this kind for example the uncomfortable embedding of elements such as motorways, litter and electricity pylons into the landscape have been a feature of this book. The modern engagement with calendar customs can be seen as an enlarged projection of this uneasy relationship. The festival is a dialectical form which is capable of carrying many often opposing meanings. Through its function as a critique of the everyday, it has been demonstrated that the festive form can have the double function of both destabilising and reinforcing societal structures. In this way it can also reveal the contradictory forces of the modern response to tradition and the complex nature of the performance of the village.

The 'performance of the village' is a phrase used by photographer Anna Fox (Fox 2009) to describe her interest in documenting contemporary village life through its engagement with calendar customs. Fox's images work to complicate notions around the modern non-metropolitan relationship to the past by drawing to the surface both its embeddedness within the rural everyday and its uncomfortable and contradictory nature.

PERFORMING THE VILLAGE

Anna Fox is unusual in the world of contemporary photography in that much of her work is made in and about rural places. This in itself is perhaps not so unusual, rather it is her refusal to see these places as unpopulated landscapes, instead determinedly focusing on what it is like to live in non-metropolitan places. She accesses the social relations and performances which constitute a community, and shows something of the felt experience of village life.

Her engagement with the rural has ranged from the hyper-staged series *Country Girls* (1996–2001) (Plate 7), to what feel like stolen documentary glimpses of a rural community in *The Village* (1991–1993) (Plate 8). In *Country Girls* Fox worked with childhood friend and musician Alison Goldfrapp, to create a series of striking images that explore the claustrophobia resulting from the very limited options for self-identification that seemed available to them as rural girls and women. In this series Goldfrapp assumes the twin characters of repressed 'country lady' in wax jacket and pearls, and vulnerable 'good time girl', drunkenly staggering down dark country lanes in party frock and very high heels. At certain points these characters become interchangeable, we never see the face of the party girl – she could be the 'country lady' performing as her alter ego and, in a real sense she is the same person, as Goldfrapp plays both parts. As the photographs take a darker turn the woman is fragmented, only parts of her appear in each image and it is clear that she has become a victim of some rural horror. These are images that make reference to the tragic fate of the now legendary Fanny Adams, a young girl who was violently murdered 1867 in Alton (Williams 2007: p. 215), a small Hampshire town which played a significant role in both women's childhoods and formative years.

With its exaggerated costumes and wigs, *Country Girls* makes explicit the fascination with performance that runs through Fox's work.[6] However, in *The Village* series such performances are not directly constructed by the artist, but are instead made visible through a combination of framing and lighting techniques that render everyday situations strange, and reveal an unexpected texture of fairytale violence. *The Village* represents an investigation into the public and private spheres of a small West Sussex community in which Fox's grandmother lived and mother was brought up. Here as in *Country Girls* it is the women of the village who are centre stage, caught in the act with mouths open, seemingly shouting, screaming, eating, about to tear into to each other. One particularly memorable image from this series shows a bride with her bridesmaid engaging in the final preparations for the big day. The image is a fragment, only hands and a mouth and big puffy sleeves are visible, all except for an enormous pair of silver scissors that seem to be heading for the Bride's back, as she is restrained by her friend clawing at her hair.[7]

That the underside of the chocolate box rural is a sinister, insular realm of unhealthy repression and physical and emotional violence is not a new idea. However, Fox's images contribute differently to this account, accessing both the performance and behind the scenes – the public and the private, the conscious and unconscious – a tactic that makes visible the intricate construction and ritualised performance of the modern village. These ideas are enacted to full effect in a series of images taken behind the scenes of performers in costume, preparing to play their roles in the annual tradition of the village play – an entertainment in which the story of the village of Selbourne is performed to an audience of residents. These photographs are at once completely familiar – evoking terrible school plays and am-dram productions, while refracting a confusing multitude of possibilities for public and private performances of the village.

Selbourne is where Fox grew up, it is a small Hampshire village, a few miles away from Alton. In 1999 she returned to live in the village and embarked upon a personal chronicle of contemporary village life seen through its customs and traditions in the series *Back to the Village* (1999–2008) (Plate 9). The photographs in this series take the form of portraits; the villagers meet the gaze of the camera head on, sometimes staring through the eyeholes in masks, they are always in costume yet away from the festive action. Many of the images relate to calendar customs with which we are all familiar such as Halloween, Christmas and bonfire night. But the series also records the performers in traditions that are specific to the village, such as the annual Pram Race – a fancy dress charity event.[8]

Fox cites the early photographer, Sir Benjamin Stone as an inspiration for this series (Williams 2007: p. 220). During the last years of the 1800s and the early 1900s Stone toured the country taking hundreds of photographs of customs and pageants, building a fascinating archive of festive practices at this time (Ford 1974) (Figure 5.4). In addition to their shared subject matter there are also formal similarities between the two photographer's work: given the limitations of early photography it is no surprise to find Stone's photographs are often very staged,

5.4   Benjamin Stone, *Hare Pie Scrambling and Bottle Kicking*, 1905. Courtesy of Library of Birmingham, Sir Benjamin Stone Photographic Collection.

with most or all of the participants looking at the camera, posed self consciously, but even a hundred years later this is also a feature of Fox's images. The festive participants are caught at a moment where they are not participating, some stay in character, like the little boys acting out gruesome Halloween fantasies, others awkwardly revert to a performance of themselves.

The awkwardness captured in Fox's portraits speaks of the strange circularity of an event in which a village performs itself to itself (literally in the case of the annual play about the history of Selbourne). As discussed above, the re-invented calendar custom predominantly focuses on the opportunity for the village to implicitly perform its present day social structure and importantly, to perform its relationship with the past. In these images something of the 'violence' of these performances is revealed. The images capture the participants in a resigned, joyless, 'celebration', where the festive subverting of everyday rules of engagement produce an unease which is often intensified through the uncanny use of masks and costumes. To return to Victor Turner's notions of cultural performance:

> Where the same person(s) are both subject and object, violence has to be done to common sense ways of classifying the world and society. The 'self' is split up in the middle – it is something that one both is and one sees and, furthermore, acts upon as though it were another (Turner 1987: p. 25).

The performance of the village is enacted by the village to the village, one is and one sees, and in this seeing one changes again. Turner argues that the festive performance is reflexive in that through the doing and the seeing identities and relationships are worked and re-worked. In non-metropolitan calendar customs identity is certainly in play, but whether this reflexive nature is entirely positive is not clear. The identities that are being performed have a desperate rigidity to them, where aspects of difference are smoothed away. The village wants to represent itself as the type of village where community is strong and active and where tradition is upheld, in this anxious clinging to tradition, the festive energies so often lauded by Bakhtin (1984 [1964]) and his followers are focussed on keeping up appearances.

A further layer of complexity is added to the idea of the village showing itself to itself – or reflexive reflection, by Fox's insistence on an autobiographical approach. She is also part of this village, and her images are themselves embroiled in this representational circularity. They form a personal archive of the village's attempts to archive itself, but they are also objects/images out there in the world which accumulate wider cultural resonances.

For her autobiographical subject matter she has been compared to other female photographers of her generation such as Nan Goldin (Chandler 2007: p. 15), who blurs the boundaries between public and private, creating an intimate record of the world she inhabits.[9] While Fox might share Goldin's forthright observational technique, her subject matter differs greatly from what Chandler characterised as Goldin's 'attractively damaged urban subcultures' (Chandler 2007: p. 16). Perhaps a more interesting comparison in relation to the alignment of rural observation and personal archiving can be found with an earlier resident of Fox's village Selbourne, the eighteenth century naturalist Gilbert White. White is best remembered for *A Natural History of Selbourne* (2007 [1789]), which is based upon his detailed observation of the flora and fauna of the village.[10] There are parallels to be made between the naturalist's dissection of specimens and the documentary photographer's gaze, not least in the perceived violence of these acts. A section from White's writings accesses a combination of vivid colour, violence and sharp observation, which is also present in Fox's images:

> A Pair of honey buzzards … built them a large shallow nest, composed of twigs and lined with dead beechen leaves, upon a tall slender beech near the middle of Selbourne-hanger, in the summer of 1780. In the middle of the month of June a bold boy climbed this tree, though standing on so steep and dizzy a situation, and brought down an egg, the only one in the nest, which had been sat on for some time and contained the embrio of a young bird. The egg was … dotted at each end with small red spots, and surrounded in the middle with a broad bloody zone. The hen bird was shot … This specimen contained in its craw some limbs of frogs and many grey snails with shells. The irides of the eyes of this bird were of a beautiful bright yellow colour (White 2007 [1789]: p. 100).[11]

The parallels between the act of photographing and violence are well known, perhaps most vividly articulated by Susan Sontag in her account of documentary photography (1979 [1971]: p. 12). In his commentary on the new forms of colour documentary photography that emerged in the UK in the 1980s Mellor sees the use of colour as a new form of violence:

> brazen new colour photography [had the potential] to destroy past frameworks, in this case Left Humanist consensus around conventional documentary. The photographs came before the reader in a hot, estranging glare … colour took on a violence and insolence never seen before in British photography (Mellor 2007: p. 130).

Anna Fox is part of the second generation of documentary photographers working with the harsh colours and disjointed framing that was so shocking in the work of Martin Parr and Paul Graham.[12] Her continued use of a direct flash which is hand held and therefore easily directed at her subjects is redolent of this highly distinctive style and continues to define how her images look (Fox 2009). Every detail and imperfection becomes visible and colours are heightened to hyper-real levels. In the case of *Back to the Village* this has the effect of creating an unforgiving clarity that makes any clichéd romanticism around the non-metropolitan impossible.

Back to the Village can also be usefully examined in relation to the work of photographers Tony Ray-Jones and Homer Sykes. In 1967 Tony Ray-Jones embarked upon a photographic journey around the UK with his wife in a Dormobile Camper van (Mellor 2008: p. 66). He documented both traditional calendar customs together with seasonal events often associated with the metropolitan elite rather than rural communities, such as Opera at Glyndebourne and the Henley Regatta. The resulting photographs became the exhibition *The English Seen* (1969) at the Institute of Contemporary Arts (ICA) and published posthumously as the book *A Day Off: An English Journal* (1974). In common with Fox, Ray-Jones' images reveal an inherent absurdity in these practices by looking behind the scenes for material. Rather than focusing on the performance of the festival as the central event, Ray-Jones looks awry, recording all the extraneous paraphernalia that you as an

5.5   Tony Ray-Jones, *Herne Bay Carnival*, 1967.

5.6   Tony Ray-Jones, York Mystery Players, 1969.

observer or participant are supposed to ignore. He records the grumpy faced child instead of the smiling performer, and the medieval Mummers sunbathing (Figures 5.5 and 5.6). Caught out of character but still in costume, the comic strangeness of these performances becomes evident.

Despite working within a few years of Ray-Jones, in the same black and white format, and on occasion documenting the same events, Homer Sykes' images have a different feel. Sykes set off on his own expedition to document the calendar customs of the UK (Mellor 2007: p. 14), which resulted in a publication *Once a Year* (1977) and a touring exhibition *Traditional British Calendar Customs*. Sykes documented 81 different calendar customs making dynamic images of the action paired with valuable written commentary on the history and current day practice of the events. Sykes' images primarily centre on the performance itself. Even when preparations for the festivals are shown, the participants seem to be wholly absorbed in the task at hand, there is no distance between them and the event. Each image is full of energy and excitement. Rather than dealing in the perhaps easy absurdity of these events, Sykes' images work to situate these customs within the everyday – the strange becomes everyday rather than the more travelled inversion of the everyday becoming strange. One striking example of this can be found in his images of *The Burry Man*. In this custom, carried out in South Queensferry, Lothian, a resident is dressed in a woollen suit which is then entirely covered in burrs, the effect is one of creating a hybrid of man and cactus, *The Burry Man* then walks the boundaries of the town, calling at all the pubs along the way. Sykes' photographs serve to situate these events firmly with the register of the ordinary as he shows

5.7   *The Burry Man*, 1977. © Homer Sykes.

this creature seated on bar stool, drinking his whisky through a straw (Figure 5.7), and walking down a cold wet tarmac road with a little kid in wellies.

These differences result from the artists' varying conceptualisations of their projects. Ray-Jones had just returned to the UK from study and work in America (Roberts 2005: p. 7), and his perspective is one of distanced observer. Mellor points out that 'this series belonged to a recognizable twentieth century strategy deployed by foreign visitors – or exiled, but returning – photographers, of representing British culture through piquant and peculiar embodiments' (Mellor 2008: p. 61).[13]

Significantly, Mellor also notes a phrase from Ray-Jones' diary citing that his intention was to be 'Dedicated to the Insanity of Modernity' (Mellor 2008: p. 61). This intention was reflected in many of his pictures through moments which track the absurdities resulting from the desperate and incongruous clinging to tradition, invented or otherwise, that seems to characterise these events.

Sykes was also engaged in the modern preoccupation with tradition, but more particularly with the concern that practices thought of as 'traditional customs' were under threat of dying out. In this way his project becomes historical, concerned with recording these aspects of rural culture for future generations. In their introduction to *Once a Year* Folklore scholars Paul and Georgina Smith make the function of these images clear:

> Photographs such as those in this collection play an important part in research into cultural traditions as a whole. They contain a store of information on the way in which particular customs are practised, and thus provide a base from which researchers can identify changes which have taken place in the form of customs over the years (Smith 1977: 12).

In this way Sykes' work borders on the ethnographic, it can be seen as contributing to the study and (photographic) preservation of tradition.

Anna Fox's approach negotiates between the differences in Ray-Jones' and Sykes' projects. Her images access both sides of the modern contradictions of tradition. They show such traditions to be both strange and firmly situated in the everyday – indeed, as distorted performances of the non-metropolitan everyday. Like Sykes and Stone, she is building an archive, one that is specific to her own village detailing the local engagement with certain calendar customs and traditions, she states that:

> When I came back to Selbourne, I became increasingly aware of how extraordinary the ritual of life in the countryside is. I had been looking at the photographs made by Benjamin Stone as he travelled around Britain recording customs and festivals in the 1900s. This inspired me to make a record of my own (Fox quoted in Williams 2007: p. 220).

However, her approach also has similarities with Ray-Jones in that she focuses her attention behind the scenes; her isolation of the participants from the events shows their hastily constructed costumes out of context, speaking of the absurdity of such enactments. However, her subjects are not mocked in the same way as Ray-Jones, and her images communicate something of the significance of these events. In relation to an image showing bonfire night guys with paper plate faces, uncannily sprawled on village hall chairs, Val Williams notes that:

> *These creations, so badly made, so menacing, are ideal subjects for Fox's*
> *continuing survey of village life, asserting as they do, the importance of custom,*
> *yet at the same time illustrating its degradations (Williams 2007: p. 216).*

This statement is important in that it accesses the contradictory yet intertwined characteristics of modernity as both the demise of tradition and its restless resurrection, a dialectic which is adeptly communicated in Fox's images.

This dialectic: the decline of tradition and its fervent performance is explored in the following sections in relation to the *Folk Archive* project by artists Jeremy Deller and Alan Kane. Like Anna Fox, whose intention is to record the rituals of contemporary village life, Deller and Kane's project is also driven by the archival impulse that we have seen stemming from anxieties around loss. Folk art is often thought to be dead, the conditions for its production being lost to a pre-1914 arcadia (a concept that is explored in more detail below). However, Deller and Kane's project presents a challenge to this nostalgic formulation by actively seeking out contemporary folk art practices. In the process of re-defining what constitutes folk art in the twenty-first century, the collection also goes some way towards presenting an alternative picture of national identity, one that brings the non-metropolitan to the fore. The Tichborne Dole and the work of the photographers analysed in the first part of this chapter demonstrated the micro-negotiations between the ancient and the modern that characterise the non-metropolitan living. The final section will look at how certain aspects of the *Folk Archive* also access these tensions and in addition make visible the simultaneity of the local and the global.

ELECTRIC FOLK

'"Folk" here has gone electric' was the response of curator and critic Tom Morton (Morton 2005: p. 133) to the *Folk Archive*, a project by artists Jeremy Deller and Alan Kane. His phrasing draws on the moment in 1965 which Bob Dylan was said to have 'gone electric', leading to criticism that he was betraying his folksy roots. As we have seen in the previous chapter, 1965 was also the year in which the members of Binsted WI 'went electric', or at least chose to represent their village with the emblem of an electricity pylon. Electricity and folk have an uncomfortable relationship, the outcry prompted by Dylan's turn toward amplification is a testament to this discomfort, as is the strangeness of the embroidered pylon on the cover of the Binsted scrapbook.

Electricity signifies modernity, interconnectedness, urbanity, industrialisation, consumerism and noise, all numerous counterpoints to folk's perceived archaism, insularity, rurality, community, home-made/hand-made qualities. But it is precisely juxtapositions such as these which complicate received notions of terms like folk.

Folk generally means people or the people. Definitions of folk art are notoriously mutable, it also goes under the sobriquets: vernacular art, popular art, traditional art, and unsophisticated art.[14] Catherine Lambert and Enid Marx, collectors and writers on folk art struggled to compose a suitable definition, but emphasised its relationship to the everyday:

Popular and Traditional Art ... is hard to define though easy enough to recognise when seen. It is the art which ordinary people have, from time immemorial, introduced into their everyday lives (Lambert and Marx 1945: p. 7).[15]

In their publication on the subject of 1951, they decide to settle on the term Popular Art to describe predominantly handmade items created by 'non-artists', a term which as Miller points out is at odds with the parallel development of Pop Art at this time, which took as its material the mass produced ephemera of the burgeoning post war consumer society (Miller 2005: p. 150). However, this homonym is perhaps not as inappropriate as it first appears, as folk and pop both share certain associations with subversion and rebellion, the use of materials that were readily to hand and the adoption of an alternative position to mainstream society.[16]

The words folk and mass also have a certain resonance with regard to the people, the popular, the non-specialist, the everyday. And there are comparisons to be made between the Mass-Observation archive (detailed in Chapter 3) and the *Folk Archive*. They are both examples of collecting information about ourselves, from ourselves – an anthropology of ourselves. Deller and Kane said that one of their aims for the *Folk Archive* was to:

highlight and preserve some of the undervalued cultural production of individuals in the face of the increasingly aggressive consumer society we inhabit and investigate how this production may be adapting to a rapidly changing world (Button and Esche 2000: p. 91).

This statement sounds remarkably anthropological in scope and ambition, a position that they sought to distance themselves from as the project evolved (Slyce 2005: p. 76). It also accesses the archival impulse seen in Sykes' anxious attempts to record folk practices for future generations. Both the Mass-Observation Archive and the *Folk Archive* projects also aimed to capture an alternative picture of Britain, one that ran contrary to that which was portrayed in the press and official mediums. Finally, both are fragmentary, using collage as a methodology to access forms of representation that highlight collective diversity and simultaneity of different voices, worlds and temporalities.

The *Folk Archive* maybe accredited to Deller and Kane, however the artefacts of which it is comprised are made by 'others' in every sense of the word. It has taken many forms over the past decade but is best known in its incarnation as a major exhibition which toured venues in the UK and Europe in 2005. The archive contains handmade objects, together with photographs and films documenting folk art practices. What constitutes folk art and what is included in the archive is entirely designated by the artists.

In describing any archive or collection, particularly one that finds its material in the realm of the everyday, it falls to the writer to provide some sort of list of what the archive holds, such lists are inevitably selections which can communicate more about the author's areas of interest than the rationale or scope of the archive itself. However, a list is nevertheless necessary to develop a context for discussion. While

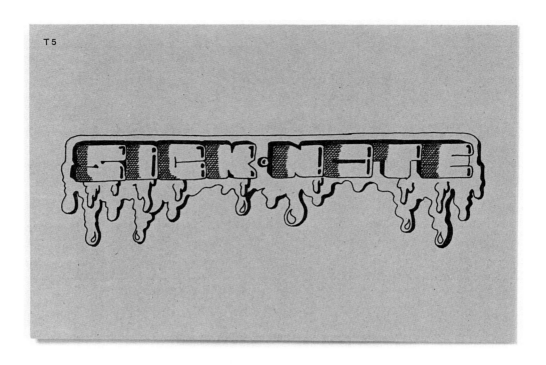

5.8   Sick note envelopes by Dean Briggs, part of Folk Archive by Jeremy Deller and Alan Kane.

the Mass-Observation founders handily provided an inventory of possible subjects including everything from bathroom behaviour to the sex lives of midwives (Harrisson *et al.* 1937), the initiators of the folk art have issued no such manifesto of content, leaving each visitor to compile their own top ten, here is mine: a set of envelopes from a job centre in Cornwall used to contain the day's sick notes on which the security guard makes intricate daily drawings (Figure 5.8), flower arrangements by members of the Women's Institute, photographs of animals made inexpertly out of vegetables for a village fête competition, green velvet shorts with floral embroidery used for traditional Cumberland wrestling, photographs of the tar-barrel rolling festival at Ottery St. Mary in Devon (Plate 10), a scarecrow dressed as Michael Jackson, a home-made toy wooden cooker, a photograph of young women dressed up as old women for a hen night, a motor cycle helmet painted to look like a skull, a knitted tea cosy that looks like a house with boarded up windows, a full sized figure of the Burry Man.

NON-METROPOLITAN ETHNOGRAPHY

The *Folk Archive* can be viewed in the context of a re-invigoration of interest in everyday creativity amongst contemporary artists. Two examples of a similar investigations into the vernacular include Richard Wentworth's photographic series *Making do and Getting By* (1970–ongoing), and Russian artist Vladimir Arkhipov's collection of contemporary Russian folk art objects *Home-Made* (1994– ongoing).[17] Wentworth's photographs document moments of everyday creativity in the sense that they record inconspicuous improvisations made by 'non-artists', usually involving the changed use of an everyday object. They demonstrate how the daily is made up of minute negotiations with the objects that surround us in order to live with and between the functionality of what we are given: A door held open by a Wellington boot – its toe jammed between door and floor, the wing of a car hastily 'repaired' with a piece of carpet and some tape, the space between drain pipe and wall pleasingly wedged with Styrofoam cups – aesthetically functional in lieu of a bin. Instances that are perhaps less formalised than the WI scrapbooks but once again speak of bricolage as a practice of creative inventiveness with whatever is at hand (de Certeau 1988: p. xix).

While Wentworth's images stand in for the fleeting conjunction of the objects he records, Arkhipov finds himself overwhelmed by the stubborn actuality of the things he collects, which have become what he terms *The People's Museum of Home-Made Objects*.[18] This collection consists of home-made objects from the Soviet Union. Unavailable in mass-produced form due to the severe shortages of consumer products suffered in the USSR during this period, each object represents a creative response to an everyday problem improvised from what was to hand. In contrast to much of what is thought of as folk art, both traditionally and in Deller and Kane's collection, few pieces have a decorative element, although all display a distinctive aesthetic of makeshift necessity. Each piece is accompanied by a testimonial from its owner or maker.

The *Folk Archive* and projects such as those by Wentworth and Arkihpov have marked a shift in the role of the artist, who becomes more involved in the processes of documentation, collection and curation, than in the production of objects. This way of working – collecting and observing the social practices and material cultures of a society or community – was notably problematised as the 'ethnographic turn' in art practice by Hal Foster. Foster argues that Benjamin's notion of the 'Author as Producer' (1970 [1934]) has, in contemporary times, found its parallel with the 'artist as ethnographer' (Foster 1996: p. 172). That whilst for Benjamin what was at stake was economic relations, now the contested ground is that of cultural relations. Foster argues that 'it is the cultural and/or ethnic other in whose name the committed artist most often struggles' (Foster 1996: p. 173). This is a way of working which foregrounds the notion of a cultural elsewhere, which represents the potential for transformation or subversion of what is presumed the cultural norm or mainstream. For the *Folk Archive*, elsewhere is the non-metropolitan, the amateur, the ordinary, the everyday and the popular, conceived as a resistive alternative to the corporate and media blanding of the nation. But what does it mean to represent something as diverse as the non-metropolitan (or anti-metropolitan as the artists termed it below) through a collection of material culture and practice?

Employing Foster's tracing of the development of artists adopting ethnographic concerns, and the ensuing problematics of representation and display, Dan Smith is critical of Deller and Kane for what he perceives as their lack of critical engagement with the systems of representation employed by the *Folk Archive*. 'The representation of the commonplace is only justifiable if adequately theorised. This is to counteract the possibility of such practices becoming purely exploitative – either ethically or commercially' (Smith 2006: p. 3). By presenting their collections in the form of an archive, displayed in traditionally museological format and exhibited in mainstream art gallery spaces, it could be argued that Deller and Kane are taking an uncritical position with regard to the established ways of looking, categorising and establishing forms of knowledge. Smith asserts that 'by taking a more straightforward [documentary] approach and by artificially homogenising the contents of *Folk Archive*, Deller and Kane risk aligning themselves with the wordless power of institutional authority' (Smith 2006: p. 3).

There are two criticisms here, one, that the material in the archive has been homogenised and two, that in becoming part of an archive it has relinquished its power to the authority of the institution, and has therefore lost its voice, its individuality and is open to exploitation. In relation to the accusation of homogenisation, a counter position would be to argue that Deller and Kane have grouped a diverse range of practices under the banner of folk art in order to complicate existing marginal notions of what this term constitutes. These objects and practices are distinctive and strong, they resist any attempt at museological rationalisation, and on encountering the *Folk Archive* the visitor is overwhelmed by a multiple patchwork of diversity. Rather than a rationalist attempt at categorisation the *Folk Archive* could instead be thought of as employing collage as its primary methodology. The grouping of the archive as a collection puts these fragmentary practices into play with one another, while still enabling the individuality of each to be maintained. They represent different geographies – from the intensely rural Westmoreland wrestling costumes, to the inner city Notting Hill Carnival costumes; different temporalities – from the very old customs like the Burry Man festival to the newly invented tradition of the Scarecrow Festival in Wray, Lancashire; and different realities from the homemade tattoo guns made by prisoners, to the homemade cakes entered into village fete competitions. All represent forms of everyday creativity yet all maintain their specificity and distinctiveness.

With regard to Smith's second point that the archive subjugates the power of the artefacts, such arguments have been played out in the many discourses surrounding institutional critique (Albero and Stimson 2009; Welchman 2006), however in this case they could be thought of as evidence of a metro-centric position which assumes a kind of innocence or purity around the non-metropolitan, that can become subject to the corruption of the metropolitan gaze.[19] Smith continues 'The images in the archive become objects of a secondary voyeurism, which preys upon, and claims superiority to, a more naïve and primary act of looking' (Smith 2006: p. 4). This is a classic relationship of power – the metropolitan audience looking at the material culture of the non-metropolitan. What is interesting here is that it assumes a naivety and a primariness that is as much a part of the myth of the non-metropolitan as it is the myth of the primitive (Hiller 1991), placing the non-metropolitan in the sphere of victimhood once more. In the chapters on Driving and Litter we saw how this familiar narrative placed the non-metropolitan as a 'natural' place which is subject to the myriad pollutions of modernity, Smith's analysis seems to follow this well trodden path. It shows an unwillingness to acknowledge that contemporary folk art and practices are made for and by an audience that is already practicing a form of secondary voyeurism. Experience as makers or consumers of folk art is already mediated, be it through the lens of tourism, perceived notions of heritage, or mass-media representations of what constitutes the non-metropolitan. There is no naïve non-metropolitan gaze. These objects and practices were made to be looked at, they are powerful and interesting, and are conceptually and materially unmoved by their either their inclusion in the archive or the metropolitan gaze.

ALTERNATIVE STORIES

Deller and Kane cite the inspiration for compiling the archive as a response to UK government plans to celebrate the millennium, in particular the exhibits inside the specially built Millennium Dome. They felt frustrated that the content of the dome with its 'zones' sponsored by companies such as Ford, McDonald's, and Tesco did not sufficiently represent the cultural identities and energies that characterise contemporary Britain.[20]

> We both love fetes, fairs, parades and the like – we've always been excited by that side of British Life ... And then in 1999 we were having a conversation about what would be in the [Millennium] Dome, and we just knew that there wasn't going to be anything that reflected that side of British life. And there wasn't. It was very corporate and inhuman even – like a big trade fair for newbritain.com with a lot of

video projections and LCD screens and touch sensitive stuff. But there was very little that was actually made by hands – it was all steel, plastic, and glass. There was very little there to engage you with the world. There was nothing actually living in it or anything that actually suggested life (Deller quoted in Slyce 2003: p. 75).

It was not just the handmade but also the non-metropolitan that was absent from the representation of Britain in the Millennium Dome. This was markedly different from the Dome's predecessor The Festival of Britain, which 50 years earlier had made the relationship between the country, nature and 'the land' itself central to its displays (Figure 5.9). In addition running alongside the Festival of Britain the Whitechapel Gallery held the exhibition *Black Eyes and Lemonade* (1951), curated by Barbara Jones, which was a celebration of British folk and vernacular arts. The absence of acknowledgement of this relationship in the Millennium Dome creates a picture of a neo-liberal homogeneous nation where difference, or local distinctiveness, does not even appear in its usual guise of heritage or nostalgia.

5.9 The Country Exhibition plan from the Festival of Britain Programme, 1951. Licensed under the Open Government Licence v.2.0.

The Dome was a bland space of a future, in which all the knots of difference have been untangled and all the unevenness of the hand-made had been eliminated. The *Folk Archive* presents an alternative picture of modern Britain, one that foregrounds the non-metropolitan. In an interview with the artists Sam Jacob notes that:

The Folk Archive represents another Britain. Jeremy keeps mentioning that it largely involves 'the rural', which is something that Alan consistently disputes.

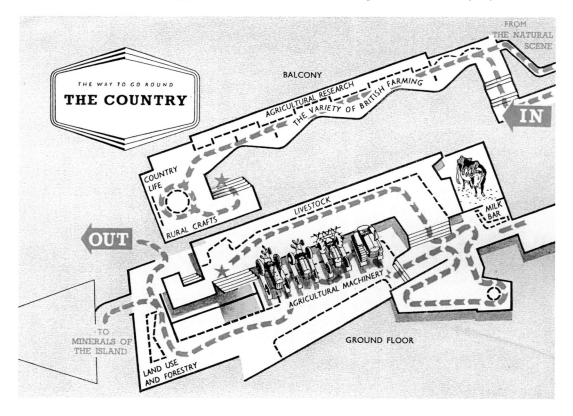

> They do agree that the Britain the Archive is drawn from is decidedly anti-
> metropolitan (Jacob 2005: p. 76).

What the practices and objects held in the Archive demonstrate is that this anti-metropolitan realm is creative, in flux, influenced by mainstream popular and global cultures but also by the past. This is in contrast to the ways in which the non-metropolitan, and indeed folk art are often conceptualised, occupying the same non-specific nostalgic past. The image of folk art is so much aligned with the past that it is often declared to be dead.

James Ayre's authoritative survey British Folk Art, seems to see its production as ceasing around 1900, with the author giving it a prelapsarian status 'Today we view this work as the product of a Garden of Eden before the Fall' (Ayres 1977: p. 6). Writing in 1951 Lambert and Marx, also predict its demise:

> The 'innocent eye' is disappearing in England, not, we think, entirely due to
> mechanisation, but rather from changing social habits, bringing a certain lack
> of initiative and interest in things with a distinctive individual character. As the
> countryside becomes more urbanised and we buy more from chain stores, the
> country craftsmen are dying out and with them that individuality in design and
> decoration that gave life to the old popular art. This is not a thing that can be
> artificially revived; to try and do so would be to get the antithesis of the genuine
> tradition (Lambert and Marx 1951: p. vi).

This quote could seem like an accurate forecast of the development of global consumerism of the past five decades, and explain the representation of the nation in exhibitions such as the Millennium Dome and through the media more generally. Deller and Kane's project however aims to re-situate folk art as a contemporary practice, demonstrating that what is needed is a re-thinking of what constitutes post millennium folk art. For Deller and Kane, folk art is not necessarily about skilled craftsmen turning out objects with a certain aesthetic, it is about adopting an attitude of creative involvement with the world, or the community in which you live. This re-definition complicates the short hand thinking which places folk art in the generic past, and instead acknowledges it as a set of contemporary practices which have been adapted to express current concerns and contexts of everyday life in Britain. Re-thinking what constitutes the contemporary practice of folk art and festivals brings with it complications which surfaced in relation to Anna Fox's rendering of current community celebrations, and my own experiences of the Tichborne Dole. Both these accounts of the contemporary festive experience draw out the awkward performances that take place in order for a community to enact its rural credentials and its connection with the past. Barbara Jones (also speaking of the death of folk art) seems to anticipate debates around preservation through performance or the performance of the village as referred to above, 'Most of the folk arts are dead, or self-consciously preserved by societies' (Jones 1951: p. 9). Jones' statement prompts the question: what is the difference between a practice being 'self-consciously preserved' and actively engaged in? In the documentation which is amassed around such events, it is difficult to determine.

This is a difference which has also become implicit in commentary around the Folk Archive. To return to Morton:

At the entrance of the archive's recent Barbican outing stood a Michael Jackson
Scarecrow, a plush toy monkey perched on its shoulder and a vindicated grin
on its lips … This is one of a number of works in the show that were informed by
Pop culture, and that saved it from being a compendium of archaic practices –
barrel-rolling, gurning, mummers' plays – that have survived into the present day
(Morton 2005: p. 133).

Morton here is perhaps deliberately, unattuned to the various uses and implications
of 'pop' culture in relation to folk art. Aficionados of that past such as Marx and
Lambert might well argue that the archaic practices he describes are indeed
forms of 'popular art' in themselves. However, leaving this aside what is interesting
about this comment is the perceived difference between archaic practices that
have survived and more contemporary or modern manifestations of folk. This
is an interesting border to explore, in trying to rethink the rural out of a generic
arcadia and into the modern: could these older, specifically rural activities, also be
perceived as contemporary rather than archaic? Or perhaps more accurately as
both simultaneously.

It can be argued that everyday life is at its most palpable – that it is driven
out into the open – in moments of crisis. This was a strategy explored by Mass-
Observation in relation to the Abdication crisis and the destruction by fire of the
Crystal Palace in 1936, and the Munich Crisis in 1939 (see Highmore 2002a: pp.
85–6). Such instances need not necessarily be crises on a national or international
scale – the fall of governments or nature disasters – rather they may characterised
by moments where the interplay of the different identities, timescales or realties
of which the everyday is constituted are made apparent. We have seen this occur
when certain elements of the WI scrapbooks showed different timescales or
realities being played out in relation to the antiquated circumstances of the village
post office in comparison to the newly designed David Gentleman stamps and
their connection to modern art and societal change. In relation to the interplay
of different identities in everyday life Kristin Ross writes that 'the moments when
everyday life becomes most vivid or tangible are the moments when most people
find themselves living more than one life' (Ross 1992: p. 63). In his description of the
how the experience of living simultaneous, bewildering or conflicting identities can
characterise the everyday of certain groups more radically than others, Highmore
gives the example of:

Young Chinese adults walking the streets of Beijing with dyed blond hair, listening
to Chinese and US pop on personal stereos, experiencing the conflicting tensions
of school, then going home to eat a traditional meal in the family apartment
(Highmore 2002b: p. 18).

The English village is obviously a very different environment from the streets of
Beijing, however I would like to suggest that the non-metropolitan festival could
also be an arena which brings these conflicting identities to the surface. For
instance the Tar Barrel Rolling festival, celebrated each 5 November in Ottery St.
Mary, Devon (documented by Sykes and included in the Folk Archive, Plate 10),
the event involves running through the village (dangerously) carrying a tar coated
barrel which has been set alight. Generations of children and adults take part and

barrels are often named to commemorate deceased family members. Before going out to participate in this tradition it is possible that teenagers from the village may have been watching television, surfing the internet or playing on a networked games console against other teenagers anywhere in the world. In preparation they may take a swig of globally super-branded soft drink, pull on their equally branded sweatshirt and ask their friends to film the barrel run on their mobile phones, uploading the footage to YouTube and Facebook before the festival is over. Participation in historic traditions like the Tar Barrel Rolling can generate an overlay of different temporalities, on one level it may be a self-conscious re-enactment, a performance of a connection with the past, on another level however it may be experienced as a bodily, immersive, engagement with ritual – perhaps more so with an event such as Tar Barrel Rolling (compared to the Tichborne Dole for example, as it is very difficult to run a flaming tar barrel through the streets in a detached or half hearted manner). At the same time it is clear that the participants, contemporary village residents are not isolated from the modern world. Lambert and Marx were right in that the 'innocent eye' has disappeared, but folk art has not.

Through examining contemporary manifestations of folk art the *Folk Archive* reveals the non-metropolitan to be an active, creative site of fluid change and modernity, it shows the interconnectedness of rural relationships with global flows of media and commerce, and that these aspects are also intertwined with the archaic, and the old weird rural. The *Folk Archive* reveals the non-metropolitan as a complicated place, at once attuned to a globalised mass media and ancient practices and traditions. A place where creativity is embedded in the ordinary, sometimes as a slapdash necessity in the service of an exuberant night out, and sometimes as the product of many hours of skilled craft and design. The *Folk Archive* does indeed electrify folk in that it begins a process of re-thinking both folk art as a contemporary practice and the non-metropolitan as an active site of modernity.

NOTES

1   London's V&A Museum organised a summer fete each year between 1999–2009. Described as 'A contemporary take on the traditional English fete' (ICO Design 2009), it was intended to bring together the design community and offer them the opportunity to inventively appropriate the fete aesthetic. This metropolitan enthusiasm for the rural fete aesthetic has been exploited/driven by designer Cath Kidston (1999) whose use of bunting spread like a plague across the interior design sector during this decade.

2   Calendar customs are traditional activities that take place on a specific day each year.

3   Lady Mabella's curse ran that should the dole ever be stopped then seven sons would be born to the house, followed immediately by a generation of seven daughters, after which the Tichborne name would die out and the ancient house fall into ruin. In 1794 the dole was stopped due to alleged misuse by vagabonds and in 1803 part of the house did indeed subside. The curse seemed to have been fulfilled when Sir Henry Tichborne who succeeded to the baronetcy in 1821(one of seven brothers), produced seven daughters, the dole was then re-established, but the family continued to be troubled and were subject to an inheritance scandal in the famous case of the Tichborne Claimant (Sykes 1977: p. 36).

4   Events such as The Abbots Bromley Horn Dance in Staffordshire, Hare Pie Scrambling and Bottle Kicking in Leicestershire, and Shrovetide Football in Derbyshire all encompass elements that mark out the boundaries of a community. The Hare Pie, and Horn Dance traditions also involve the village church and priests as sites of authority and power (Hogg 1971: pp. 32, 54, 80; Sykes 1977: pp. 34, 43, 122).

5   Shrove Tuesday is also a popular time for carnival to take place, signalling the last day of feasting before the entry into Lent, the tradition of Mardi Gras, means Fat Tuesday (Lindhal 2004: p. 126).

6   Fox's series *Pictures of Linda* (1983–ongoing) also makes this connection clear, it documents Fox's long term friend, musician, Linda Lunas, who when they met was a singer in an Alton punk band called Fashionable Living Death. These images record Linda's many different guises over the years, using extravagant costume to assume different identities.

7   When shown in a gallery installation *The Village* also comprises a series of 20 black and white photographs of gardens, a booth in which colour images of the residents (as detailed above) as projected with an accompanying soundtrack of whispered quotes from the women of the village and from a BBC Sound Effects recording called *Sounds of the Village*.

8   Events like this which may appear to be modern inventions often originate from much older summer celebrations and are examples of the evolution of calendar customs.

9   This autobiographical concern has been a feature of Fox's work throughout her career, not only the series relating to non-metropolitan themes. Notably *41 Hewitt Road* (1996–1999) and *Cockroach Diary* (1996–1999) document her own spiralling domestic disorder.

10 A publication compiled from White's correspondence with the zoologist Thomas Pennant and the lawyer, antiquary and naturalist, the Honourable Daines Barrington. White also made notable contributions to the study of the phenomenon of hibernation in animals, and is thought to be the first person to recognise the harvest mouse as a separate species.

11 A hanger is a Hampshire and West Sussex term for a wooded hill.

12 Fox studied photography in the mid-1980s at West Surrey College of Art and Design at Farnham, under the tutelage of Martin Parr and Paul Graham (Chandler 2007: p. 15).

13 A tradition that notably includes Bill Brandt's *The English at Home* (1936).

14 Compton Verney collection of British Folk Art have recently explored the different meanings of the word by launching a public competition to define the idea of *folk* (Compton Verney 2010).

15 Enid Marx was a designer who trained at the RCA in the interwar years, she was an author and illustrator of children's books, a book designer, a printmaker, a textile designer and a painter. Together with her friend and co-author Catherine Lambert she amassed a great collection of folk art which she used as inspiration for her designs: The Marx-Lambert collection is housed at Compton Verney.

16 It is also worth noting that in her book on folk art Barbara Jones includes items that may also have captured the attention of artists concerned with popular culture of the time, such as the design of sweets and their packaging – liquorice pipes, sherbet fountains and pink seaside rock (Jones 1951: p. 111).

17 For further information on Wentworth's project see Bush (2001) and for Archipov's collection see Archipov (2006).

18   'There are over a thousand items in my collection today … They represent an astonishing part of modern folk material culture but unfortunately, are under constant threat of ruin, because I do not have the means at my disposal for their proper storage' (Arkhipov 2006: p. 7).

19   For further discussion of the problematic of Folk Art and archival practise see Myrone (2009).

20   Zones sponsored by corporations were: Skyscape (Sky Television), Learning (Tesco), Work (Manpower), Body (Boots, L'Oreal and Roche), Journey (Ford), Shared Ground (Camelot Group plc.), Home Planet (British Airways and BAA), Self Portrait (Marks and Spencer), Faith (various trusts and foundations), Mind (British Aerospace and Marconi), Our Town and Learning Experience Centre (MacDonald's), Money (City of London and a consortium of City interests) (Millennium Experience 2000).

6

Conclusion: Limbo Dancing

6.1 Bampton Morris Dancing, Bampton, Oxfordshire, 1977. © Homer Sykes.

In a lecture called *When was Modernism?* Raymond Williams asserted that:

> *We must search out and counterpose an alternative tradition taken from the neglected works left in the wide margin of the century, a tradition which may address itself not to this by now exploitable because quite inhuman rewriting of the past, but for all our sakes, to a modern future in which community may be imagined again (Williams 1987: p. 52).*

In this address he demonstrates how the modernist tradition in literature and art is a product of an ideological construction that privileges narratives of isolation, alienation and the anonymous relocation to urban centres, as central to what constitutes prevailing notions of the modern. He calls for a re-evaluation of this tradition and as such, a rethinking of modernity itself. For Williams, this alternative way of thinking modernity will start with an exploration of the 'wide margins of the century'. In these margins lie traditions, practices, and artefacts of visual and written culture and that have been consigned to limbo: 'a condition of neglect or oblivion to which persons or things are consigned when regarded as outworn, useless, or absurd' (Oxford English Dictionary). It is within these wide margins, this area of limbo, that this book has been situated, in an exploration of the marginal terrain of the non-metropolitan.

The main concern of this study has been to challenge the way we think about the rural. My intention has been to move from the passive aesthetic register of the landscape, towards a re-imagining of the countryside as an active, inhabited and practised realm. The preceding chapters have been diverse in their subject matter, each one taking as its theme a knot, a troublesome spot that prevents a smooth rendering of a countryside situated in a pre-modern past, instead forcing a re-evaluation of the rural as a complicated and at times uncomfortable site of modernity.

Central to my thinking has been a desire to complicate the distinction between the city and the country, acknowledging not only their inter-related nature, but also the multiple degrees of what might be considered 'country'. In part, this smudging of the two terms has been achieved through the use of the word non-metropolitan. This anti-definition works to designate manifold locations, but perhaps most usefully those places which, although far from urban, find it difficult to identify as rural. This difficulty in identification is not because these places are not situated in rural locations, it is because they are very likely to also possess features associated with the urban, such as motorways, litter, power stations and large new housing developments. These factors make the term rural an uncomfortable fit, given the connotations of the isolated picturesque that this term engenders. This book moves towards redefining the rural as a multiple terrain, a definition which rather than seeing motorways etc. as urban incursions, acknowledges that they are a significant part of what constitutes an understanding of the modern rural. The designation of non-metropolitan contributes to the vocabulary that can be used to think about the rural opening up new geographical and theoretical terrain. It works to defamiliarise the habitual sense of the rural and provides a space for thinking about places that themselves evade attempts at convenient definition.

Working within the realm of the repeated practices and performances that constitute the everyday has enabled me to, in effect, repopulate the rural as an arena for theoretical and visual analysis, enriching the field of everyday life studies by providing a much needed non-metropolitan alternative to the more frequently travelled routes which centre on (western) urban experience. In *Everyday Life and Cultural Theory* (2002a), Ben Highmore identifies necessary new directions for everyday life studies, stating that 'a focus on everyday life would insist on the uneven experiences of modernity on an international and intranational scale for instance, the different everydays of rural and urban communities' (Highmore 2002a: p. 177). I hope that this study contributes towards an intranational perspective, by shifting the focus towards the English rural and the non-metropolitan sphere as a realm with its own spaces, practices and aesthetics of everyday life, shaped by uneven and at times anxious engagements with modernity.

Key to this changed perspective has been to recast the rural as an active site of modernity, as an alternative to engaging with a narrative of the rural as a victim of forms of modernity imposed from elsewhere. Developing a conception of the non-metropolitan as having its own agency within the narrative of modernity has revealed different ways of telling this story. In exploring the wide margin of the non-metropolitan, different ideas around what constitutes modernity and what constitutes the everyday, different images and different practices become important. One of the important areas of difference that has become apparent through this marginal perspective has been the recurring tension between the ancient and the modern.

The photograph at the beginning of this chapter is one of the images Homer Sykes made to document the Morris-dancing which takes place in Bampton, Oxfordshire each Spring Bank Holiday. Morris-dancing is not specific to Oxfordshire, it is a familiar practice in many rural places.[1] Sykes chose to document the Bampton dancers because of the long history of Morris in the village. The Morris men flapping their handkerchiefs, their legs garlanded with flowers, are redolent of the sort of generic, nostalgic, summer-time, countryside which has been mass produced and marketed as a national image in so many ways that it is almost difficult to take it seriously as anything other than an expression of the clichéd national picturesque, like cricket on the green or the white cliffs of Dover. However, this image should not simply be dismissed as belonging to the raft of cultural production that re-inscribes the rural as 'of the past'. Sykes' commentary which accompanies each image in his archive of calendar customs *Once a Year* (1977) reminds us that Morris-dancing is not simply an invention of the tourist industry or Sunday night television, used as a short hand way of signalling the benign continuity of the countryside. Instead he shows it to be a practice dating back well over 600 years, which has been subject to a number of dynamic changes reflecting the wider socio-political changes of a society in thrall to modernity. First recorded in the time of Henry VII, it achieved great popularity under Henry VIII when it became a staple component of many seasonal festivals. In the seventeenth century it was prohibited along with the celebration of religious feasts by the Puritans. Gradually it once again became popular but lacked its initial vigour and meaning. During the industrial revolution and the associated depopulation of the countryside it went into decline in and some rural areas never really recovered but in Bampton the tradition has persisted with particular vitality, its form going through several incarnations as successive generations re-define its purpose and territory.

Aside from Sykes' commentary the image itself also accesses something of the complexity of the rural, visually registering the everyday negotiations of the ancient and modern. Describing Sykes' festival images Val Williams writes that the dancers are:

> caught at a moment between an old way of life and a new ... Sykes' Morris Men
> are cheerful youths, their hair long and bushy, [they] seem aware of the absurdity
> of their activity, half way between modernity and antiquity (Williams and Bright
> 2007: p. 17).

There may be an inference here that this feeling of suspension between the old and new is specific to this period in time – that the late seventies in particular, is a point in which a transition between an old and new Britain was taking place. However, as this thesis demonstrates this condition has been a constant characteristic of non-metropolitan experience, evidenced in the tensions played out between development and preservation in Nairn's *Subtopia*, and the *Shell County Guides* detailed Chapter 2; in the anxieties generated by changing occupancies of the countryside in Chapter 3; in relation to the different timescales in evidence in the WI scrapbooks in Chapter 4, as well as in the festive practices explored in Chapter 5.

Williams' remarks have the dancers occupying a suspended region halfway between two times, two ways of being, antiquity and modernity, whereas the image has them literally suspended, caught with their feet off the ground – they hover. While their dance has them momentarily suspended in the air, the photograph has them in a more permanent fix, suspended forever. Their costume is old, Morris-dancing is old, Bampton is old, yet it is impossible to mistake this image as coming from any other time than the 1970s. Under the traditional hat the men's hair is abundant in the style of the times, the car in the background is undeniably of that decade, the fact of the car itself places this image within the last century, and the fact of the photograph places the image within the last 150 years. What is happening here is a temporal collage, different points in time are being simultaneously overlaid. The timescale of the 1970s, the present day when this photograph was taken pulls in one direction, while the antiquity of the traditional costumes and movements pull in another, while the dancers perform along this tightrope. Adding to this multilayering of time is that this photograph itself is now an artefact, a piece of the past, archaic in its own way as images from a previous era always are.

This temporal collage, the simultaneity of the ancient and the modern, as this study has shown is important in thinking about how the non-metropolitan everyday is experienced. The grace of the dancers silently suspended above the ground belies the tension and anxiety that lived experience and negotiation of such temporal simultaneity engenders. The moment of suspension captured in this image is a moment that happens again and again in the non-metropolitan arena, in some ways it is taken for granted – inscribed into the daily, in others this tension results in extreme behaviour and rhetoric, as evidenced for example in the CPRE's image of modernity as a creeping menace in the form of a giant octopus (Williams-Ellis 1928).

By examining the practices of driving, littering, creating scrapbooks and the celebration of festivals through the lens of the visual, this study has brought to light a set of rural aesthetics which are intrinsically related to, but quite different from the habitual image of a lightly and attractively populated landscape. Chapter 2 reveals an unexpected aesthetic of speed in the countryside. Andrew Cross' film *3 hours from here* (2004), takes the form of a somnambulist's gaze at the modern rural, whisked through time and space as the passive passenger in a northward bound HGV, there are plenty of rolling green hills here, but in this vision they are motorway embankments. Similarly *Country Life* magazine, with its juxtaposition of adverts for fast cars and pieces on the preservation of ancient windmills, together with montage aesthetics of *The Shell Guides*, work to speed up and fragment experience of the countryside.

The link between landscape and ownership has been made by many commentators (Rose 1993; Daniels 1994; Wolff 1993) most famously perhaps around the image of Gainsborough's *Mr and Mrs Andrews*, in which the portrait genre merged with the landscape to create an image of a man and his possessions: his wife and his land.

In Chapter 3, this traditional aesthetic of ownership was explored in an unusual direction through an examination the visual aspects of littering in the countryside. In the drawings made by the litter trail observers an obsession with the recording of detail can be seen, registering the anxiety inherent in their suspicions of a potential invasion of their landscape by enemy forces. The posters produced by the Keep Britain Tidy Campaign also register this anxiety around changes in who inhabits the countryside, by tying the rural to the country as a whole through their use of nationalist symbols of Britannia and the lion. Whereas Stephen Willat's photographic and film work *Dangerous Pathway* (1999) contributes to this visual narrative of ownership, by mapping littering practices as potentially resistive activity which enacts a form of ownership working as a contrary system to that of the economic ownership of the farmer or the stewardship of the concerned litter picker.

Scrapbooks are personal archives with their own aesthetic. The WI scrapbooks examined in Chapter 4 traverse the territory between the private and the public archive. Created communally, the scrapbooks both document and are physically constructed from their creator's daily lives. These visual artefacts represent specific personal experiences of the non-metropolitan everyday in the 1960s home and village, but also, importantly they are pieces of a national collage which together builds a multi-vocal rurality. This patchwork of the daily is replete with the contrasts that characterise the unevenness of modernity so evocative of the non-metropolitan experience.

The embroidered collage from the front cover of the Binsted scrapbook, showing elements representing the village's agricultural production intertwined in a design with an electricity pylon is a striking example of how such contrasts become integrated into the visual and conceptual image of the a modern rural.

Folk art and calendar customs are perhaps as clichéd a rural aesthetic as landscape, and are often written about as practices situated in the familiar non-specific past of the rural. Chapter 5 examined contemporary folk art practices, through the lens of archiving and performance. The photographic archival projects of Anna Fox, Homer Sykes and Tony Ray-Jones reveal an aesthetic of strangeness of the non-metropolitan everyday but one that is shot through with a knowing performativity. The villagers portrayed in Fox's images grit their teeth through their badly made masks and costumes, acknowledging their role in the grim performance of the village and their own connections to the past. Jeremy Deller and Allan Kane's *Folk Archive* disrupted the idea of folk art as situated in the past or the countryside. Their photographs of contemporary folk practices together with the current re-enactments of older traditions reveal a slap-dash vibrancy and lazy exuberance. Dubious practices, like drawing in the dirt on the back of white vans might be skilfully undertaken, while re-iterations of traditional practices are often executed with a rushed enthusiasm rather than the traditionally valorised amateur expertise.

One element that draws these varied non-metropolitan aesthetics together is a concern with collage. And it is this visual similarity that has significantly contributed to this conceptualisation of the non-metropolitan everyday and specifically its dissonant relationship with modernity. Lucy Lippard's notion of collage in its broadest sense as 'the juxtaposition of unlike realities to create a new reality' (Lippard [1981] 1996: p. 16) (discussed in Chapter 4) is enacted in the contrasting edges of things which seem to butt up against or sometimes overlay each other in non-metropolitan space. It is at these junctures where an A road scythes the edge of a burial mound, or a stiletto moulders under a tree, or a pylon is embroidered in silver thread, where the jolt of the edge is felt and a new conception of what constitutes the rural can begin to be explored.

FUTURE DIRECTIONS

The areas of investigation on which this book has focused were chosen because they represent stumbling points which productively problematise the idea of the rural space as being outside the processes of modernity. These moments have opened out a field in which the different rhythms and routines of the non-metropolitan everyday and by extension different experiences of modernity invite further exploration. To build on the work carried out by this thesis it would be valuable to examine how visual cultures can complicate two of the more persistent narratives associated with the rural: that it is identified with or situated in the past, and that it is a stable place founded on continuity as opposed to the transience of the city.

The first of these: that the countryside belongs to the past, I think, could be explored by looking at forms of economic engagement with the land, specifically the practices of agriculture and coal mining. There is a mirroring effect of the two industries, farming is wholly identified with the rural and it is often necessary to remind ourselves that it is actually an industry which has often been at the forefront of developments in mechanical, biological and chemical technologies. Whereas mining is so often associated with heavy industry that it is easy to forget the rural locations of many of the pits and the rural nature of the communities they supported. These two areas of production have at various times in the past century been major employers in rural areas, shaping community's economic and social structures. During the twentieth century both of these industries were subject to immense changes effecting their position as employers: the mass closure of pits in the 1980s and the development of new technologies together with intensive farming methods leading to a radical decrease in the need for agricultural labour. This rapid decline in everyday visibility, if not economic power, means that in many ways they exist now most powerfully in the realm of memory.

Two examples of visual culture which could act as interesting points of analysis for exploring the theme of memory in relation to mining and agriculture are

Jeremy Deller's *Battle of Orgreave* (2001) and Peter Hall's film of Ronald Blythe's book *Akenfield* (2005 [1969]). Neither source provides an easy rendering of the rural as situated in a comfortable past, instead they question the ways in which the past might be re-inscribed into the present. Deller's film documents a re-enactment staged by the artist of the violent clashes between police and striking miners that took place in the South Yorkshire village of Orgreave in 1984. While *Akenfield* tells the parallel stories of multiple generations of agricultural workers in a Suffolk village, based on the memories of the villagers as told to the author Ronald Blythe.

Both sources extend the notion of connection with the past through re-enactment and performance building on the exploration of these themes carried out in Chapter 4 of this study. Deller's re-enactment was staged by police officers and miners who had taken part in the original event, supported by amateur battle re-enacters, while the characters in the film *Akenfield* were played by people living in the village in which it was set. This aspect of physical re-enactment of the non-metropolitan past indicates that there is fertile ground to be investigated around forms of memory played out through bodily engagement. At the beginning of this book I referred to the tradition of beating the bounds, in which, legend has it, boys had their heads hit against boundary stones in order that they should remember the village's borders. Surely there is a visual resonance to be found between physical violence and the operation of memory in the clashes between the police and miners in Deller's film (Figure 6.2). In a similar way to Syke's Morris dancer, these scenes seem to invigorate the non-metropolitan realm as place that is not situated in the past, but maintains a dynamic engagement with it.

6.2   Jeremy Deller's re-enactment of the Battle of Orgreave. Filmed for Channel 4, directed by Mike Figgis and produced by Artangel, 2001. © Martin Jenkinson www.pressphotos.co.uk

The second of the persistent narratives: that the countryside is a stable place founded on continuity as opposed to the transience of the city, could be examined through works such as Jordan Baseman's *I hate Boston and Boston hates me* (2006), and *Witch Hunt* (2009) by Delaine Le Bas (Plate 11). Baseman's film was originally made for *Beacon*, however it was withdrawn by the artist after the local and national press condemned it as a 'race-hate video' (Norfolk 2006).[2] It centres on an interview with a female migrant agricultural worker from Portugal, one of the estimated 5,000 Portuguese residents of Boston, who come to the town to work as fruit and vegetable pickers and packers. The woman recounts instances of racial abuse suffered by her daughter and talks about the difficulties of making friends and fitting in in Boston. Her voice is combined with a visual of the flat Lincolnshire landscape; in the distance stand the severe verticals of pylons, in the foreground a flag pole flying the cross of St. George. The winds from the East, from the North Sea and mainland Europe blow the flag outwards causing its emblem – the word ENGLAND, to be read backwards.

This work forefronts the changes in population that have often characterised the non-metropolitan realm, from depopulation during the industrial revolution to the influx of middle class second home owners of more recent times. It reveals the other side of often lauded notion of community, that of insularity and ignorance. Representations of the rural often trade heavily on a denial of change and an instance of the rural as a point of continuity. So it is perhaps inevitable that any evidence of instability is suppressed in this carefully built up rural construction, with any signs of the mutability of such long established conceits greeted with anxiety, anger and hatred. *I hate Boston and Boston hates me*, builds on the anxieties enacted in Chapter 3 of this thesis regarding the perceived invasions of outsiders, here the fears were sublimated in concerns over litter, however this piece shows how such tensions can force extreme behaviours. While addressing the insularity of community it also demonstrates the embroilment of the non-metropolitan in global currents that facilitate and rely upon the large scale movement of goods, money and people, at the same time showing how these meta-rhythms are played out in everyday experience.

The idea of transience and hostility as a counterpoint to continuity and community are also explored in the work of Delaine Le Bas, which is inspired by her experiences as part of the British Roma community. Her work is particularly interesting because the idea of gypsies can often be part of a romanticised notion of the countryside, a paradoxical concept that embodies a static view of the rural past through a transient community. Often utilising personalised and traditional folk art aesthetics, Le Bas' installations reveal the overt and covert violence that marks the relationship between travelling families and the more permanent countryside residents. Interestingly her work also accesses the restriction and isolation felt by women in Roma communities, adding a multilayered critique of very specific non-metropolitan experience.

In thinking about modes of artistic engagement with the non-metropolitan a significant area for future inquiry are the cultural ventures that work to reinvigorate the rural, not simply as the subject of artworks but also as a site of artistic production. In England one of the most interesting in their critical and reflexive approach to working rurally is Grizedale Arts situated in Grizedale Forest in the Lake District. Grizedale has a long history as a venue for artists' residencies starting in the 1970s with land art inspired sculptures being made in response to the location and situated within the forest in an informal sculpture trail. In 1999 under the new directorship of Adam Sutherland, it became apparent that something more than the straightforward interpretation of the rural context offered by this environmental/land art approach, i.e. 'nature = wild = good' (Griffin 2009: p. 21) needed to evolve in order to acknowledge the rural as a space of complexity. Sutherland built up relationships with contemporary artists who were also interested in working within and more often than not disrupting unwritten codes which surround how we think of and inhabit the countryside. For Grizedale the past ten years have been characterised by difficulty, but productive difficulty. Changing the way the organisation operated and opening up the rural as a site for contemporary artistic engagement has resulted in some challenging questions:

> Is there an intrinsic value of culture? Can artists be of use in a rural community? What does it mean to engage with a community? Do artists really want to puncture their cultural enclave and why should communities care if they do or not? (Hudson 2010).

Some challenging art works were created some of which became indistinguishable from the everyday practices and social structures of the village of Satterthwaite in which Grizedale resides, with artists organising car boot sales and taking part in the village's party to celebrate the Queen's Golden Jubilee. Of course it has also engendered some challenging reactions, notably the village collectively voting to burn down a billboard, erected by Grizedale Arts, along with the image it was displaying.

What is remarkable about Grizedale is that these knotty problems define the organisation's practice, they are honest about the complexities of the rural environment and with that open eyed honesty, create dynamic engagements.

> We adopted an ideology that saw the rural context as complex, contrary, inspiring, relevant to the wider world and potentially useful – a contributor. This may sound simplistic, but the evidence was all around us; the rural idyll was there to perform a role for an urban notion of rural life, fantasy of what life could be like (Sutherland 2009: p. 41).

With tongue in cheek they identify themselves as being of the cultural margins 'and there is no shortage of them in the UK' Sutherland notes (Griffin 2009: p. 133). Finally then we return to the margins, where this study has remained rooted throughout, there is so much to explore in this rich non-metropolitan terrain. Grizedale's ambition to see the rural with new eyes, as both a complex site and a cultural contributor, would seem to exemplify the aims of this book and point the way towards new ways of rethinking the rural.

NOTES

1   It also has connections with urban areas, for example there is a strong Morris-dancing tradition in Blackheath in London, which dates back to times when Blackheath was a rural village. Cities also host Morris and folk dancing festivals where various groups come together and dance in competition with each other.

2   Beacon is a site specific exhibition that has taken place at various locations around Lincolnshire on an annual basis since 2004, see Plowman (2006).

Bibliography

3 Hours from Here, 2004. [DVD]. Directed by Andrew Cross. London: Film and Video Umbrella.

Ades, D., 1993. *Photomontage*. Rev. ed. London: Thames and Hudson.

Akenfield, 1974. [Film]. Directed by Peter Hall. London: Angle Films Limited.

Ashby, W.R., 1964. *An Introduction to Cybernetics*. London: Methuen.

Alberro, A. and Stimson, B. (eds), 2009. *Institutional Critique: An Anthology of Artist's Writings*. London and Cambridge, MA: MIT Press.

Alpers, S., Apter, E., Armstrong, C., Buck-Morss, S., Conley, T., Crary, J., Crow, T., Gunning, T., Holly, M.A., Jay, M., Kaufmann, T.D., Kolbowski S., Lavin, S., Melville, S., Molesworth, H., Moxey, K., Rodowick, D.N., Waite G. and Wood, C., 1996. Visual Cultures Questionnaire. *October*, (77), Summer, pp. 25–70.

Andrews, M., 1997. *The Acceptable Face of Feminism: The Women's Institute as a Social Movement*. London: Lawrence & Wishart.

Arkhipov, V., 2006. *Home-Made: Contemporary Russian Folk Archive*. London: Fuel.

Augé, M., 1995. *Non-places: Introduction to an Anthropology of Supermodernity*. Translated from French by J. Howe. London: Verso.

Ayres, J., 1977. *British Folk Art*. London: Barrie & Jenkins Ltd.

Bakhtin, M., 1984 [1968]. *Rabelais and his World*. Translated from French by H. Iswolsky. Bloomington, IN: Indiana University Press.

Barker, F., Hulme, P. and Iversen, M. (eds), 1992. *Postmodernism and the Re-reading of Modernity*. Manchester: Manchester University Press, pp. 46–65.

BBC, 2004. Country Faces 'Passive Apartheid'. Available at: http://news.bbc.co.uk/1/hi/uk/3725524.stm [accessed 22 April 2011].

BBC, 2014. BBC Coverage of Rural Affairs in the UK. Available at: http://downloads.bbc.co.uk/bbctrust/assets/files/pdf/our_work/rural_impartiality/rural_impartiality.pdf [accessed 28 September 2014].

Bell, D., 1997. Anti-Idyll: Rural Horror. In: P. Cloke and J. Little (eds), *Contested Countryside Cultures: Otherness, Marginalisation and Rurality*. London: Routledge, pp. 94–108.

Benjamin, W., 1970 [1934]. Author as Producer. Translated from German by J. Heckman. *New Left Review*, i(62), July–August, pp. 83–96.

Benjamin, W., 1999 [1955]. *Illuminations*. Translated from German by H. Zorn. London: Pimlico.

Betjeman, J., 1934. *Cornwall, Illustrated in a Series of Views, of Castles, Seats of Nobility, Mines, Picturesque Scenery, Towns, Public Buildings, Churches, Antiquities &c*. London: Architectural Press.

Betjeman, J., 1935. *Devon*. London: Architectural Press.

Biswell, A., 2009. The Age of Anxiety. In: T. Brennan (ed.), *English Anxieties*. Brighton: Photoworks and Ffotogallery, pp. 25–8.

Blake, W., 1804. Preface. In: E.R.D. Maclagen and A.G.B. Russell (eds), 1907. *The Poetic Works of William Blake: Milton*. London: A.H. Bullen, p. xix.

Blanchot, M., 1987. Everyday Speech. Translated from French by S. Hanson. *Yale French Studies*, (73), pp. 12–20.

Blood on Satan's Claw, 1971. [Film]. Directed by Piers Haggard. London: Tigon Pictures.

Blythe, R., 2005 [1969]. *Akenfield Portrait of a Country Village*. London: Allen Lane.

Bode, S., 2004. *An English Journey*. London: Film and Video Umbrella.

Bone, S., 1938. *West Coast of Scotland: Skye to Oban – A Shell Guide*. London: Faber and Faber.

Borland, S., 2008. Cathedral Bans Popular Hymn Jerusalem. *Times Online*, 9 April. Available at: http://www.telegraph.co.uk/news/uknews/1584578/Cathedral-bans-popular-hymn-Jerusalem.html [accessed 5 June 2010].

Borsay, P., 2006. *A History of Leisure*. Basingstoke and New York: Palgrave Macmillan.

Bridge, G. and Watson, S. (eds), 2010. *The Blackwell City Reader*. Oxford and Malden, MA: Wiley and Blackwell.

Bristow, F.W., 2009. *UK Pylon Designs*. Available at: http://www.gorge.org/pylons/structure.shtml [accessed 25 September 2010].

British Council, 2009. *Folk Archive Online*. Available at: http://www.britishcouncil.org/folkarchive/folk.html [accessed 6 May 2011].

Brunsdon, C., 2004. Taste and Time on Television. *Screen*, 2(45), Summer, pp. 115–29.

Bryant, B., 1996. *Twyford Down: Roads, Campaigning and Environmental Law*. London and New York: E&FN Spon.

Burke, P., 1978. *Popular Culture in Early Modern Europe*. London: Temple Smith Ltd.

Burke, P., 1995. The Invention of Leisure in Early Modern Europe. *Past and Present*, 146, pp. 136–50.

Bush, K., 2001. *Richard Wentworth/Eugène Atget*. London: Photographers Gallery and Lisson Gallery.

Butcher, A.C., 1996. *Mid-Hants Railway in Colour*. Shepperton: Ian Alan.

Button, V. and Esche, C., 2000. *Intelligence: New British Art 2000*. London: Tate Gallery.

Calder, A. and Sheridan, D. (eds), 1985. *Speak for Yourself a Mass-Observation Anthology 1937–1949*. Oxford: Oxford University Press.

Calendar Girls, 2003. [Film]. Directed by Nigel Cole. London: Beuna Vista International UK.

A Canterbury Tale, 1944. [Film]. Directed by Michael Powell. London: The Archers.

Carlin, B., 2004. Rural 'apartheid keeps blacks out of countryside'. *The Telegraph*, 9 October. Available at: http://www.telegraph.co.uk/news/uknews/1473711/Rural-apartheid-keeps-blacks-out-of-countryside.html [accessed 22 April 2011].

Castello di Rivoli, 2000. *Quotidiana: The Continuity of the Everyday in 20th Century Art*. Milan: Charta.

Chandler, D., 2007. Vile Bodies. In: V. Williams (ed.), *Anna Fox Photographs 1983–2007*. Brighton: Photoworks, pp. 15–25.

Chaney, D., 1990. Subtopia in Gateshead: The Metro Centre as a Cultural Form. *Theory, Culture & Society*, November, (7), pp. 49–68.

Clarke, J. and Critcher, C., 1985. *The Devil Makes Work: Leisure in Capitalist Britain*. Basingstoke: Palgrave Macmillan.

Clifford, S. and King, A., 2006. *England in Particular: A Celebration of the Commonplace, the Local, the Vernacular and the Distinctive*. London: Hodder and Stoughton.

Coast: Series 3, 2005. [DVD]. Directed by Oliver Clarke. Bristol: BBC and Open University.

Compton Verney, 2010. *What the Folk Say*. Available at: http://www.comptonverney.org.uk/modules/events/event.aspx?e=70&title=what_the_folk_say__contemporary_artist_interventions [accessed 5 May 2011].

Connor, S., 2001. 'A Door Half Open to Surprise': Charles Madge's Imminences. *New Formations*, (44), pp. 52–62.

Connor, S., 2011. *Smear Campaigns*. Available at: http://www.stevenconnor.com/smearcampaigns/ [accessed 30 July 2014].

Corbin, A., 1998. The Auditory Markers of the Village. In: M. Bull and L. Back (eds), 2003. *The Auditory Culture Reader*. Oxford: Berg, pp. 117–26.

Crick Village, 2014. *Crick Village Website*. Available at: http://www.crick.org.uk/index.html [accessed 29 July 2014].

Daily Telegraph, 2011a. Safe Pools Save Native Crayfish. *Daily Telegraph*, 16 March, p. 34.

Daily Telegraph, 2011b. Rowers to Help Tackle Killer Shrimp in Rivers. *Daily Telegraph*, 29 March, p. 32.

Daniels, S., 1994. *Fields of Vision: Landscape Imagery and National Identity in England and the United States*. Cambridge: Polity Press.

Darwent, C., 2009. Beating the Bounds, Tate Britain. *The Independent*, 13 September. Available at: http://www.independent.co.uk/arts-entertainment/art/reviews/beating-the-bounds-tate-britain-london-1786338.html [accessed 2 April 2011].

Davis, S., 2009. Pylons and Our Precious Countryside. *Guardian*, 31 October, p. 37.

de Beauvoir, S., 1953 [1949]. *The Second Sex*. Harmondsworth: Penguin Books.

de Certeau, M., 1984. *The Practice of Everyday Life*. Translated from French by S. Randall. Berkley, CA: University of California Press.

de Certeau, M., Giard, L. and Mayol, P., 1994. *The Practice of Everyday Life, Volume Two: Living and Cooking*. Rev. ed. Translated from French by T.J. Tomasik. London and Minneapolis, MN: University of Minnesota Press.

Deliverance, 1972. [Film]. Directed by John Boorman. Los Angeles, CA: Warner Bros. Pictures.

Deller, J. and Kane, A., 2008. *Folk Archive*. London: Book Works.

Derbyshire, D., 2011. The New Knotweeds: Warning Over More Alien Plants Set to Wreak Havoc. *Daily Mail*, 1 March. Available at: http://www.dailymail.co.uk/sciencetech/article-1361668/The-new-knotweed-Warning-alien-plants-set-wreak-havoc.html [accessed 4 May 2011].

Dickinson, P., 2008. *Lord Berners: Composer, Writer, Painter*. Woodbridge: The Boydell Press.

DIRFT, 2010. *A Second Phase Build to Suit Opportunities at the UK's Premier Road and Rail Distribution Hub*. Available at: http://www.prologisrfidirft.co.uk/index.html [accessed 25 August 2010].

Douglas, M., 1991 [1966]. *Purity and Danger: An Analysis of the Concepts of Pollution and Taboo*. London: Routledge.

Drabble, M., 1997. Introduction. In: J.B. Priestley, *English Journey: Being a Rambling but Truthful Account … During a Journey through England during the Autumn of the Year 1933*. London: The Folio Society, pp. 7–13.

During, S., 1999. *Cultural Studies Reader*. London and New York: Routledge.

Edensor, T., 2002. *National Identity, Popular Culture and Everyday Life*. Oxford: Berg.

Edensor, T., 2003. Defamiliarizing the Mundane Roadscape. *Space and Culture*, (6), pp. 151–68.

Edensor, T., 2004. Automobility and National Identity: Representation, Geography, and Driving Practice. *Theory, Culture & Society*, 21(4–5), pp. 101–20.

Excess Baggage, 2009. [Radio Programme]BBC Radio 4. Saturday, 7 February.

Felski, R., 1999. The Invention of Everyday Life. *New Formations*, (39), pp. 15–31.

Fisher, M., 1964. Scrapbooks Competition: What, Where, When, How and Why. *Home and Country*, September, pp. 294–5.

Foley, M., 2012. *Embracing the Ordinary: Lessons from the Champions of Everyday Life*. London: Simon and Schuster.

Ford, C., 1974. *Sir Benjamin Stone 1838–1914: Victorian People, Places and Things Surveyed by a Master Photographer*. London: The National Portrait Gallery.

Foster, H. 1996. *Return of the Real: The Avant-Garde at the End of the Century*. Cambridge, MA: MIT Press.

Fox, A., 2009. *Artist's Talk*. Presentation given at The Winchester Gallery, 20 January.

Friedan, B., 1992 [1963]. *The Feminine Mystique*. Reprint. Harmondsworth: Penguin Books.

Freud, S., 1975 [1901]. *The Psychopathology of Everyday Life*. Translated by A. Tyson. Harmondsworth: Penguin.

Gardiner, M.E., 2000. *Critiques of Everyday Life*. London and New York: Routledge.

Gas Council, 1961. Pilot's Family gets Jet-Age Heating. [Advertisement] *Woman's Realm*, February, p. 58.

Giard, L., 1994. The Nourishing Arts. In: M. de Certeau, L. Giard, and P. Mayol, *The Practice of Everyday Life Volume II: Living and Cooking*. Rev. ed. Translated from French by T.J. Tomasik. London and Minneapolis, MN: University of Minnesota Press, pp. 151–69.

Gottmann, J., 1961. *Megalopolis: The Urbanized Northeastern Seaboard of the United States*. London and Cambridge, MA: MIT Press.

Greer, G., 1970. *The Female Eunuch*. London: Paladin.

Griffin, J., 2009. *Grizedale Arts: Adding Complexity to Confusion*. Grizedale: Grizedale Books.

Guardian, The, 2009. Electricity Lines: Power to the People. *The Guardian*, 28 October, p. 32.

Gumpert, L. (ed.), 1997. *The Art of the Everyday: The Quotidian in Postwar French Culture*. London and New York: New York University Press.

The Hairy Bakers – Tea Time Treats, 2008. [TV Programme]. BBC 2, Monday, 25 August.

Hardyment, C., 1988. *From Mangle to Microwave: The Mechanisation of Household Work*. Cambridge: Polity Press.

Harootunian, H., 2000. *History's Disquiet: Modernity, Cultural Practice, and the Question of Everyday Life*. Chichester and New York: Columbia University Press.

Harris, A., 2010. *Romantic Moderns: English Writers, Artists and the Imagination from Virginia Woolf to John Piper*. London: Thames and Hudson.

Harrison, J., 1964. Report from the N.F.W.I., 43rd Annual General Meeting. *Home and Country*, July, p. 227.

Harrisson, T., Jennings, H. and Madge, C., 1937. Anthropology at Home. *The New Statesman and Nation*, 30 January, p. 155.

Harrisson, T. and Madge, C., 1986 [1939]. *Britain by Mass-Observation*. London: Cresset Library.

Hatherley, O., 2009. *Militant Modernism*. London: Zero Books.

Hawkins, G., 2001. Plastic Bags: Living with Rubbish. *International Journal of Cultural Studies*, 4(5), pp. 5–23.

Hawkins, G., 2006. *The Ethics of Waste: How we Relate to Rubbish*. Oxford: Rowman and Littlefield Publishers Inc.

Heathcote, D., 2011. *A Shell Eye on England*. Faringdon: Libri Publishing.

Hewison, R., 1987. *The Heritage Industry: Britain in a Climate of Decline*. London: Methuen.

Hewitson, J., 2010. Young Hip and Part of the WI: The Women's Institute has Come of Age. *The Telegraph*, 17 July, p. 10.

Hewitt, J., 1998. *The Shell Poster Book*. London: Profile Books Ltd.

Highmore, B., 2002a. *Everyday Life and Cultural Theory: An Introduction*. London and New York: Routledge.

Highmore, B., 2002b. *The Everyday Life Reader*. London and New York: Routledge.

Hill, C., 1984. *The World Turned Upside Down: Radical Ideas During the English Revolution*. London: Penguin.

Hiller, S., 1991. *The Myth of Primitivism*. London and New York: Routledge.

Hobhouse, C., 1935. *Shell Guide to Derbyshire, a Series of Views, of Castles, Seats of Nobility, Mines, Picturesque Scenery, Towns, Public Buildings, Churches, Antiquities &c*. London: Architectural Press.

Hobsbawm, E. and Ranger, T. (eds), 2000 [1983]. *The Invention of Tradition*. New ed. Cambridge and New York: Cambridge University Press.

Hogg, G., 1971. *Customs and Traditions of England*. Newton Abbot: David & Charles.

Holloway, L. and Kneafsey, M., 2000. Reading the Space of the Framers Market: A Case Study from the United Kingdom. *Sociologia Ruralis*, 40(3), pp. 285–99.

Holt, Y., 2003. *British Artists and the Modernist Landscape*. Aldershot: Ashgate.

Hubble, N., 2006. *Mass-Observation and Everyday Life: Culture, History, Theory*. Basingstoke and New York: Palgrave Macmillan.

Hudson, A., 2010. *Grizedale Arts*. Presentation given at Modus Operandi Agrestis Symposium, Tullie House, Carlisle, 11 November.

Humphrey, C., 2001. *The Politics of Carnival*. Manchester: Manchester University Press.

Hutton, R., 1996. *The Stations of the Sun: A History of the Ritual Year in Britain*. Oxford: Oxford University Press.

Hyams, E., 1977. *The Changing Face of Britain*. St. Albans: Paladin.

ICO Design, 2008. *V&A: Flap to Freedom Environment*. Available at: http://www.icodesign. co.uk/project/V%26A%3A+Flap+to+Freedom+Environment [accessed 28 September 2014].

Jack, C., 2005. *Blowin' in the Wind: A Short History of Litter in the Twentieth Century*. Available at: http://www.cehp.stir.ac.uk/research-centre/resources/reports-papers/documents/jack-litter-web.pdf [accessed 18 April 2011].

Jacob, S., 2005. Jeremy Deller and Alan Kane's Folk Archive. *Modern Painters*, May, pp. 74–7.

James Smith, D., 2010. England's Green and Prejudiced Land. *Sunday Times Magazine*, 8 August, p. 16.

Jam and Jerusalem, 2006. [TV Programme]. BBC 1, Friday, 24 November.

Jeanne Dielman, 23 Quai du Commerce, 1080 Bruxelles, 1975. [Film]. Directed by Chantal Ackerman. France and Belgium: Ministère de la Culture Française de Belgique, Paradise Films, Unité Trois.

Jennings, H., 1985. *Pandæmonium: 1660–1886 the Coming of the Machine as Seen by Contemporary Observers*. London: Andre Deutsch.

Jennings, H. and Madge, C., 1937. *May the Twelfth: Mass Observation Day Surveys 1937*. London: Faber and Faber.

Jennings, P., 1961. *I Said Oddly Diddle I?* London: Max Reinhardt.

Jennings, P., 1968. *The Living Village*. London: Hodder and Stoughton.

Joad, C.E.M., 1937. The Peoples Claim. In: C. William-Ellis (ed.), *Britain and the Beast*. London: J.M. Dent and Sons Ltd, pp. 67–103.

Johnson, L. and Lloyd, J., 2004. *Sentenced to Everyday Life*. Oxford and New York: Berg.

Johnstone, S. (ed.), 2008. *The Everyday: Documents of Contemporary Art*. London and Cambridge, MA: Whitechapel and MIT Press.

Jones, B., 1951. *The Unsophisticated Arts*. London: The Architectural Press.

Kaplan, A. and Ross, K., 1987. Introduction. *Yale French Studies*, (73), pp. 1–4.

Keep Britain Tidy Campaign, 2010. *Keep Britain Tidy*. Available at: http://www.keepbritaintidy.org [accessed 4 June 2010].

Kern, S., 2003. *The Culture of Time and Space*. Cambridge, MA: Harvard University Press.

Kidston, C., 1999. *Vintage Style: A New Approach to Home Decorating*. London: Ebury.

Koshar, R., 1998. What Ought to be Seen: Tourists' Guidebooks and National Identity in Modern Europe and Germany. *Journal of Contemporary History*, 3(33), July, pp. 323–40.

Kristeva, J., 1982. *Powers of Horror: An Essay on Abjection*. Translated from French by S. Roudiez. New York: Columbia University Press.

Lambert, C. and Marx, E., 1945. *English Popular and Traditional Art*. London: Collins.

Lefebvre, H., 1995 [1962]. *Introduction to Modernity: Twelve Preludes September 1959–May 1961*. Translated from French by J. Moore. London and New York: Verso.

Lefebvre, H., 2004 [1992]. *Rhythmanalysis: Space, Time and Everyday Life*. Translated from French by S. Elden and G. More. London and New York: Continuum.

Lefebvre, H., 2008 [1958]. *Critique of Everyday Life: Volume 1*. Translated from French by J. Moore. London: Verso.

Lefebvre, H., 2009 [1971]. *Everyday Life in the Modern World*. New ed. Translated from French by S. Rabinovitch. New Brunswick: Transaction Editions.

Lethbridge, T.C., 1957. *Gogmagog: The Buried Gods*. London: Routledge and Kegan Paul.

Lethbridge, T.C., 1976. *The Power of the Pendulum*. London: Routledge.

Lindhal, C., 2004. 'That's My Day' Cajun Country Mardi Gras in Basile, Louisiana, USA. In: B. Mauldin (ed.), *Carnival*. London: Thames and Hudson, pp. 121–43.

Lippard, L., 1981. Hot Potatoes: Art and Politics in 1980. In: J. Bird, B. Curtis, M. Mash, T. Putnam, G. Robertson, S. Stafford, and L. Tickner (eds), *The BLOCK Reader in Visual Culture* (1996). London and New York: Routledge, pp. 7–20.

Lock, M.M. and J. Farquhar (eds), 2007. *Beyond the Body Proper: Reading the Anthropology of Material Life*. London and Durham, NC: Duke University Press.

Listen to Britain, 1942. [Film]. Directed by Humphrey Jennings and Stewart McAllister. London: Crow Film Unit.

Lowenthal, D., 1994. European Landscapes as National Symbols. In: D. Hooson (ed.), *Geography and National Identity*. Oxford: Blackwell, pp. 15–38.

Lupton, D., 1999. Monsters in Metal Cocoons: 'Road Rage' and Cyborg Bodies. *Body and Society*, 5(1), pp. 57–72.

Lupton, E. and Miller, J.A., 1992. *The Bathroom, the Kitchen, and the Aesthetics of Waste: A Process of Elimination*. New York: Kiosk.

Lyon Biennale, 2009. *The Spectacle of the Everyday*. Dijon: Les Presses du Reel.

Madge, C., 1937. Anthropology at Home. *The New Statesman and Nation*, 2 January, p. 12.

Madge, C. and Harrisson, T., 1937. *Mass-Observation*. London: Frederick Muller.

Marcus, L., 2001. Introduction: The Project of Mass-Observation. *New Formations*, (44), Autumn, pp. 5–20.

Marin, L., 1984. *Utopics: Spatial Play*. Translated from French by R.A. Vollrath. New Jersey: Humanities Press and London: MacMillan Press.

Marinetti, F.T., 1996 [1909]. The Foundation and Manifesto of Futurism. In: C. Harrison and P. Wood (eds), *Art in Theory 1900–1990: An Anthology of Changing Ideas*. Oxford and Cambridge, MA: Blackwell Publishers Ltd, pp. 145–9.

Marr, A., 2007. *A History of Modern Britain*. London: Pan Macmillan.

Mason, C., 2008. *A Computer in the Art Room: The Origins of British Computer Arts 1950–1980*. Hindrigham: JJG Publishing.

Matless, D., 1998. *Landscape and Englishness*. London: Reaktion Books Ltd.

Mawson, C., 2010. *The Shell County Guides Website*. Available at: http://www.shellcounty
    guides.co.uk [accessed 6 April 2001].

McCall, C., 1943. *Women's Institutes*. London: William Collins.

McKay, G., 1996. *Senseless Acts of Beauty: Cultures of Resistance since the Sixties*.London and
    New York: Verso.

Meads, J., 2014. *An Encyclopaedia of Myself*. London: Fourth Estate.

Mellor, D., 1987. *Paradise Lost: The Neo-Romantic Imagination in Britain 1935–55*. London:
    Lund Humphries.

Mellor, D.A., 2007. *No Such Thing as Society: Photography in Britain 1967–87*. London:
    Hayward Publishing.

Mellor, D.A., 2008. Living Briefly in an Old Country: Tony Ray-Jones, 1966–70. *Visual Culture
    in Britain*, 9(2), pp. 61–74.

Merriman, P., 2004. Driving Places: Marc Augé, Non-Places, and the Geographies of
    England's M1 Motorway. *Theory, Culture and Society*, 21(4–5), pp. 145–67.

Merriman, P., 2006. A New Look at the English Landscape: Landscape Architecture,
    Movement and the Aesthetics of Motorways in Early Postwar Britain. *Cultural
    Geographies*, 1(13), pp. 78–105.

Miller, J., 2005. Poets of Their Own Affairs. In: J. Deller and A. Kane (eds), *Folk Archive*.
    London: Book Works, pp. 149–52.

Millennium Experience, 2000. *The Dome*. Leaflet guide to the Millennium Dome.

Minton, A. 2009. *Ground Control: Fear and Happiness in the Twenty-First Century City*. London:
    Penguin.

Mitchell, W.J.T., 1994. *Picture Theory*. London and Chicago, IL: University of Chicago Press.

Mitford, N., 1945. *The Pursuit of Love*. London: The Reprint Society.

Mirzoeff, N. (ed.), 1998. *Visual Culture Reader*. London and New York: Routledge.

MoDA (Museum of Domestic Design and Architecture), 2008. *The Shell Guides: Surrealism,
    Modernism and Tourism*. Exhibition interpretative text, 4 March–2 November.

Montagu, J. (ed.), 2003. *Paul Nash: Modern Artist, Ancient Landscape*. London: Tate
    Publishing.

Moran, J., 2005. *Reading the Everyday*. London and New York: Routledge.

Moran, J., 2007. A Life Less Ordinary. *New Formations*, 61, Summer, pp. 166–71.

Moran, J., 2009. *On Roads: A Hidden History*. London: Profile.

More, T. Sir, 1986 [1516]. *Utopia*. Translated from Latin by P. Turner. London: Penguin.

Morton, H.V., 1927. *In Search of England*. London: Methuen.

Morton, H.V., 1931. *The Call of England*. 7th ed. London: Methuen.

Morton, H.V., 1942. *I Saw Two Englands*. London: Methuen.

Morton, T., 2005. Folk Archive. *Frieze*, (93) September, pp. 133–4.

Muir, D.N., 2009. *Gentleman on Stamps: The David Gentleman Album*. Available at: http://
    www.postalheritage.org.uk [accessed 29 November 2009].

Mumford, L., 1940. *The Culture of Cities*. London: Secker and Warburg.

Naipaul, V.S., 2002 [1987]. *The Enigma of Arrival*. London: Picador.

Nairn, I., 1955. *Outrage*. London: The Architectural Press.

Nash, J., 1937. *Bucks (Shell Guide)*. London: B.T. Batsford.

Nash, P., 1936a. *Dorset (Shell Guide)*. London: Architectural Press.

Nash, P., 1936b [2000]. Swanage or Seaside Surrealism. In: A. Causey (ed.), *Paul Nash: Writings on Art*. Oxford and New York: Oxford University Press, pp. 125–9.

Natural England, 2011. *Look After Your Land with Environmental Stewardship*. Available at: http://www.naturalengland.org.uk/Images/layl_tcm6–25342.pdf [accessed 16 April 2011].

Neal, S. and Agyeman J. (eds), 2006. *The New Countryside?: Ethnicity, Nation and Exclusion in Contemporary Rural Britain*. Bristol: The Policy Press.

Neal, S. and Walters S., 2008. Rural Be/longing and Rural Social Organisations: Conviviality and Community Making in the English Countryside. *Sociology*, (42), pp. 279–97.

Norfolk, A., 2006. Artist's 'Race-Hate' Video Divides Troubled Town. *The Times* 16 August. Available at: http://www.timesonline.co.uk/tol/news/uk/article613629.ece [accessed 12 May 2011].

O'Reilly, S., 2008. Collage: Diversions, Contradictions and Anomalies. In: B. Craig (ed.), *Collage: Assembling Contemporary*. London: Blackdog Publishing Ltd, pp. 8–19.

Oakley, A., 1974. *The Housewife*. Harmondsworth: Penguin Books.

Obrist, H.U., 2009. *Stephen Willats Interviewed by Hans Ulrich Obrist on the Abitare Magazine Website*. Available at: http://www.abitare.it/en/highlights/hans-ulrich-obrist-intervista-stephen-willats [accessed 10 February 2010].

Observer, The, 1966. Self Portrait of a Village (Colour supplement). *The Observer*, 21 August, pp. 3–8.

Orwell, G., 1941. *The Lion and the Unicorn: Socialism and the English Genius*. London: Secker and Warburg.

Oxford English Dictionary, 2010. Oxford: Oxford University Press.

Pawley, M., 1988. The Sheds that Ate the World. *Blueprint*, (45), pp. 20–22.

Paxman, J., 2007. *The English: A Portrait of a People*. London: Penguin Books.

Peakland Heritage, 2011. *Smedley's Hydro*. Available at: http://www.peaklandheritage.org.uk/index.asp?peakkey=31401221 [accessed 8 August 2011].

Pidd, H., 2009. Mother Would Approve: University Students Join WI. *The Guardian*, 10 November. Available at: http://www.guardian.co.uk/education/2009/nov/06/womens-institute-university-students [accessed: 6 May 2011].

Piper, J., 1938. *Oxon*. London. B.T. Batsford.

Plowman, J., 2006. *No Place, Like Home*. Lincoln: B. Press.

Pollard, I., 2004. *Postcards Home*. London: Chris Boot and Autograph.

Priestley, J.B., 1997 [1934]. *English Journey: Being a Rambling but Truthful Account of What One Man Saw and Heard and Felt and thought During a Journey through England During the Autumn of the Year 1933*. London: the Folio Society.

Pugh, M., 2000. *Women and the Women's Movement in Britain 1949–1999*. Basingstoke: Macmillan Press.

Radio On, 2008 [Film]. Directed by Chris Petit. London: BFI.

Ray-Jones, T., 1974. *A Day Off: An English Journal by Tony Ray-Jones*. London: Thames and Hudson.

Raynor, J., 1937. *Towards a Dictionary of the County of Southampton, Commonly Hampshire or Hants, by John Raynor, Shell Guide*. London: Batsford.

Rees, E., 2011. Bushy-tailed bandits ready to go native. *The Daily Telegraph*, 26 March, p. 12.

Renfrew, C. and Bahn, P., 1994. *Archaeology: Theories, Methods, Practices*. London: Thames and Hudson.

Roberts, R., 2005. *Tony Ray-Jones*. Halifax: Chris Boot.

Robin Redreast: A Play for Today, 2013. [DVD]. Directed by James McTaggart. London: BFI.

Robinson in Space, 1997. [DVD]. Directed by Patrick Keiller. London: BFI.

Robinson in Ruins, 2010. [DVD]. Directed by Patrick Keiller. London: BFI.

Robinson, J., 2011. *A Force to be Reckoned With: A History of the Women's Institute*. London: Virago.

Rogoff, I., 1998. Studying Visual Culture. In: N. Mirzoeff (ed.), *Visual Culture Reader*. London and New York: Routledge.

Rogers, A., 1989. People in the Countryside. In: G.E. Mingay (ed.), *The Rural Idyll*. London: Routledge.

Rose, G., 1993. *Feminism and Geography*. Cambridge: Polity Press.

Ross, K., 1992. Watching the Detectives. In F. Barker, P. Hulme, and M. Iverson (eds), *Postmodernism and Re-reading Modernity*. Manchester: Manchester University Press, pp. 46–65.

Ross, K., 1995. *Fast Cars, Clean Bodies: Decolonization and the Re-ordering of French Culture*. London: MIT Press.

Sanghera, S., 2009. Another Country. *The Times*, 20 June, pp. 32–9.

Sanghera, S., 2010. The Odd Appeal of Antique Britain on Sunday Night TV. *The Times*, 20 October, p. 3.

Schor, N., 1992. Cartes Postals: Representing Paris 1900. *Critical Inquiry*, 18(2), pp. 188–244.

The Secret Life of the National Grid, 2010. [TV Programme]. BBC 4, Wednesday 17 November.

Shelburne Museum, 2014. *Museum Story*. Available at: http://shelburnemuseum.org/visit/about-the-museum/museum-story [accessed 28 July 2014].

Sheringham, M., 2006. *Everyday Life: Theories and Practices from Surrealism to the Present*. Oxford and New York: Oxford University Press.

Short, B. (ed.), 1992. *The English Rural Community: Image and Analysis*. Cambridge: Cambridge University Press.

Shove, E. and Southerton, D., 2000. Defrosting the Freezer: From Novelty to Convenience, a Narrative of Normalization. *Journal of Material Culture*, 5(3), pp. 301–19.

Simmel, G., 1997 [1902]. The Metropolis and Mental Life. In: D. Frisby and M. Featherstone (eds), *Simmel on Culture*. London: Sage Publications, pp. 174–85.

Simmel, G., 2004 [1900]. *The Philosophy of Money*. Edited by D. Frisby. Translated from German by T. Bottomore and D. Frisby from a first draft by K. Mengelberg. London: Routledge.

Sinclair, I., 2002. *London Orbital: A Walk Around the 25*. London: Penguin.

Slyce, J., 2003. Jeremy Deller: Fables of the Reconstruction. *Flash Art*, January–February, pp. 75–7.

Smith, D., 2006. Folk Art? *Art Monthly*, (299), September, pp. 1–3.

Smith, D.E., 1988. *The Everyday World as Problematic: A Feminist Sociology*. Milton Keynes: Open University Press.

Smith, L., 2004. Villagers Bristle at Accusation of Rural Prejudice. *The Guardian*, Saturday, 9 October. Available at: http://www.guardian.co.uk/society/2004/oct/09/raceintheuk. ruralaffairs [accessed 22 April 2011].

Smith, P. and Smith, G., 1977. Introduction. In: H. Sykes, *Once a Year: Some Traditional British Customs*. London: Gordon Fraser, pp. 9–12.

Solnit, R., 2002. *Wanderlust: A History of Walking*. London: Verso.

Sontag, S., 1979 [1971]. *On Photography*. London and New York: Penguin Books.

Spalding, F., 1994. *British Art Since 1900*. London: Thames and Hudson.

Spence, J. and Holland, P. (eds), 1991. *Family Snaps: The Meaning of Domestic Photography*. London: Virago Press Limited.

Spender, S., 1933. *Poems*. London: Faber and Faber.

Stallabrass, J., 1996. *Gargantua: Manufactured Mass Culture*. London: Verso.

Straw Dogs, 1971. [Film]. Directed by Sam Peckinpah. Los Angeles, CA: ABC Pictures.

Summers, J., 2013. *Jambusters*. London: Simon and Schuster.

Sutherland, A., 2009. 2000. In: J. Griffin (ed.), *Grizedale Arts: Adding Complexity to Confusion*. Grizedale: Grizedale Books, pp. 41–58.

Sykes, H., 1977. *Once a Year: Some Traditional British Customs*. London: Gordon Fraser.

Sykes, J., 1964. The Wirescape. *Home and Country*, July, pp. 235–6.

Szeman, I. and Kaposy, T. (eds), 2011. *Cultural Theory: An Anthology*. Oxford and Malden, MA: Wiley and Blackwell.

Taylor, J., 1971. The Price of Independence: Reconciling the Car with Civilised Living. *Country Life*, 14 October, pp. 981–4.

Taylor, J., 1994. *A Dream of England: Landscape, Photography and the Tourist's Imagination*. Manchester: Manchester University Press.

Taylor-Martin, P., 1983. *John Betjeman: His Life and Work*. London: Allen Lane.

Tate Britain, 2009. *Beating the Bounds*. Exhibition leaflet, 5 September–13 December. London: Tate.

Tate, W.E., 1983 [1946]. *The Parish Chest: A Study of the Records of Parochial Administration in England*. Cambridge: Cambridge University Press.

Texas Chainsaw Massacre, 1974. [Film]. Directed by Toby Hooper. Los Angeles, CA: Vortex.

Times, The, 1930. Litter in the New Forest. *The Times*, 8 September, p. 9.

Turner, V., 1987. *The Anthropology of Performance*. New York: PAJ Publications.

Turner, W.J., 1947. *Exmoor Village: A General Account Based on Factual Information from Mass Observation*. London: George G. Harrap and Co.

Urry, J., 1995. *Consuming Places*. London and New York: Routledge.

Wallis, C. (ed.), 2009. *Richard Long: Heaven and Earth*. London: Tate Publishing.

Wander, P., 2009 [1984]. Introduction to the Transaction Edition. In: H. Lefebvre, *Everyday Life in the Modern World*. Translated from French by S. Rabinovitch. New Brunswick: Transaction Editions.

Webb, B. and Skipworth, P., 2007. *E. McKnight Kauffer: Design*. Woodbridge: Antique Collectors Club.

Weightman, G., 2011. *Children of the Light: How Electricity Changed Britain Forever*. London: Atlantic Books.

Welchman, J.C. (ed.), 2006. *Institutional Critique and After: SoCCAS Symposium Vol. II*. Zurich: JRP Editions.

Went the Day Well, 1942. [Film]. Directed by Alberto Cavalcanti. London: Ealing Studios.

The Wickerman, 1973. [Film]. Directed by Robert Hardy. London: British Lion Film Corporation.

Witchfinder General, 1968. [Film]. Directed by Michael Reeves. London: Tigon British Film Productions.

White, G., 2007 [1789]. *The Illustrated Natural History of Selbourne*. London: Thames and Hudson.

Willats, S., 1978. *The Lurky Place*. London: Lisson Gallery.

Willats, S., 1996. *Between Buildings and People*. London: Academy Editions.

Williams-Ellis, C., 1928. *England and the Octopus*. London: CPRE.

Williams-Ellis, C. (ed.), 1937. *Britain and the Beast*. London: J.M. Dent and Sons.

Williams, R., 1987. When was Modernism? *New Left Review*, i/175, May–June, 1989, pp. 48–52.

Williams, R., 1989 [1976]. *Keywords: A Vocabulary of Culture and Society*. London: Fontana.

Williams, R., 1993 [1973]. *The Country and the City*. London: Hogarth Press.

Williams, V., 2007. *Anna Fox: Photographs 1983–2007*. Brighton: Photoworks.

Williams, V. and Bright, S., 2007. *How We Are: Photography Britain*. London: Tate Publishing.

Wolff, J., 1993. *The Social Production of Art*. London: Macmillan.

Women's Institute, 2009. *Homepage*. Available at: http://www.thewi.org.uk [accessed 29 November 2009].

Women's Institute, 2011a. *Denman College Brochure*. Available at: http://www.thewi.org.uk/FindACourse.aspx?id=2693 [accessed 25 April 2011].

Women's Institute, 2011b. *WI Life*. Available at: http://www.thewi.org.uk/standard.aspx?id=142 [accessed 25 April 2011].

Wright, P., 1985. *On Living in an Old Country*. London and New York: Verso.

Wyndham Lewis, P., 1914 [1996]. 'Our Vortex'. In: C. Harrison and P. Wood (eds), *Art in Theory 1900–1990: An Anthology of Changing Ideas*. Oxford and Cambridge, MA: Blackwell Publishers Ltd, pp. 154–6.

Wyndham Lewis, P., 1921 [1996]. The Children of the New Epoch. In: C. Harrison and P. Wood (eds), *Art in Theory 1900–1990: An Anthology of Changing Ideas*. Oxford and Cambridge, MA: Blackwell Publishers Ltd, pp. 244–5.

Young, R., 2010. The Pattern Under the Plough. *Sight and Sound*, August, pp. 16–22.

ARCHIVAL SOURCES

East Sussex County Archives, *Burwash Village Scrapbook* (1965).

East Sussex County Archives, *Crowborough St. Johns Village Scrapbook* (1965).

Hampshire County Archives, *Binsted Village Scrapbook* (1965).

Hampshire County Archives, *Micheldever Village Scrapbook* (1965).

Mass Observation Archive (University of Sussex), Replies to Spring 1995 directive.

Mass Observation Archive (University of Sussex), Topic Collection: Wall Chalkings (1/A).

National Federation of Women's Institutes Archive, *Home and Country* (1954a), 'Member's Letters', September, p. 149.

National Federation of Women's Institutes Archive, *Home and Country* (1954b), 'AGM Report', July, p. 123.

National Federation of Women's Institutes Archive, *Home and Country* (1965), 'You and Your Refrigerator', June, p. 234.

National Federation of Women's Institutes Archive: *Home and Country* (1966), 'Membership Numbers', March, p. 152.

National Federation of Women's Institutes Archive: *Golden Jubilee and Scrapbook competition* (1964–69), 5FWI/B/2/1/123.

National Federation of Women's Institutes Archive: *Golden Jubilee General* (1965), 5FWI/F/3/36.

Sheet Women's Institute: *Sheet Village Scrapbook* (1965).

Index